S0-BSR-009

N

SECR

THE NEW SECRETARY

How to Handle People As Well As You Handle Paper

Dianna Booher

Facts On File Publications
New York, New York • Oxford, England

The New Secretary: How to Handle
People As Well As You Handle Paper

Library of Congress Cataloging-in-Publication Data

Booher, Dianna Daniels.
The new secretary.

Bibliography: p.
1. Secretaries. 2. Office practice. 3. Business etiquette. I. Title.
HF5547.5.B615 1985 651.3 85-15864
ISBN 0-8160-1160-5

Printed in the United States of America

10 9 8 7 6 5 4 3 2 1

Composition by Facts On File/Circle Graphics
Printed by R.R. Donnelley & Sons Co.

CONTENTS

Part Two
Cooperating with Clients and Customers

Part Three
Preparing Yourself to Meet the Challenges

ACKNOWLEDGMENTS

I'd like to thank the following secretaries, administrative assistants, office managers, and directors (as well as all those who wished to remain anonymous) for their invaluable insights into both the problems and the solutions of working with people to become more productive:

Jan Baker, Administrative Assistant
Shirley Barnett, Secretary
Virginia Bedford, Administrative Assistant
Leanne Berry, Office Manager
Eulonda Dreher, Administrative Assistant
Yvette Harris, Administrative Assistant
Judy Hewitt, Office Manager
Agnes Knott, Executive Secretary
Jane Madding, Secretary
Marlene McCray, Administrative Assistant
Patti McFee, Director of Certification and Records
Elsie Pecena, Administrative Services Supervisor
Lynn Runnels, Secretary
Mary Dee Sims, Executive Secretary
Nancy Strand, Administrative Services Supervisor
Reba B. Strickland, CPS, Executive Assistant

Dortha Strong, CPS, Executive Secretary
Sandra Walker, Executive Secretary
Marcia Wiseman, Administrative Assistant

Because it's cumbersome to continue listing all the various titles these "people" persons hold in different companies, I'll use secretary generally throughout this book.

One last note: Because statistics tell us that 99 percent of all secretaries in the U.S. are women, I will be using the female gender pronoun when speaking of secretaries. However, all suggestions and discussions apply equally to men serving in the same capacity.

INTRODUCTION

This book does not deal with typing, filing, or making photocopies. Rather, this is a desk manual on people skills for those, whatever their titles—secretaries, executive secretaries, administrative assistants, executive assistants, administrative office managers—who are spending most of their time shuffling people rather than paper.

As the training director for a large oil tool company recently told me: "In our division alone, we hire approximately 29 new secretaries a month. The turnover is tremendous. We're getting people who can type and file, but they've had no experience in dealing with people or getting along in the business world. By the time we send them to all the seminars to make them productive, they've become frustrated and quit or moved on."

When I hear executives speak glowingly of their secretaries they mention skills relating to planning, organizing, coordinating, communicating, and handling subordinates, superiors, and peers to get work done. So why don't they speak of typing speed, filing system, or expense-report accuracy? These skills and tasks are assumed. Anyone who markets herself as a secretary has these minimum skills, which have been required of secretaries for the past few decades. Office automation has freed the modern secretary from the drudge work.

As management experts have noted, it's the secretary with the ability to handle people well who distinguishes herself in today's corporate office. And organizations are just now realizing the enormous potential of their secretaries who are capable and willing to take on administrative responsibilities and PR functions formerly handled by their bosses.

Of course, managers have known all along that their own effectiveness centers on their ability to communicate and to motivate people to productivity. Various corporate and university studies show that these managers spend anywhere from 75 to 90 percent of their time relating to people (Reber, *Behavioral Insights for Supervision*, p. 138). Consequently, companies spend thousands of dollars to teach their executives skills in oral presentations, writing, listening, supervision, participative goal setting, and such. Yet their secretaries deal with far more people in the average week, having to employ all the same skills—judging, praising, criticizing, accepting, understanding, screening, instructing, and learning—without the help of equal training! And not only is the secretary's own reputation at stake; her people skills directly reflect on her boss and her company.

Therefore, bosses and companies must begin to recognize their secretaries as valuable resources for relating to others inside and outside the organization.

According to the U.S. Bureau of Labor Statistics, our country's 3.9 million secretaries represent the largest segment of the white-collar work force. And the latest Labor Department studies reveal that during the next dozen or so years, secretaries will comprise the third fastest-growing job category in the U.S.

Like managers and management experts, students entering the business world for the first time already perceive the importance of their ability to work with people. The CPC Foundation, a research arm of the College Placement Council, recently sponsored a study entitled, "Career Values of the New Lifestyle Professionals." Nearly 2,000 graduating seniors at 50 institutions across the U.S. responded to the questionnaire about keys to career success, among other topics. Students ranked the ability to work with people as the top determinant in job success (*Training and Development Journal*, July 1984, p. 14).

Basically, there are only three areas of concern in relating to people: yourself, other people, and the methods you use to influence others. And these methods have little to do with the frequently touted adjective, "charisma"; human-relations techniques can be learned.

But, some ask, isn't good human relations just common sense? Yes, a large part is. However, as you may have noticed, common sense is not all that common. Therefore, this desk manual on people skills belongs on the reference shelf beside the secretarial handbooks covering syllabication, proper salutations, and semiblock typing format.

part one

CONTRIBUTING TO THE TEAM EFFORT

chapter 1

GETTING ON YOUR BOSS'S TEAM

"A secretarial job is a little like marriage," says administrative assistant Virginia Bedford. "You have to have a union of personalities and goals. Your technical skills are least important. You should never work your own program; your program becomes the boss's and the company's program. You read the other person carefully and you do things his way with a great deal of depth and sincerity. If you are in basic disagreement, you're working for the wrong boss."

The boss relationship sets the tone for how you handle all other business relationships—with clients and customers, with vendors and suppliers, with your boss's superiors, with your peers, and with your subordinates. And it is your responsibility as much as your boss's to create and maintain an effective working relationship.

Much of what you may think about your boss is a self-fulfilling prophecy. All you have to do to change your work relationship is to change the way you regard him or her. For example, many books or seminars set up a you-against-them attitude; they label and describe bosses in the following, derogatory ways:

The Silent Boss: Produces anxiety; rarely gives praise or feedback at all; explains very little, never tells you what's coming next.

The Slave-Driver: Assigns work without consideration for the stress that deadlines and difficult tasks bring.

The "Nice Guy": Overuses his or her charm to talk you into extra work or personal favors.

The Critic: Nothing or no one pleases.

The Daydreamer: Head in the clouds, can't be bothered with day-to-day operations. Only concerned with the "big picture."

The Default Boss: Leaves you alone to fend for yourself.

The Public-Executor Boss: Humiliates you in public.

The Bull-of-the-Woods: Authoritarian who dominates completely.

The Great-Gray Abdicator: Takes no responsibility for things getting done.

The Climber: Ruthless; interested in only what you and others can do for him or her.

The Robot: Everything is "by the book"; closed to any suggestions from you.

The Pacifier: No backbone to anybody about anything; accommodates whoever screams loudest.

The Fighter: Has attitude that he or she is up against the world; sulky, hostile, revengeful; always involved in a conflict.

The Entertainer: Wants to be liked by others; becomes a backslapper and storyteller to keep everybody happy.

The Cold Loner: Distant; powerful; secretive; distrustful.

The Queen Bee: Has a negative attitude about other women in the organization and enjoys her status as one of the few who have made it to management. Acts tough and insensitive.

The Mother Figure: Treats everyone as her children; delegates little; invades others' privacy; smothers employees.

Is it any wonder that if you peg your boss on one of these negative nails, you'll not be able to develop a productive working relationship? The idea is to realize that bosses don't fit into categories so easily. They are individuals affected by upbringing, education, and home life, just as you are. And despite different personalities and work styles—even because of them—with a little confidence, consideration, and communication, boss and secretary can form a productive team.

New Boss

Don't begin the new relationship thinking that the new boss is out to get you. Probably he or she is hoping things will work out as much as you are. If things gel between you, it'll be a lot easier than having to suffer the disfavor around the office of transferring or firing you. So assume that you will be compatible until things prove otherwise.

How to treat the new boss? Don't come on as guardian of the mint in the beginning. Be willing to explain office procedures and what information or reports are due to whom on what date. Give her a list of regularly scheduled meetings—where, when, and why. Introduce her to the people around the office, later adding positive sketches that will help her get to know each. Let her know who the real power people are and how things get done informally. Clue her in on her superior's preferences for certain reports or information, as well as any personal information of a nonprivate nature such as hobbies and sports. Provide her with company policy manuals, annual reports, or any desk manuals available for the position.

Appreciate her problem in being new and recognize the necessity for time to get her bearings on things before you throw new problems at her. Assume procedures will continue as they have until she questions them or suggests changes.

Show your willingness to explain and to answer questions, but don't usurp authority if she wishes to change things. Convey the message that you are capable of keeping operations running smoothly until she gets her feet on the ground, but that you are also flexible and open to new ideas or responsibilities.

Finally, express genuine compliments when you think the boss has done an outstanding job of assuming the reins. When she does something ineffectively, withhold comments until she asks for your feedback.

Finding Out Your Boss's Goals and Priorities

Knowing your boss is paramount. What is his standing in the company? What pressures or deadlines does he have? Observe how he schedules his work, delegates responsibility to you and others, contributes and leads in meetings, takes and offers criticism, takes and gives praise, decides which option to take, deals with complainers and apple polishers, asks for favors, researches solutions, controls emotions, reacts to stress, hires someone, fires someone, plays politics, shows his loyalty. What does he regard as good performance? Does he welcome or dislike conferring with subordinates?

A secretary to a vice-president of a large oil company characterizes her "team" relationship with her boss this way:

> He had never had a secretary to work *with* him; he'd always had people who were dingy. He used to give dictation and spell t-h-e, and it was driving me crazy. He appreciated the fact that I said, Hey, I went to college, and if I can't spell something I certainly can look it up. I've told him that he's brilliant but that he doesn't have a lot of common sense. He can go far, but he needs me to deal with all the things he doesn't know how to or want to deal with. I'm people-oriented, and so I can get things done that he needs done. He's taught me a lot—protocol, dealing with presidents of other countries and from other cultures...That doesn't mean we always agree, however. He wants me to be understated, and that's not my personality. If I were understated, we'd never get anything done. He's very passive—maybe things will get done or maybe they won't. I get things done for him.

Study your boss likewise; learn how your personality and skills complement his.

Predict his reactions to various situations and then analyze why you were right or wrong in your prediction. Pinpoint what it is about both his behavior and yours that makes you less effective as a team.

Of course, this understanding comes after weeks, months, and even years of observation, but you can begin learning immediately.

Marlene McCray says that the first thing she does after learning she has a new position is to schedule a long conference with her boss. She asks what his priorities and goals are, as well as what her responsibilities are. She explains what responsibilities she has handled in the past and asks which the boss wants her to assume in the new position: "I always tell him that I want him to tell me when I don't do something exactly the way he wants. I tell him I want to please. That always starts us off right."

"I always go in and say, 'Let's talk about what you do and how I can help you get it done,'" explains another secretary, Sandra Walker. "I usually say to my boss, 'I don't want to work *for* you; I want to work *with* you.' All my bosses have responded well to that."

Another assistant suggests reading your boss's job description to find out what he or she is supposed to be doing. That is particularly helpful if you frequently misjudge which of your projects your boss says has priority.

One of the best ways to learn and maintain your boss's priorities is to arrange a daily conference. Two minutes may be all that's necessary to compare notes on scheduled meetings and appointments, and then to outline what he will be working on and what you will be working on during the day. Mention any notes you have in your tickler file about projects that need to be started with a few phone calls or written requests for information from others. Always make note of any special "must-do's" and deadlines of which either of you may have been unaware.

In addition to the daily conferences, ask for new appraisals once or twice a year. Ask what the boss sees as your current strengths and weaknesses and in what areas she'd like you to assume more or less responsibility. Insist on this appraisal as essential to meeting your mutual goals of productivity. "Some people can't handle having a superior to report to," explains another secretary. "If you feel less about yourself because you report to someone, you're in the wrong job to be secretary."

You may occasionally run into a do-it-myselfer boss who takes care of his own mail, takes his own calls, schedules his own meetings. If that is the case, you may need to learn to anticipate his needs and do them first. Be one step ahead in order for him to discover ways you can be of help with little or no supervision.

An executive secretary to a CEO explains that this was her method in taking over her boss's routine correspondence. "When he would get letters congratulating him on his new position, I prepared acknowledgment letters ready for his signature and attached them to the incoming letters. He liked them, signed them, and I've been handling his correspondence ever since."

Bosses usually permit you to assume as much authority as you have the knowledge and ability to handle. Simply don't take control of things he prefers to do himself and don't manipulate. The idea is to assume the things that are bothersome to him.

Gaining Credibility as Your Boss's Representative

The key to your being accepted as your boss's representative is to have others see you and your boss as a team, and, fortunately, you have much control over how others see you in this role. Specifically, you want to be informed and you want to help your boss keep you informed so that you can readily deal with routine matters.

Once people learn that you are "in the know," they will sense that you can take care of their problems, often coming to you for a judgment on a situation rather than going to your superior.

How do you start this process? First, try not to be offended by the impersonal attitude that many people have toward secretaries—that is, treating them as part of the furniture. But to change this treatment, as best you can, start with the boss. Show him that you appreciate being introduced to visitors. His introduction makes the other person acknowledge you as part of the team.

Second, to encourage your boss to keep you informed, when he makes a comment such as, "I need to call so-and-so to see how he's coming on that project," offer to get in touch with the appropriate person yourself. Or, offer to write a letter for your boss's signature. For example, "May I tell so-and-so that you approve of this?" And when he gives you that approval, then you can write, speak, or telephone with authority to that person. It will be natural, of course, for you to follow up and for that person to approach any necessary follow-up with you rather than with the boss.

In fact, one secretary to a CEO says that frequently her boss tells visitors and co-workers who call him that he knows absolutely nothing about a particular situation—that they will have to contact her for all the details. If you can show your boss your appreciation when he introduces you and when he turns problems and situations over to you, you will begin to be treated truly as his representative.

Third, to gain credibility as his representative, it is essential that you read all of your boss's correspondence. Don't simply glance at the letterhead and signature at the bottom, noting that it's a first-class letter and, therefore, should go to his desk. Read and underline key ideas. First of all, this time-management technique will speed your boss's own reading and help him quickly grasp key points. Second, it will keep you aware so that you can handle routine matters and questions. Generally, the more questions you can answer, the more questions directed to you, and the more judgments you can make with regard to how situations are handled.

Finally, make contacts with other departments on your boss's behalf. For example, when you send something to the company newsletter, a trade publication or journal, submit it as if you are handling all the details yourself. There is no need for your boss to get involved as long as you have his specific approval for the overall project. You need not pass on the idea to the other departments that you have to check every detail with a superior. And the sooner the boss delegates that authority to you for complete judgment on the situation, the sooner others will see the boss's confidence in you and will begin to relax about your ability to handle those situations.

A final thought: Don't forget that as the boss's representative you naturally will have to take some of the blame. Some jobs have built-in responsibility for accepting the blame, and the secretary's job falls in that category. When you apologize for a mistake that your superior has made, rather than saying, "Yes, I'll inform my boss of his mistake," instead say, "We're sorry; we'll try to avoid that next time." The other person will know that you're not accepting all the blame for yourself but that you see yourself and your boss as a team and that you take responsibility for correcting situations just as he or she would.

Managing Your Boss's Time

Where time is concerned, think of yourself as the coach with the whistle while the boss runs the track during workouts. You must be able to coordinate projects, appointments, and visitors to allow your boss adequate working time, thinking time, and planning time.

Keep a calendar at least a year in advance to record such things as field trips, vacations, conventions, monthly meetings of professional organizations, presentations to upper management, annual or quarterly report due dates.

Then during the weekly and/or daily conferences you can adjust schedules and remind the boss of upcoming major events toward and around which she must work.

Use a reminder system for daily appointments or meetings such as small tent cards for his desk with meeting name and time or color-coded notes that will stand out from the slush pile of papers and ongoing projects in his work area.

Finally, managing your boss's time means you must learn who and what should have access to your boss and which people and projects need to be routed elsewhere. If too many staff people seem to be dropping in to see your boss, perhaps you should suggest that he schedule staff meetings more frequently so that everyone can discuss problems or projects with him and ask questions all at one time.

Additional motives for some people who drop by frequently are to get reassurance that they are on the right track with projects, to keep visible themselves, to "get the latest" on ongoing mutual projects. In cases where these motives exist, you perhaps can step in and take care of these reassurances, pass on acknowledgment that the boss knows of their work and frustrations, or give out nonconfidential updates on mutual projects.

In other words, discern if your boss's open-door policy is to be taken literally, and then try to carry out her wishes while making the best use of her time.

(See Chapter 10 for more specific information on managing your own time, as well as that of your boss.)

Being a Good Sounding Board

Your boss may not want to confide in his superiors until he has a good solution to a problem; talking with peers may create jealousies, raise competition, or violate confidentiality; and discussing matters with other subordinates may create unrest. Therefore, a secretary is the most likely person a boss turns to for honest evaluation and discussion of problems and plans.

Being a good confidante is often like being a good journalist; you learn to investigate and ask questions about who, what, when, where, why, and how. You listen for gaps in logic or missing information, challenge unjustified assumptions, point out tangent trails to the same result, turn problems into puzzles to be solved, or warn of dangers lurking out of sight along the paths your boss may propose to take. Make notes as he or she talks so you can ask questions or check further information. Notes also enable you to mull over your initial response and come back with later reactions.

Although positive feedback reassures a boss, negative feedback, too, provides the same function. When you keep him from making a mistake, your negative feedback becomes positive in the end.

A secretary to a vice-president shares this example of being an effective sounding board for her boss: The company had decided to quit subsidizing employee transportation costs such as parking reimbursements and van pools. The idea had been approved throughout top management, and the secretary had been asked to type the memo announcing the new policy. But after typing the memo ready for signature, she went in to her boss and pointed out how relatively little the company would be saving and what a big cost the new policy would have in employee morale. The boss reexamined his decision, agreed, and canceled his plans.

Psychologists and sociologists have conducted numerous studies that verify that bosses have a higher regard for those who at first may disagree and then later agree than those subordinates who always agree no matter what (Tarrant, *How to Negotiate a Raise*, pp. 52, 54; Kleinke, *First Impressions*, p. 121). But, of course, you must be careful about going to the other extreme and always playing devil's advocate; your boss may no longer take your reactions seriously.

In giving negative feedback, however, don't cast doubt on the boss's basic reasoning or decision-making process. And if he decides to proceed with plans that eventually fail, don't remind him of pitfalls you warned against. It's also not a good idea to point out problems with a decision when it's too late to change the situation.

Offering Suggestions to Your Boss

According to Wesley Wiksell in his book on oral communications, *Do They Understand You?* (p. 91), the first-ranked problem with which 222 supervisors in a well-known company felt they needed more help was how to *sell* ideas to their own bosses. Wiksell points out the absurdity of bosses having to be sold on ideas. Leaders grab ideas.

Often the problem is not that the boss is closed to suggestions, but that a secretary either has not presented an effective suggestion or has not presented a suggestion effectively. Let's investigate both possibilities:

An effective suggestion hinges on your thorough understanding of the situation: Make sure you know the goal, the criteria for evaluating ideas, and the why behind the way things are currently done. Only then can you cull the workable suggestions from all the others that may spring into your mind.

On the other hand, your boss's acceptance of your suggestion may simply be a matter of presenting the idea effectively. Remember that change and new ideas are best accepted when presented in small, retractable steps.

Second, don't worry about who gets credit for your idea. You may want to plant the seed of your suggestion by simply asking a question: "I was thinking the last time we compiled that report that there had to be a better way. Then the thought struck me that...Do you think that might have some possibilities?" Let your boss expand and modify the idea, and, if her ego demands, turn it into her own idea. What do you care, if the new procedure makes your work easier?

For example, an executive secretary relates that she used to have to type all meeting agendas, invite the attendees, send out the reminders, arrange the catering details, as well as be on hand during the meeting to be gofer for this or that information and to deliver messages to attendees. She suggested, and management agreed, that since the company had so many meetings someone be hired solely to coordinate meetings company-wide. Her boss got credit for the idea, but she began to get her other work done.

Third, decide if your idea would be better received informally through conversation or formally in a memo. Some bosses are more oriented to the written word and take those suggestions more seriously—as if by writing the idea, the secretary expects more serious consideration. Conversations are soon forgotten; verbal suggestions go unaccepted or acted upon simply because they are often lost in the haystack of other topics rather than because the suggestions are judged unworkable.

Additionally, writing a suggestion leaves the boss an open door—he can mention the situation to you again and get more details or he can drop the matter without having to explain himself or to worry about hurting your feelings with a turndown. End your suggestion memo with a nonpushy statement such as, "If you want to discuss why..., let me know and I'll try to get more information about..."

If you decide to discuss the matter rather than to write a memo, make sure you have his attention and then prepare him for the discussion. Tell him what you're going to talk about; point out immediately how the subject or problem relates to you and him; and then give him the suggestion, followed by details.

Fourth, offering suggestions by way of explaining consequences can be effective. One secretary to a vice-president explains that she had a boss who never let her read his mail or telexes; thus, he wasted much time that could have been spent more productively elsewhere. However, after being out of town on business, he would come into the office and ask what had been going on in his absence. The secretary simply answered that since she didn't read the mail she didn't know. Then she suggested that if she could open and read the mail *before* forwarding it to the administrative assistant, she could stay better informed, as well as flag things for him and pull necessary files. He okayed the more effective procedure.

Finally, give your boss time to think over the suggestion before expecting an answer. "I never walk into my boss's office expecting him to adopt my viewpoint or new solution in toto," explains an office manager for an insurance agency. "More often I realize we'll end up with a compromise. I feel like I have input that he may not have; he also has more experience than I have. What I do is offer my suggestion, give him any unknown facts, explain my reasoning, and then tell him I don't want an immediate answer. I usually say that I'll get back to him in a few days to evaluate and discuss it. When he's not under pressure, he can give it more serious attention, piggy-back the idea, and sometimes improve on it."

Accepting Blame and Learning from Error

"Certain jobs carry with them the responsibility for accepting the blame, and I know that," says one secretary to the CEO of a large oil company.

If you're of that mindset, you're fortunate because blame will not throw you off stride. But not everyone feels that way, and unfortunately, we all make mistakes. Judy Martin in her *Miss Manners Guide to Excruciatingly Correct Behavior* (p.422), has this to say about accepting responsibility for all those mistakes:

> Nobody is taking any blame for anything any longer. The new battle cry is "It's not my fault." Perhaps it's not. But Miss Manners, who believes that collective civilization is more important to the public happiness than a lot of little satisfied psyches bumping up against one another, does not like the result. She believes that if each one of us were to accept graciously a small portion of blame, it wouldn't all be hanging there, clogging up the air.

But accepting blame for mistakes you didn't make is not as easy and pleasant as witty Miss Manners would have us believe.

First of all, accepting the blame for some errors may seriously damage your reputation or credibility in doing a job. Therefore, accepting the blame should not always be an admission of guilt. It may simply mean apologizing for the action itself.

And don't mistake a negative reaction to bad news as a personal attack; make sure the "criticism" really is criticism of you or your work before you undertake to correct it.

If the matter is a small one, you may choose to ignore "getting blamed" altogether. But with more serious mistakes, accept the blame but don't admit guilt:

> "I don't believe it's my error, but I will be happy to take care of correcting the situation."
>
> "That's true. The figures should have been rechecked before they left the office. I'll see that they are double-checked next time."
>
> "Yes, someone should have made the copy before it left the file. I'm sorry for the inconvenience. Would you like me to see if I can find a copy in another department?"
>
> "We're sorry. I'll make sure everyone gets another copy of the accepted procedure before the next meeting."
>
> "I wasn't involved in that project; however, I think I can help you find the information you need to straighten out the problem."

Any of these statements are more gracious and more flattering to you than something like, "I didn't do it." Or, "Don't blame me for that." Or, "You'll have to talk to Sharon about that. That's her job."

So much for accepting the blame for a mistake you didn't actually make. Now let's move on to the harder kind—those situations where you were clearly in error. Some are "understandable" because of rushed, pressured work. Some are "honest mistakes" due to lack of knowledge or missing information. Some are "no-no" mistakes that should have never been made, such as misspellings or inaccurate phone messages.

With the understandable or honest mistakes, admitting error is easier. First, be up front about the error. Second, as soon as you catch the mistake, bring it to someone's attention who either can correct it or can lessen the damage. A delay in reporting the situation usually adds to the repercussions. Third, never laugh off or play down the error. When you do that, you force your boss to be more forceful in pointing out the seriousness of your error and in persuading you not to make the same mistake again. Fourth, emphasize that you intend to turn the mistake into a learning situation.

Use phrases such as, "Yes, I'm aware that that report was not set up in the functional format we've used in the past. Can you tell me where I can find an example to follow?" Or, "I realize I didn't handle the visitor appropriately. Would you give me some guidelines about which of the sales reps you do always want to see?"

Oscar Wilde once wrote that "experience is the name everyone gives to his mistakes."' The tendency, however, especially for new secretaries, is to think that one error will have a more far-reaching result that it actually has. But the secretaries I interviewed offer reassurances that such is not the case.

Some of the more serious mistakes that these secretaries were able to turn into learning experiences and recover from follow:

"I interviewed someone and hired her on the spot. Then I went in to my boss and told him what I thought about the woman. My boss said, 'When are you going to have her back for a second interview?' And I said, 'I already hired her.' He was shocked. I was supposed to have let her come back for a second interview and talk to the person she was going to report to."

"When I was first assigned accounting chores, I explained that I didn't know anything about accounting, but they insisted I could learn. I tried to calculate something with decimals and didn't get it right because I'd missed out on decimals in fourth grade and had never learned them. And when I asked for help with this particular decimal problem, my supervisor only gave me cursory help. She took the report—without checking it—and sent it on to her boss, who only glanced at it and sent it to the board of directors. Then this boss was called down for my mistake in the board meeting and came back and chewed me out good. By this time the president had received his copy and called me up to his office. He shoved the paper in my face and said that such-and-such part cost 3.5 cents, not $3.50. He asked if I knew who in the hell made such a stupid mistake. All I could do was cry and say, 'I did.' And then I told him if they'd hired more competent help instead of people like me, things like this wouldn't happen. Well, he got over it, but it took me a long time. And I did learn my decimals."

"We give other doctors a discount when they come in. The discount amount was written at one place as one amount and somewhere else at another figure. And I just gave this particular doctor a figure off the top of my head and undercharged him $1,000. I learned to check the facts."

"When I first started working for my supervisor, I had not met his boss. About all I knew was that my boss had two kids. This person, who sounded like a small child, called one day and asked, 'Is Mickey (her supervisor) there?' And thinking it was his son, I said in a cutesy, baby voice: 'Yes, he is, darling.' Well, he (the caller) came out of his office, down the hall, and around the corner to where I was: 'That was real cute.' I apologized all over the place. Believe me, I learned not to be flippant on the phone."

"I learned never to side with someone until you know all the issues. A student came into the office and said she'd moved out of the district but wanted to finish the school year where she was. I gave her an okay, without checking the details, and then sent her the approval form. Later I found out other extenuating circumstances and we had to retract that approval."

"My boss once said to me, 'Jeannie, how many years would let this sit here without filing?' Well, I got up and filed everything in the entire office. Then he humored me and said I'd done so much good that I was going to get promoted straight to heaven."

If these mistakes and criticisms illustrate one point, it's this: Most errors are redeemable—if you're willing to admit the mistake or weakness and turn it into a learning situation. Accepting criticism and owning up to mistakes comes with self-confidence.

Pointing Out Your Boss's Mistakes

Learn *when* to point out; timing can be everything. *When* we look at things often determines *how* we look at things. Be careful that you don't choose a Monday morning, a five-minute breather between appointments, or a high-pressure moment on some other front.

Learn *what* to point out. Is it necessary to point out a grammatical error in his rough draft when you can simply correct it? Is the situation correctable even if the boss knows about it? Are you sure the matter is a mistake in your boss's eyes?

Learn *how* to point out. Tact is in order when pointing out anyone's mistake. The following comments may work well in getting the mistake corrected and letting the boss save face:

"Did I misunderstand you about this? Did you say...?"

"I think I must have misunderstood your directions. Would you explain this again?"

"Can you explain to me why these two figures don't match? Are they supposed to?"

"If I had known such-and-such, I could have handled this situation differently. (Explain the repercussions of something.) Perhaps next time, if you would..."

"Could we look this over again? I'd feel better with one more check; I've penciled in some question marks here and there. Just initial the changes to be made."

"I typed this section of the report in two different formats just so you can compare one more time. (The boss instructed you to do it one specific way.) Which way did you want it?"

Covering Your Boss's Bloopers

The secretaries I interviewed insisted that their bosses make few mistakes. But when pressed, they commented on the following occasions when they find it necessary to cover for their bosses:

Tardiness: "When he's late to meetings or appointments, I offer excuses that he was 'delayed unexpectedly' or 'got tied up on a pressing problem.'"

Unreturned Phone Calls: "When he doesn't return a phone call and the caller phones again to ask why, I apologize with, 'I'm sorry; we must have mislaid that message.'"

Out of the Office: "When she's not in in the mornings, I tell callers that she's 'not at her desk' rather than that she overslept, which is usually what's happened."

Anger: "If my boss dictates an angry letter or memo, I usually hold it a few hours or even overnight. That gives him a chance to change his mind."

Hasty Decisions: "If I think he's made a hasty decision, I go in and ask if he's sure that's what he wants done. He usually knows my manner enough and respects my opinion well enough that he'll rethink the situation."

Rudeness: "I cover for my boss when others comment on his unfriendliness by telling them that he's preoccupied with such-and-such situation."

"Occasionally I intervene for him with a patient and put a softer interpretation on his actions or words. For example, we have a patient who could have had a few cheap fillings, but now he has to have a root canal and crowns and those things cost big bucks. My boss lectured this patient about letting his dental work go too long and the patient called me later and said he wasn't coming back. My boss had made the patient feel like a small child. He'd told him, 'You've got a bombed-out mouth; if you'd have come in sooner, etc.' He also told the patient that because he was a salesman, he needed to get rid of those stains on his front teeth to improve his self-confidence. So I had to apologize to the patient and explain that the dentist was only concerned about him but was not a very good communicator. Then I went in and talked to my boss and explained how the patient had taken his lecture and suggested he call the patient and apologize—which he did."

Remember that covering for a boss's blind spots can be a way to demonstrate loyalty and improve relationships with other departments or clients. Secretaries attest that bosses are appreciative of the effort.

Flagging Your Boss's Accomplishments

Almost anything you do has the potential for making your boss look good. Your being courteous, being timely with requested information, and being correct are all taken as accomplishments of your boss because she has had the good taste to have you as her representative.

Specifically, you can mention to others outstanding projects and results and your supervisor's efforts in each situation. However, be careful not to embarrass a boss by giving too glowing a report in her presence. Also, be aware of creating jealousy and increasing competition among your boss's colleagues. And never reveal anything confidential, even for a "good cause" such as making your boss look good.

Also, remember that when you flag your boss's accomplishments, there's the "quality by association" principle at work; if she looks good, you look good. Conducive to your own success is a successful and rapidly rising boss.

Relaying Complaints and "Scuttlebutt" to Your Boss

The secretarial grapevine has a negative reputation, especially among bosses. And if you find your boss tells you as little as possible about her thinking and her work, possibly it is her fear that you are participating in the grapevine too closely.

Nevertheless, bosses have learned to respect the grapevine system because usually the information is based on some fact. The problem is that the facts have been distorted by everyone's speculating on missing details and/or adding interpretations of the situation. The boss knows, however, that news from the grapevine, even complaints, can be useful to her.

For example, news from the grapevine gives her advance warning on things. If funds for a certain project are going to be cut, she perhaps will decide to put her work on hold for a few days. In the case of complaints, a boss who learns of the dissatisfaction informally and quickly through the grapevine can sometimes settle a brewing problem before it explodes.

As secretary, you then become a filter. You want to stay tuned to the grapevine as a service to your boss, but not to participate other than to give publicly available facts when asked. Most certainly, when you hear complaints or rumors, you should not interpret them, reveal your reaction to them, or speculate to others on how your boss will react.

The second thing you need to remember, as a filter, is that you must be aware of how people will "use" you to get messages to your boss. An administrative assistant in a large personnel department explains that she asks directly: "Would you like for me to pass that on to Mr. Brown?" She says that sometimes the complainer answers affirmatively and acts relieved. At other times, he clears his throat, shuffles his feet, and says to "forget it." In that case, the complainer knows his ruse hasn't worked and that the secretary hasn't been taken in.

As far as "indirect" complaints and other scuttlebutt, here are some guidelines to consider before passing comments on to your boss:

1. Would this be considered a "tiny tale" and give the impression that you did not know how to sift the trivial from the serious matters that need attention?
2. Is the solution to the complaint within your own realm of authority? If so, correct the problem yourself.
3. Would your boss expect you to pass this on as part of your job responsibilities in making him more aware and capable of performing his duties?
4. Will this situation or problem likely recur, or is this a complaint about past action only?
5. Is the problem or situation solvable?
6. Will there possibly be repercussions that your boss will have to deal with later?
7. Is hearing complaints and rumors a priority for your boss? (For example, a director of nursing may want to hear patients' complaints as part of her goal of improved hospital care.)
8. Can you make your boss aware of a problem without passing on a complaint as such? ("Ms. Wynn, we've got some morale

problems in this department." Or, "Mr. Oakley, off the record, I think you probably need to spend a little time with Mary Ann in the next few days." Most bosses will pick up on your hint and follow up for themselves, respecting your sense of propriety.)

9. Can you change the wording of a complaint to make it less offensive before passing it on?

Some secretaries fail to pass on scuttlebutt because they dread being the bearer of bad news. If this is the case, remind yourself during a boss's angry reaction that he is angry at the news, not you.

Finally, watch any impulses to manipulate your boss into action by your own interpretation from looks, innocent comments, or actions from others.

As a filter for complaints or grapevine rumors, you control valuable information. Consider that as just another vital role you play on your boss's team.

Showing Your Loyalty

Some secretaries confuse loyalty with overwork. If they work in a highly stressful situation with top-priority projects, they may come to think of loyalty as doing anything and everything the boss asks without regard for the consequences of mental or physical health or personal relationships.

Although productivity plays a part, there are numerous ways to show loyalty to your boss. One way, of course, is through deferential statements: "Okay, Ms. Crowder, I'll do it your way. You've certainly had more experience than I have." Deferring to superior knowledge or experience is not a demeaning act, but one of good judgment and subordination. One office manager explains her deference this way: "I felt divided loyalty when a peer of mine got fired. I wanted to give her another chance. But I had to remember that I didn't have first-hand knowledge as my manager did."

A second way to show loyalty is to handle the matters the boss hates—performance appraisals for those who report to you, administrative trivia, first drafts of detailed reports, calling security when someone takes the boss's reserved parking space.

Another way to reveal loyalty is through your comments to others inside and outside the office. Never agree outwardly with another who criticizes your boss or his work. One secretary says that she often hears complaints when her boss turns someone down for a raise: "It's hard to defend his decision when I identify with the person. It's difficult to reassure them (the subordinate) with a compliment and say, 'Take this to Safeway and buy some bread.'" But if you can't defend the boss's decision, at least remain neutral.

Complimenting a boss is another way to show your loyalty and respect. If you don't feel comfortable with a direct statement to her about the merit of her work, say so indirectly to a third party within her hearing. Or, demonstrate your compliment by quoting her favorite clichés or adopting her way of doing things. Imitation is a genuine form of praise and loyalty.

Keeping your boss informed is still another method of showing loyalty. Bosses are not always as tuned in to the "people part" of their productivity as you are. An executive secretary at an oil company commented on a particularly threatening situation: "We had another person in the office who felt that he should have my boss's job. He was a little overbearing. He would tell everybody that I was his secretary, and I had to continually correct that. He would promise information to others that he wasn't authorized to deliver. He would try to go around my boss to get things out. I felt loyalty to my boss, and although he knew of the situation, I kept him informed."

A final way to show loyalty, and the most important, is to make the boss look good—whether that's by catching mistakes in work before it goes out, by suggesting alternative ideas and solutions, or by passing on credit for work you actually did. When the boss looks good, you look good.

(For matters of divided loyalty between boss, peer, and company, see Chapter 11.)

How to Say "No"

Rarely will you have to say "no" to a boss if you understand the difference between a request and an order. Some bosses disguise requests as orders with statements such as, "I want this typed by noon." It's then up to you to turn the order into a request.

First of all, level with your supervisor that a certain deadline is impossible to meet under present circumstances. Make a statement such as, "This will take approximately two hours; which other letters here would you like me to delay to work this in?" You've turned the order into a problem-solving situation and let him call the punches. If he says he needs them all done and insists that you will have time, then continue to pursue the matter in your own problem-solving mode: "I'll call another department and see if someone can send over temporary help. If not, which of these projects would you like me to give first priority?"

When you are sure you are unable to accommodate the request, say so. Keeping quiet misleads the boss into thinking you will be able to do what she has asked.

Be sure you always give your reason for not being able to do something, and make sure it is specific and unarguable. "I can't work late tomorrow because I am having out-of-town guests for dinner."

On occasion, you can try the I-have-a-better-suggestion approach. When the boss says that she wants the company picnic catered at the headquarters site rather than in the nearby park, suggest that you call the caterer and ask which arrangement will allow quicker service at the lower cost before she makes the final decision.

When the boss resists your alternative approaches, insists "you can do it" about impossible tasks, and ignores your warnings about deadlines, ask the boss how long she thinks a certain project will take or how much it will cost. Then keep track of your time and at the end of the work, let her know how long each step took "in order to improve planning and coordination the next time" or to explain why the work is late.

Turning even intended orders into requests can help your boss save face. If he issues an order for you to work overtime and you say "no," he loses face by backing down. When you can do so, help him by turning the order into a request:

> "I'd like you to stay a couple of hours tonight to finish those budget figures for tomorrow's meeting."
>
> "I'm sorry that I can't tonight; I have to pick up my sister at the airport. But I could arrange to come in earlier in the morning." (Or, "I could ask the temporary agency to send someone over.")

If all your attempts to turn the order into a request fail and you recognize that the situation is truly an order, then you must decide whether to comply or suffer the consequences.

Working for More Than One Boss

A survey from *BIZ*, a bimonthly publication of Xerox Learning Systems, of more than 890 executive secretaries reveals that they work for from two to five bosses. And the higher their rank, the more likely secretaries are to work for multiple bosses. Relieved of much of the routine typing and filing that clerks do, these secretaries have more time to devote to the larger public-relations functions for these high-level bosses.

Often these bosses head multiple divisions or subsidiaries and are of different rank, situations which further complicate the picture. As one secretary explains, "Working for two bosses means you have to be really with it. I'm not just working with two people; it's two people and four divisions. You have to organize in your mind."

The primary area of concern in dealing with more than one boss is conflict in scheduling work: Secretaries report handling work for multiple bosses in one of several ways: 1)first come first served; 2)division of time—half a day for each or certain days of the week for each; 3)priority of projects; 4)rank of boss.

But even these four guidelines create problems when there is a "rush" matter or when both projects seem top priority. Secretaries can sometimes determine priorities for themselves. One way is to outline priorities as you see them (highest priority—an immediate phone call to start a project, make plane reservations, etc.; second priority—correspondence; routine—monthly reports, etc.) and reveal these priorities to the boss requesting work.

And if you will not be able to accommodate the boss in the usual turnaround time, give him an estimate of when he can expect you to have the project completed. This is far better than "surprising" him with the delay. With forewarning about any scheduling conflict in your work, he may be able to rearrange his schedule around your timetable.

If there is still disagreement about what you have perceived to be top priority, then ask both supervisors involved to make the decision about the conflict and tell you how to proceed.

Another major concern of those who work for multiple bosses is fearing that they may show favoritism to a boss they like better. At all costs, keep this possibility in the back of your mind and make sure it never affects your work schedule.

One last tip in working for more than one boss—you may have to resort to reading moods and personalities. One secretary says she works for two supervisors of equal rank, "one who likes to think he's boss and another who's mature enough that he couldn't care less." When the first supervisor issues priorities that create no problems, she and the more agreeable supervisor try to accommodate the other one and keep him happy.

Dealing with Your Boss's Boss

The most prevalent concern here is contradictory instructions. One philosophy involves the concept of "he's my boss's boss, so what he says goes for both of us." The other philosophy is "I work for Ms. Smith. What she says goes; if there are problems from above, then she'll have to handle it."

Tact is definitely in order here. I suggest that when you receive contradictory instructions from your boss's superior that you relay those instructions to your own boss and ask for her direction: "Mr. Tensly suggested that we compile the information in this format rather than the one you and I talked about earlier. Which do you want me to follow?" Such a statement lets your boss save face by making the final decision and also prevents her from making a mistake in sending her superior something unsatisfactory.

Another secretary explains that she usually uses humor or at least a light touch to help her boss save face when his boss overrides his decisions: "Mr. Jones wants it done this way—do you think we should make him happy this time?"

Another concern in dealing with your boss's boss is making requests of the superior. Again, tact is in order so as not to convey the idea that your boss is giving the higher boss orders: When calling a superior to a meeting, requesting missing information, or asking for project approval, make the issue a request, not a demand: "Mr. Black asked me to call and find out if we can pick up your Hinburg information in about half an hour." Or, "Mr. Black has scheduled the meeting for 3:00; will you be able to be here?"

A third concern is your own day-to-day relationship with higher-ups. Some secretaries violate protocol by becoming too familiar with higher-ups simply because they see them in their boss's office often. That is not to say that you don't greet superiors warmly, make pleasant conversation when invited, or take an interest in their business or home situation. But it does mean that you don't offend by taking the lead in initiating personal comments or inquiries that indicate that you consider the higher-up your peer.

Particularly, this distinction is important when others are around. Some secretaries take this opportunity with the higher-up to impress others about their own close working relationship with the top brass. Top executives are usually on to that game and resent being used in this way.

Fourth, you are an important part of dealing with your boss's superior in that you can help cultivate their relationship. As you read, learn to clip cartoons or articles that would be of interest to the higher-up and supply them to your boss to forward to his superior. Also, when the higher-up drops by to visit, make it a point to remember personal preferences and accommodate him, such as bringing decaffeinated coffee. Your thoughtfulness will reflect favorably on both you and the boss.

Finally, remember that respecting the chain-of-command is paramount. Never take the opportunity to go over your boss's head about something you want simply because the higher-up is frequently available.

Socializing with the Boss

If there is little socializing with your boss, don't take the situation personally. Bosses sometimes have a fear of being unable to command respect from subordinates with whom they become too friendly or informal.

Protocol insists that all socializing should be at the request of the superior, not vice versa. And when your boss does ask you to lunch or dinner, she will pay the tab, particularly when the discussion centers on business matters.

Particularly avoid anything that would be considered a sexual come-on for the sake of your own career. If a boss does let you know that he has other-than-business interests in you, be firm about your turndowns while protecting your working relationship. You may try several not-so-subtle answers to his invitations, all of which allow him to save face. You can say your life is "just too busy" with outside classes, children, other relatives, and hobbies. You can claim interest in another relationship. Or, you can be honest about your feelings about dating someone with whom you work and the effect that socializing may have on your own and your boss's effectiveness on the job.

Remember that rumors start easily, particularly when you are tempted to flaunt a close relationship with your boss. Best to keep an emotional distance in your relationship. You want to be cordial, but not personal.

Gifts for the Boss

When the occasion for a gift arises—such as birthdays, promotions, holidays—stick with work-related items such as pen-and-pencil sets, desk-top gadgets, decorative items, cards, food, or beverages. Avoid personal items.

Let your boss set the precedent about whether you should consider giving a gift at all. And remember that your boss's gift to you in no way obligates you to reciprocate—rarely will the boss expect a gift in return.

How to Treat the Boss's Spouse or Other Relatives

Establish access according to your boss's directions. Don't assume that if the spouse calls, your boss always wants you to "put her through." Sometimes this is the case, but not always. When screening, however, it's best not to appear to pry: Try something like, "Would you like for me to give him (or her) any message?" If the spouse doesn't explain the reason for the call, leave it at that.

A few bosses have problems with relatives who "check in" too often. If you gather from the boss's facial expression or his failure to return the calls that he resents being checked on, make sure that you don't give out more information than he wants you to give.

With callers other than relatives, secretaries follow the routine safeguards about confidentiality and tact with the usual comments such as, "He's not at his desk at the moment." But with relatives, the secretary tends to be more accommodating and to give out more specific information. If you are in doubt about handling such calls from relatives, observe the boss's reactions and actions. If you are still in doubt, you can ask your boss for more guidance in a tactful manner: "Would you like for me to handle your husband's calls in the same manner as those of other callers, or do you want me to be more specific about the information I give out?"

Another troublesome situation is the spouse who thinks you are her assistant also. She brings in a personal Christmas mailing list for you to address or a paper for graduate school for you to type. Most such work requests, however, will come indirectly through your boss. If that's the case, turn the order into a request and follow the suggestions under "How to Say No." If you don't mind doing the work, let your boss know that other priority items will have to be put aside.

At parties or other social occasions, don't ignore the boss's spouse. There is a tendency for your boss to ignore his wife, thinking she doesn't know or care about the details of the latest project with which you may be involved. However, you shouldn't make the same mistake. If you exclude the spouse and wax on eloquently about the project in an exclusive way, you are bound to build resentment.

Dealing with What Irritates the Boss About You

Bosses don't usually keep their irritations to themselves. Secretaries I've talked with seem to be very aware of things they do to cause the boss displeasure. Here are the most frequently mentioned irritants, along with guidelines for minimizing them:

Interruptions: Bosses don't like to be interrupted with questions during their thinking, planning, or working time. Try to keep a list of all questions you need to ask and messages you need to deliver for appropriate times such as the daily conference or just before lunch or at the end of the day. Then when the boss is free, catch her and ask her all the questions at once.

Also, try handling most of the questions or comments with notes. As you read the mail or a report, underline and mark questions about your expected action in the margins. Or write notes and leave them on her desk at the end of the day. She can then answer before she goes home in the evening or begins work the next day.

When you must interrupt, make sure your thoughts are organized and you make the discussion as brief as possible. Have available all the information she may need in giving you a directive.

Catching her in the right mood has much to do with the response you get. Make sure you don't interrupt when she is under a pressing deadline.

Never interrupt for something you can find out for yourself with minimal effort. You probably identify with the irritation if you've ever called a department store to ask if it stocks a particular item. The salesclerk drops the phone to go check the shelf. She comes back and tells you that she does carry the item in stock. You ask the price. She didn't notice. You wait while she goes back to check. She comes back to the phone to tell you the price. You ask if they have blue and red. She didn't notice. She goes back to the shelf. You ask if they have several in stock. She didn't notice. She makes a fourth trip to the shelf. She comes back to tell you they have exactly four.

Be thorough in providing the pertinent details and salient points before you get the boss's attention. If you are habitually thorough, your boss will soon learn that if you have interrupted, the interruption is a necessity.

Of course, you also must use your discretion about what you should dig up for yourself and what you should ask your boss to provide in the interest of team productivity. For example, let's say your boss leaves you a note, asking that you find a copy of a competitor's annual report for five years earlier and then becomes involved in another project without giving you further information. It would be antiproductive for you to spend two hours on the phone and finally send a carrier over to get a copy of the old annual report from the library, when all the boss wants is a sales figure you could have gotten from your own reference files. To have interrupted him to ask why he needed the annual report would have been far more productive for both of you.

But on some interruptions you and your boss may disagree about urgency. One executive secretary who had tried to use her discretion and discovered that wasn't good enough for her boss finally spoke to him about his frowns and scowls when she interrupted:

"'Okay, if you keep frowning when I interrupt, one of these days I'm going to get something really important on my desk, and I won't interrupt you because you've scared me so much.' He has changed the way he responds to me now."

Differences in priorities: This is where the daily conference comes in. Things planned and put in priority order on Monday may need to be reshuffled on Wednesday. Stay tuned; be alert to the boss's phone calls and office conversations so you can anticipate a change of direction.

Being kept waiting:"My boss walks out of a meeting and that's my signal to call his limousine; it infuriates him if the limo isn't there by the time he gets out the front door," explains another executive secretary. How to avoid this frustration? Be one step ahead. Organize your present hour's work around the boss's upcoming hour's work.

Noise or chatter: Get up and close the boss's door when anything out of the ordinary develops out front.

Your absence from your desk: When necessary to leave your desk, tell the boss that you'll be gone for approximately x minutes. Of course, if he's busy when you leave and you want to avoid a second irritation of interrupting him, the next best thing is to leave a note on your desk saying when you will return.

Dealing with What Irritates You About the Boss

Secretaries are equally vocal about things that their bosses do that make their job more difficult, their time less productive, and their stress greater. Following are some tips for minimizing those common irritants:

Disappearing act: Secretaries say bosses have a way of vanishing, particularly after asking that a call be placed or when expecting a visitor or immediately after leaving them with a critical deadline and complicated project. And a few secretaries resent the boss's coming in late every day when they themselves are expected to be on the job sharply at 8:00.

In the latter case, resentment isn't called for. It may help you to consider that part of your job responsibility is simply availability; to be at the desk "just in case" is part of what you are paid to do. On the other hand, your boss is not necessarily paid for his or her availability but rather for results—no matter when the work gets done.

In the other disappearing acts, however, you can exert some

control. Whenever the boss walks past your desk, get in the habit of fishing for his whereabouts by making statements of your needs rather than asking questions:

"I should have your return call from Mr. Howard any moment now." (Usually a statement of such fact will bring an explanation about whereabouts and/or subtly remind him that perhaps he should stay around.) Not: "Where are you going? Mr. Howard is supposed to call in a moment." (He may view this inquiry as nosy.)

Also, you might try sign-out sheets on the back of his door or the corner of your desk. That way, at least you'll know where to reach him in emergencies.

Sarcasm: Bosses who habitually use sarcasm with others to get their work done may have difficulty in turning off the sarcasm when dealing with you. Some bosses confuse sarcasm with wit or humor and do not understand its belittling effect. To deal with a sarcastic comment, try something like: "Under that bit of humor, I think there must be something a little more serious you're trying to tell me. Want to discuss it with me?" Or, "You seem a little upset; could we discuss any changes you'd like me to make in handling this?"

Refusing to delegate enough responsibility: Secretaries say they feel that many of their talents are wasted because bosses do not give them opportunity to show how they can perform certain functions. If that's so in your case, prove yourself by taking the steps in Chapter 10 to assume more responsibilities.

Bosses often do not realize that they are overdirecting and oversupervising until you tell them directly.

Indecision: Prompt your boss on decisions by asking if there is any further information you can get for him. If he says he needs to check with someone else, offer to call that person immediately. Get him off dead center by asking probing questions about the results or alternative steps of action.

No recognition for a job well done: Some bosses are frugal with praise out of ignorance; others think praising a subordinate dilutes authority; some fear it raises expectations about more money; finally, some think that since you "should" do a good job, there's no need to compliment when you're doing only what you're supposed to do. Of course, this is hardly the case.

And while the majority of secretaries say they need no praise for doing their job because they are self-motivated and/or perceive salary and increased responsibility as rewards, they do appreciate recognition and notice.

If your boss infrequently expresses praise verbally, look for other ways she may show you that she appreciates your work. As just mentioned, raises, more authority, and more responsibility can be taken as forms of praise.

One administrative assistant expresses her boss's praise this way: "I have his confidence. I take care of practically all his finances. I can call up any of eight banks and say there's a jumbo CD coming due, and would they take $500,000 from here and put it there. And they do it. And people can talk to my boss about certain projects and he will tell them he doesn't know a thing about it, that they should check with me. That's his way of praising me."

Third, a boss may show recognition and praise by the way she treats you in front of visitors. Consider it a compliment when the boss doesn't consider you a piece of furniture but rather introduces you to her guests and asks you to sit in on meetings as a participant.

Another secretary says that her boss shows appreciation by supporting her in her career growth and making donations to her professional organizations, as well as allowing time off for her to participate in training seminars.

So before you become too discouraged about lack of verbal pats of praise, observe other ways that your boss may say you're appreciated.

And if you continue to fail to see any acknowledgment or praise of your work, ask your boss directly if he is pleased with your work and if he can comment on your strengths and weaknesses.

Personal favors: Secretaries with whom I spoke report that they have been asked to get coffee, take clothes to the laundry for repair, buy a negligee for a wife, order flowers, go home and get the cat unstuck from the garage door, go to the post office, lend money for lunch, carry out the trash, water the plants, and settle the boss's mother's estate.

Surprisingly, however, most of these secretaries say they do *not* feel demeaned in doing these chores, simply that these tasks may interrupt their other work. As one secretary put it: "My boss knows what I have to do. I figure if he knows how much I make an hour and he thinks I have time to go to the store, then I have time to go to the store."

If you prefer not to do personal chores but hate to refuse outright, try turning the boss's personal requests into give-and-take situations. For example, many secretaries say their bosses offer to bring them coffee or stop by the deli for a sandwich as often as they request their secretaries to do the same. Others say that they trade personal favors from time to time, asking a boss for time off for a school conference or a funeral or borrowing the boss's car to go shopping during the lunch hour.

Another way to minimize any resentment you may feel is to realize that your boss may do personal favors himself for his superiors such as getting tickets to the theater or a sports event. Personal favors aren't limited to secretaries.

If "household chores" or getting coffee is what it takes to keep both of you and the office functioning, then it only makes sense that the one making the least money should do the task.

If the idea of personal favors really upsets you, perhaps you should reconsider your career as secretary. One top-level secretary explains: "The more important they (the bosses) are, the more personal business you handle. You free a top executive from home responsibilities so he is free to think about the company's business."

Handling Conflict with Your Boss

Secretaries tend to deal with conflict with the boss in one of four ways:

Give-in: Whenever the boss insists on things being done a certain way, this secretary simply grits her teeth and complies—whether she finds the situation palatable or distasteful. She may think that if she countered the directive, she would displease her boss; and she cannot stand the possibility of rejection. She gives in and resigns herself to a second-best situation.

Retreat/hide: When conflict arises, the secretary takes an I'll-show-you-attitude and lets consequences take their course for what may have been a weak or wrong directive. Or, she may simply withdraw her support from the boss both emotionally and physically. She no longer is willing to "stick her neck out" and support his work with colleagues or superiors, and she may initiate only the minimal contact to deliver phone messages or files.

Walk out: Some secretaries "collect stamps" for all the wrongs or conflicts that arise with the boss without ever letting him know her feelings. Then when she reaches her "limit," she resigns or asks for a transfer to another department.

Confront: The wise secretary learns to confront her boss when there's a conflict. She doesn't think of confrontation in a negative light; confrontation can be as easy for her as the following opener: "Would you be willing to spend 10 minutes with me this afternoon on this food-facility proposal?" she asks when she is feeling frustrated that the boss hasn't given her enough authority to take the next steps and the project is lagging behind schedule.

Don't wait until a conflict smoulders and presume you have to build a legal case before you'll be heard and your feelings respected. Much conflict is created unintentionally by a boss who doesn't know how to manage her time well, who doesn't delegate enough authority, and who has a blunt manner of pointing out mistakes. Give the boss the benefit of the doubt about things that upset you and express your viewpoint of the situation.

All of the secretaries I interviewed affirmed that confrontation was the way they handled conflict and agreed that it was the most effective way to maintain a team effort. After all, if you won't stand up to your boss on important matters, how does he know you are capable of confronting others on his behalf?

Defining a Good Relationship

Some male boss-female secretary teams hit hard times simply because they are unaware of different communication styles. Researchers John E. Baird and Patricia H. Bradley ("Styles of Management Communication: A Comparative Study of Men and Women," *Communication Monographs*, June 1979, pp. 108-09) report that women exceed men in giving information, stressing interpersonal relations, being receptive to ideas, encouraging effort, showing concern, and being attentive to others. Males, on the other hand, generally exceed females in dominating, being quick to challenge others, and directing the course of conversations.

Realizing these basic differences may be the first step in pinpointing specifics that are causing resentment in male-female boss-subordinate relationships and working on changing them.

In addition to similarities or differences in communication or work styles, many secretaries equate informality with a good relationship. Informality in and of itself is not necessarily indicative of a good relationship. That's much like evaluating the telephone as either a help or a nuisance; its ringing can certainly be an interruption, but I'd hate to be caught without one in case of emergency.

Informality has its advantages when you want to discuss a good place to get a steak, but it can sure be bothersome if your boss spends half an hour "shooting the bull" from the corner of your desk when you have a deadline to meet.

A good relationship requires mutual respect, but not necessarily informality, intimacy, or fondness.

Ultimately, a good working relationship is one in which both persons can be fully productive and one in which they feel like a team rather than master and slave. You should both be supportive of each other's advancement in the organization. The secretary takes on responsibilities to free her boss to move ahead with larger assignments; while the boss, in turn, provides the secretary with knowledge, skills, and visibility.

A good secretary-boss relationship is based on openness and cooperation, not domination and deception. And it is both the secretary's and the boss's responsibility to maintain an effective working relationship.

In a way, you are your own boss, and the relationship is what you make it; you have chosen to be where you are.

chapter 2

MAKING YOUR PEERS TEAM PLAYERS WITHOUT FOULING OUT

Why should you bother to get along with your peers? After all, they can't fire you, and they don't give you performance appraisals. Time was when most secretaries worked for only one boss; they rarely came in contact with people in other departments. But most secretaries today consider themselves working for the company as well as for a particular boss. Therefore, their responsibilities involve relating to a whole team of players rather than to one coach; getting along with your peers can make your job much easier.

For one thing, your results often depend on others' contributions to your own work projects, such as compiling a departmental report. Second, co-workers can be necessary sources of information important to both you and your boss. Third, peers can make you either visible or invisible in the political arena, complementing or denigrating your efficiency with a certain project. Finally, you never know when a peer may become either your supervisor, with the clout to make your life miserable, or your subordinate, with an inclination to be an albatross around your neck.

Mistakes to Avoid as a Newcomer

Your first effort at a new job should be to get the lay of the land. Spend time learning about your new environment. When you ride in the elevator, go to lunch, pass others' desks, meet co-workers during breaks or after hours, be alert. Are the people around you happy, relaxed, bored, angry? Whom do you see talking with whom? What cliques have formed? What are the social codes? What are the attitudes about upper management? About the competition? Are things always done "by the book" or are there unwritten procedures you need to follow to get along?

Waiting for Others to Make You Feel Welcome

Don't wait; take the initiative in a low-key way. Spend some time with chitchat when it's appropriate. Ask people how they fit into the company, what their job is like, what they enjoy about it, what they dislike about it. Leave for coffee with different people each day for the first few days. At lunch don't wait for others to ask you to join them. "Where are the rest of you going for lunch? May I go along?" will get you into a group and help you learn the power structures that exist.

You may have the attitude that people should come to you because you're the one who's new. That may be true, but that doesn't always happen, because others may be as unsure of how you will react as you are about them. They don't want to risk rejection any more than you do.

When fitting into a new job, working your way into a group may seem foreboding. It's difficult to meet and form close relationships with several people at once, but most people are friendlier one-on-one. Ask about their interests or their job, and they'll be glad to fill you in because it makes them feel important.

One final tip in fitting into a group: Offer to help someone who's behind or to do a "housekeeping" job that no one else enjoys. If someone expresses a problem to you—let's say, a problem finding a new apartment across town—offer what you know. Take her problem as your problem or her interest as your interest. In other words, make yourself welcome by making yourself useful.

Getting in with the Wrong Group

"Wrong" varies in everybody's vocabulary. But by wrong, I mean becoming involved with a work group that will classify you in a way unfavorable to your success on the job. When you are new, be careful to avoid prejudices in sizing up people; keep your likes and dislikes out of the situation. Observe details about people and avoid being influenced by general impressions that lead to hasty judgments. Keep in touch with your changing opinions of people and update those impressions as often as possible. Finally, be sure that you are judging with regard to primary qualities and not superficial characteristics that others may have pointed out to you.

Generally, you'll find several cliques that have formed according to how members feel about management. There's always the clique that is supportive of management, the clique that's neutral, and the clique that complains about every move management makes. Particularly in a smaller company, you can be sure that management knows who belongs to which clique and you will be characterized accordingly.

When I suggest observing the groups around you and talking to people about how they feel about their job, that does not mean that you are quite so analytical about friends as it may seem. But it does mean that the people with whom you decide to associate have much bearing on how you do your job. It's just as easy to choose a group that you would like to be associated with as one that has a reputation with management that you would find yourself having to minimize or overcome.

Whiz-Kid Syndrome

Watch the tendency to come on too strong with what you already know about your job. Obviously you have skills that you bring to your job from other experience, but every job and office involve a different set of procedures. It's a good idea to keep quiet for the first few weeks until you find out how things are run and how you can bring your skills to the new job possibly to improve the situation. Then after you've been on the scene awhile, you can gradually introduce ways to meet office objectives more effectively. Coming across as the Whiz-Kid makes others around you feel uncomfortable.

Also, avoid sentences that begin with "At my other job, the way we did it was to..." Such statements about how nice or efficient things were back on the old job are often taken as put-downs of the new job and co-workers.

Laziness

In addition to avoiding the Whiz-Kid syndrome, neither do you want to come across as Lazy Lily—imposing on others to do your job; taking advantage of their good nature to show you around, to give you instructions, or to tell you whom to contact about the malfunctioning copy machine. In other words, taking advantage of others' helpfulness too long after you've been on the job creates resentment. Learn to "do it yourself."

Negative Opinions

Be careful about voicing opinions, particularly of other workers. You don't yet have the right to express an opinion when you've been around only a few weeks—even though you may be expressing an opinion to someone who will agree. Such negative opinions make the newcomer seem arrogant.

Cries of "It's Not in My Job Description"

Any newcomer who keeps a copy of her job description by her telephone pad is going to be in trouble. No job ever exactly fits the written description. Therefore, when others say to you, "This is part of your job," don't immediately contradict. If you think the task is one that you're not responsible for, check it out quietly with your supervisor. And if you do learn that it is one of your "unwritten" responsibilities, add it willingly, not begrudgingly.

Flippancy

When you're new to the job, don't act too self-assured and flippant: Laughing at the wrong things, being negative when other people are negative, making light of serious situations, taking advantage of breaks and lunch times.

The people who have been around longer have made a name for themselves in other areas and their indiscretions are sometimes overlooked whereas yours as a newcomer may not be. Even those who do take advantage may resent your doing so, because they may feel they've earned the right to the extras and that you haven't "put in your time."

Overfamiliarity

It's a good idea to address your superiors by last name until they ask you to do otherwise. Even though you hear others calling them by their first name, remember that they have been around longer and may have been given permission to do so. Let superiors be the ones to initiate the informality of first names. And when they do ask you to call them by first name, call them by last name in front of outsiders or support staff to whom they may not have given that same freedom.

Extracurricular Activities— To Participate or Not to Participate?

A long time ago secretaries began a job with the intention of working with the same people for five, 10, 15 years of their career. Nowadays that's no longer true; some people change jobs every couple of years. Even if that's the case for you, that does not mean, however, that you should not take the time to develop relationships on the job.

Rather, you should understand that although relationships may be temporary, they are valuable. Most of us need positive stroking just to feel good about working around other people.

Extracurricular activities provided by various companies include annual picnics, committees for civic causes such as the United Way or the annual blood drive, sports teams, individual memberships to social clubs and physical fitness clubs. Additionally, some companies offer self-development activities such as Toastmasters, the Living-Well program, foreign languages, or cooking classes.

Secretaries who take advantage of these opportunities cite several benefits from participation. First, you have a chance to meet families of those you work with and can often come to understand your colleagues better once you see their home relationships and environments. Second, contact outside the office also helps you connect a telephone voice or a signature to a face.

Third, these extracurricular activities also provide you with contacts that may prove to be learning experiences; they give you a chance to sit down with someone else one-on-one and ask how she does her job, how she has progressed through the ranks, and what advice she has for your own career objectives.

Fourth, extracurricular activities allow you to be more casual with others, to be seen in a different role than you perhaps allow yourself to be seen in the office. People begin to see you as a person rather than a department, and many secretaries say they find this helpful in getting cooperation from other departments.

Fifth, participating in sports activities or wellness programs helps you become physically fit while developing other relationships. Exercise helps you to perform better on the job and to develop a good attitude. Studies in various companies providing such activities show that absenteeism is reduced.

Finally, attending extracurricular activities such as retirement luncheons or farewell dinners can be a way of showing loyalty to your boss. Your interest in the company and staff as a whole reflects on your supervisor's own attitude toward the job. Don't underestimate the ability of extracurricular activities to make you more visible and to enhance your career, to fulfill self-esteem and social needs, and to gain cooperation from other departments.

Getting Cooperation from Other Departments

In what situations do secretaries find themselves having to get cooperation? With people who perform services around the organization—people who dust the plants, people who repair the copy machine, people who bring the coffee, people who cater the luncheons, people who handle requisitions, people who prepare the expense-reimbursement checks, people who deliver the mail, people who run errands. The list is almost endless.

Growing up on Charles Darwin's theory of the survival of the fittest, we understandably come to visualize many situations as you-against-them. But try to avoid this attitude if you expect to win cooperation. Assume that both you and the other person or department have objectives to be met and that the other person will let you do your job as long as you permit her to do hers.

Here are some guidelines to help both you and the other person or department win:

1. Don't make requests personal. If you and the other person know each other well, the other may take advantage of your relationship, insisting that "you surely understand" why he can't get a certain job done when you need it. Instead, you want to emphasize that your entire department is counting on the other individual to come through and will know if he fails. Rather than "I really need these figures by..., " use statements

such as "We really need..." or "Everybody will sure appreciate your efforts in..."

2. When you make a request, ask for a commitment about when the work will be completed or when the information will be available. Otherwise, when you have to follow up, you may seem unreasonable in your expectations.

3. Don't make your follow-ups sound like nagging; try to find a "new" reason for making contact: "I just phoned to say that we ran across a copy of...that we thought you could use in completing..."

4. Be sure to offer all the details and all the help you can to make the request simpler. Could you send over temporary help? Provide copies of past contracts? Make phone calls? In other words, don't just dump the problem and run.

5. Be a good winner. Don't pressure simply because you have the power to do so. Try to turn the situation into a win-win proposition, helping to resolve the issue so that both of you get your objectives accomplished. Take initiative in helping the other person save face when she has to "give in." Heal the wounds.

When to Pull the Boss's Rank

The easiest way, of course, to get cooperation from other departments is to pull your boss's rank. An executive secretary gives this example of a vexing problem in getting other departments to bend rigid rules:

The hospital had a new dietician on duty who would not okay a coffee pot replacement for the third floor. The patients' visitors were complaining; the patients were complaining; and the rest of the nursing staff was complaining. Yet, because the head nurse on the third floor had not gone through proper procedures to get a replacement, the dietician refused to honor her request. Having called twice, the head nurse finally gave up and called the secretary to the director of nursing. The secretary immediately called the dietary department, mentioned her boss's name, and asked that a coffee pot be delivered to the third floor. Within five minutes, the third floor had the coffee pot.

Although many secretaries have found that the quickest way to get cooperation is to pull rank, they also admit that they must learn to live with the consequences—which can involve much bitterness and many political backaches.

Most people resent a secretary who thinks that her boss's rank allows her certain personal privileges. For example, cutting in a cafeteria line because your "boss so-and-so wants you back on the job in 15 minutes" is pulling rank for unnecessary privileges.

The secretaries I interviewed named only three situations where they found it necessary to pull rank: 1) at the copy machine when their boss unexpectedly needs copies immediately; 2) unexpected travel arrangements and accommodations on the company plane; and 3) occasionally withholding paychecks from employees when they had specific orders to do so. But all secretaries emphasize that *how* they pull rank is of the utmost importance and that they never make pulling rank a habit.

They call to mind the fact that most of the executives in the company who are well liked and respected do not make an effort to impress others with their power and do not "throw their weight around." The same is true of secretaries. Secretaries who *enjoy* pulling a boss's rank to get things done need to reexamine their motives to see if they aren't doing so to massage their own egos.

And more dangerously, a secretary may be giving her boss a bad name; if that's not his manner for handling people, he probably does not wish her to handle situations in that way. Of course, this does not include some bosses who have their secretaries pull rank to get things done, but who, when people complain, act as though they didn't know that this treatment was going on. Of course, this creates a good impression for the boss and a bad impression for the secretary.

So if and when you decide it's necessary to pull rank, make sure that you go about it with the right attitude. Never be sarcastic or haughty. Don't be arbitrary; give a real *why* when you need something rather than a simple "Ms. Top Executive needs this; I have to cut in line here to make 40 copies." Rather explain, "Ms. Top Executive is in a meeting with 20 people, and they've just decided they need copies of this document. Would you please permit me to..." Again, note that the "would you please" is a much more courteous wording than just simply stating you are going to do something. Also, when you find it necessary to make a "would you please" request, always add your thanks.

Finally about pulling rank, don't cry wolf too often or people will tend to ignore the request—even when it comes from the boss. Try using your personal influence rather than your boss's power.

Offering Favors

Offer to trade a favor. On occasions when your project or request needs special attention, explain that you are aware of asking "for the moon" and then offer to trade a specific favor for special duty on your project: "If you'll hand carry this through for me, I will personally..."

Asking Favors

Another method of cultivating cooperation of another department is to ask favors. When you never ask people for favors, you keep them at arm's length, possibly leaving the impression that you consider yourself superior and hate to humble yourself to ask for help. Some secretaries avoid asking favors because they do not want to feel obligated—they do not want to feel they owe something in return. However, your asking a favor gives the other person an opportunity to feel needed.

When you do ask a favor, make sure the request is reasonable. And make the request tentative and easy for the person to do, remembering to express appreciation. Also, be careful with wording. When you pass on typing to another department, rather than "I'm too busy to handle this," or "I've got more important things to do," try instead, "I have another project that I've got to work on and this letter is very important. I want to make sure that it's done well. Therefore, I need your help."

The connotation is altogether different with such wording. Rather than the other person's begrudging you the favor, you will tend to find that she is friendlier. We all tend to be more cordial to those for whom we perform favors and extra services.

Asking for What You Want

The Bible says, "Ye have not because ye ask not." That's also a prime reason for lack of cooperation between departments. People don't "have" because they expect other people to be mind readers.

When you need cooperation, talk to the point. Say *I* when you mean *I*, *we* when you mean *we*. Say the such-and-such department rather than the vague *they*. Be specific about what you want and go directly to the person who can help you. Don't feed the information or the request through three other people with dropped hints such as, "I wish I could get so-and-so to do such-and-such."

Don't preface your request by reminding the person of all the wonderful things you've done for her in the last 48 years. Expect that she will recall those things on her own; you don't want your request to seem like a bribe or a debt.

Also stay away from *shoulds*. To tell a typist in another department that this "should have been done" one way rather than another does not sit well. Tell her that you need the work done in a certain way, and don't just expect that she *should* do what you consider any other reasonable person would do.

Don't exaggerate your needs or the consequences of not having something done as you want it. When you overstate the situation, such as by setting an impossible deadline, people will tend to disregard your real needs.

Don't threaten. Let the other person make the decision about whether she will cooperate. Again, even when you're asking for something you need, make sure that you retain the questioning tone of voice.

Remember when you ask for what you need also to give the other person an opportunity to express what he or she needs. Talk in terms of a mutual situation. "I need thus-and so, and I understand that your deadline is thus-and-so. How can we get both of these reports typed by 2:00?" Turn the situation into a problem-solving situation.

And never forget the importance of eye contact when asking for what you need. When you walk into a room or an office of four or five busy people and make a request, probably you will get little response. No one feels individually responsible in a group. Such a request is like saying, "Someone should go out for Chinese food." Few people immediately jump to volunteer even in a friendly setting. So if you expect an individual response, make eye contact with one person in the group and make it an individual favor.

Finally, don't forget to express hearty appreciation, being specific in your thanks and praise. Tell the other person what consequences she has saved you from—without being phony, of course. Then offer to cooperate in return.

Cultivating People

Cooperation on demand is difficult. Most secretaries who are successful in maintaining good interdepartmental relationships make a real effort to cultivate others over a long period of time. That means remembering others and calling them by name—not just when you want something, but when you see them in the elevator or at lunch. One secretary says that when people go to special trouble for her she takes it upon herself to send flowers from her department, to take her to lunch, to write a memo to that person's supervisor, to do small favors such as bringing a sandwich from the deli or making a special trip with an important phone message.

Maintain ongoing contact with people. Call them occasionally just to ask for their advice on an idea or to ask what's happening in their department. Keeping such a connection says that you care about them personally and how they fit into the organization.

Thoughtfulness is power.

Cooperating on a Specific Project

First, expect that your needs will differ from those of your collaborator. Ask yourself "what's in it" for both you and the other person.

Expect not only your needs to differ but also your methods. Realize that both ends of the project do not have to be handled in the same manner to result in a good product, service, or event.

You may feel comfortable in making tentative suggestions, but do so slowly at first; "read" the other person to see how open she is to your comments.

Next, face problems as they arise; don't let them build to the point of explosion before you say anything. Make a practice of both giving and getting feedback.

Finally, be willing to go more than 50 percent of the way. If you're taking responsibility for the project, be willing to do more than your "fair share."

Working with People You Don't Like

Obviously for most of us, it's easier to work with people we like. We grow up playing with our friends, not our enemies. Therefore, the first thing in working with another person you don't like personally is to get over the idea that you must like someone to work with him or her. Cooperating with someone has nothing to do with liking.

Maybe the dislike is not on your part, but on the part of the other person. You begin to notice that the person either is late to meetings or appointments with you or doesn't show up at all. She takes your messages very perfunctorily, writing down nothing more than the absolute essentials. She is very blunt on the phone and gives short yes and no replies. She takes snipes at you through humorous remarks that are not meant to be funny. She forgets to tell you little details that would help you to do your job better. All of these are ways others may express dislike of you.

To cooperate with another person despite a personal dislike, first decide what it is about the person that upsets you and try to talk about the situation. For example, you may try: "I noticed the other day that when I brought in that report you had a frustrated look on your face and had little to say. Do you want to talk about the situation?" This should give the person avenue to express feelings that she's been hiding. When you talk, be specific about the behavior, words, or actions that you noted and don't make judgmental statements. Talk only about the behavior that is acceptable or the missed deadline that was unacceptable.

Second, try to control your anger or vent it in a constructive way. If you're angry, rather than slam file drawers, purge files in a whirl of constructive, not wasted, activity.

Third, try to minimize your contact with this person. If you feel uncomfortable in each other's presence, try to write notes, leave lists for each other, or let your superior or someone else in a mutual department pass on information that you need to communicate.

Finally, try to psyche yourself up for the situation. If you can, laugh at yourself and what makes you angry; tell yourself that it's unreasonable to let another person's behavior make you unhappy all day, push you to lose your job, or cause you to be ill-tempered with other employees or clients.

If all else fails, ask yourself, "Is it worth being paid x dollars to have to speak to this person every day?"

Cooperating with Other Women

Unfortunately, as many psychologists have pointed out, women sometimes have a problem working with other women due to cultural conditioning. When teen-age girls make plans with each other and a boy later calls and asks one of them to go out, the earlier plans with the girlfriend are often canceled—as if those plans were less important.

Some women continue to have this same attitude toward other women in the business world. Because women are sometimes treated as inferior and are often paid less than their male peers, they tend to have a low self-esteem and additionally tend to view other women as inferior to men: Women's requests are not as important as men's; women's opinions are not as worthy of approval or as essential as those of men. And therefore, when a woman asks for a favor or help, another woman may consider such a request as cooperating with an inferior person.

Do your best to guard against any such prejudicial notions that you may have brought with you to the job and which may affect your cooperating with other women.

To sum up about cooperation: As an executive secretary of an oil company says, "When I need cooperation, the approach is the important thing. I always put myself in the other person's place. I try always to make her feel important in the process, that without her I would not be able to continue with what I'm doing. I think this is the key to getting other people to cooperate—to make them feel important in the work process."

Small Talk

Some people get the reputation of being loners, isolates, or aloof simply because they are shy and do not know how to chitchat.

One of the primary ways to become a better conversationalist is to read newspapers, magazines, books, company newsletters, professional journals, and memos from top management. This will give you more to talk about.

Second, be observant. Particularly notice office decor. Diplomas, certificates, awards of merit, sports trophies, plants, special knick-knacks on the desk—all of these things give you an idea of what your fellow workers are like and what might be a good conversation topic of interest to them.

After you learn the art of being observant, turning what you have observed into conversation is simply a matter of the journalist's five W's—who, what, when, where, why—and how. "Did you win this trophy in the recent tournament?" "How old was your son in that picture?" "I noted your certificate for CPR; did you attend the class through this company?" "What kind of things did the course cover?"

Another conversation topic is a mutual acquaintance. "I notice that you work very closely with so-and-so in such-and-such a department. How do your jobs relate?" Or, you may wish to mention another person you know well and relate some particular compliment about that person.

Other possible topics of conversation are new hobbies and fads or trends circulating through the company. For example, you may say, "I've noticed that almost everyone has this new kind of picture frame in the office. I wonder, have you gotten into painting these? Do you know anyone who does?" Again, use the five W's—*who* introduced the idea, *why* it caught on.

Of course, another topic of conversation that frequently comes to the rescue is any necessary information or directions: "Can you tell me how these reports should be filed?" "Can you tell me how Mr. X prefers to see the annual report—does he like to see the first draft or final draft only?" "Can you tell me which way to the so-and-so department store? I'm going shopping on my lunch hour." People like to be of help and your question gives them a connection with you and your mission.

If your approach to chitchat is always humorous, be careful. Some people feel comfortable only when cracking jokes at themselves, or, occasionally, at other people. This kind of chitchat—the pun, the off-handed flippant remark—does carry with it risk in that humor is a very subjective thing that may offend some. So make sure when you use humor in small talk that the listener takes your remarks the way you intend.

Last, when you are attempting to chitchat in a group such as in an office setting or around the lunch table, remember not to emphasize your aquaintance with certain people in the group who are better known to you. Special eye contact with only those people and personal references make the others feel as though you're conducting a one-on-one conversation. And that, of course, defeats the purpose for learning to make small talk with a group.

How to Say "No" Tactfully

Occasionally you must tell a co-worker no. This situation is not so crucial as telling your boss no; nevertheless, saying no to a peer can damage future communication lines.

Of course, you have a right to say either yes or no to a specific request and are never obligated to give a reason. All that is necessary when prodded about your answer is to repeat your no. However, to give a reason or excuse—whether or not it's a bona fide reason—comes across as courtesy.

When a child comes in and asks, "May I spend the weekend with a friend?" and you say "yes," he's gone. On the other hand, when you tell the child "no," the automatic reaction is "Why not?" Adults often react as children do. Therefore, if you want to make your "no" more palatable, state your reason.

"I was on the phone long distance with my boss who was out of town," explains an executive assistant. "And this lawyer comes out of a conference next door and hands me something and says, 'I need 10 copies.' I kept talking to my boss and the lawyer said, 'I don't think you heard me; I need 10 copies.' Well, my boss heard him and asked who was there with me. So I had to put him on hold and I said to the lawyer, 'My boss is on the line. If you need copies, the copier is right around the corner.' He looked at me kind of funny, but he did it himself. Sometimes you just have to be assertive."

An assertive "no" works. Just be sure you don't get drawn into an argument about the validity of your reason or excuse. When you answer "no," make sure that you use a friendly tone and add a smile to make it clear that there are no hard feelings, that your decision is business rather than personal.

Refusing Confidential Information

The ways people try to get confidential information from secretaries are varied and challenging. Some people make it a point always to drop by your desk when they think you're working on something confidential, and a few can read upside down as they talk with you over the typewriter. A computer screen is even more difficult to hide.

If someone asks to see confidential papers on your desk, say that you are supposed to work on them right away or that the boss needs them immediately. Then stuff them back in the file until the person leaves, or step into the boss's office with the information.

Be particularly careful when you leave your desk. Don't leave dictation pads out, half-typed letters in the typewriter, file folders open, or computer screens full.

Always be careful to destroy classified material when required. You need to shred, burn, or chemically decompose notes, carbon paper, scratch pads, typewriter ribbons, access codes, or any other item that would yield information to someone who is not easily deterred.

However, most people not having access to your paperwork will try to get information from you by direct question. Some, of course, will try to weasel things out of you with a bit of psychology. For example, they may imply that your boss really keeps important things from you, and that you're really not "in the know." The idea here is to get you to talk just to prove that you are an important person to your boss and that you do have special knowledge. Be aware of the various intimations people use to sneak such information from you.

In fact, bosses frequently cite a loose tongue as a primary reason for secretaries' lack of promotion. If your boss has a tendency to keep things from you, it may be that he or she is afraid of someone's getting confidential information from you.

Following are tips from top-notch secretaries for refusing to give out confidential information without offending people unnecessarily:

- "I never say no when someone asks for information. I always give them an answer—but not exactly the one they want."

- "I usually say, 'I'm sorry, I'm not qualified to give that information,' or 'I'm only the secretary.'"

- "I appeal to their sympathy: 'That information is confidential and I'm not allowed to discuss it. My job is on the line if I reveal this.'"

- "I use humor when people ask about meetings of the board of directors: 'What is this? Your day to get me fired?' Or, 'Gee, I'd very much like to share that little piece of business with you but I really, really need my job.'

- "'I'm sorry, it's against company policy to give you that information, but I can give you...' and I offer what information I can." (By offering information that they may already have, you have conveyed the idea that you are trying to be helpful.)

- "You may also plead time: 'I don't have all that information at this time. I'll keep your question in mind and as we gather more information possibly I'll be able to get back to you."

- "If you're afraid that people are trying to get information from you that they would never try to wriggle from your boss, you can always offer the following: 'I'm not sure that information is available. Would you like for me to discuss it with my boss and find out?' Usually that person will back off and decide that he didn't need to know that badly."

Is it a matter of great consequence to give out information to someone you think will not discuss it with others? Yes! As I talk with secretaries across the country, I hear of instances where people have been fired for giving information they considered completely nonconfidential.

For example, in some offices it's reason for termination to discuss salaries. In another, an office manager explains that two accountants began discussing money freely in front of other employees. One mentioned that a subsidiary was not doing well and that management was discussing transfer of funds from one company to the other. Both accountants lost their jobs. They were completely shocked and lamented, "Everyone else discusses it." The office manager's reply was, "When that comes to my attention, they will be dismissed also."

Remember, confidential means confidential.

Suggesting More Efficient Methods

If you are achievement-oriented, you probably find it difficult to work with people who have lower performance standards and do things less efficiently than you. And when that's the case, you often feel as though you should offer them tips on more efficient methods.

But you've also probably noticed that people don't like to be told a *better* way to do things. Therefore, you need to keep your office running as smoothly as possible but yet prevent offending others when you offer suggestions, changes, or solutions.

Try wording your tips in one of the following ways:

"I noticed how you're doing so-and-so. Why are you doing it in that particular manner?" Listen reflectively to understand the reasons; and then if your suggestion still has merit, you may offer, "Well, this is the way I have been doing that same thing and it seems to work better for me when I..."

Another method of suggesting new procedures is simply to offer to help and then *demonstrate* your method without verbally calling attention to it.

Or, you may casually observe, "I've been watching you do so-and-so; I really had a problem with that until I discovered...If you want me to show you how I finally figured it out, I'd be happy to when you have the time." With this kind of lead-in, you are leaving the follow-up to the other person.

A fourth way of offering a more efficient method is to offer it as a tip or favor: "Did you know so-and-so likes his reports presented in this format?" Speak as though you are giving an inside tip and perhaps the other person will thank you rather than feel as though you are making a correction.

A fifth way to present your idea is to imply that it originated with someone else or is meant for someone else: "This friend of mine who works for XYZ sure has improved the way they handle credits by..." An attempt to make the suggestion seem like a general one—from someone other than you to anyone in general who can use the new idea—may overcome an ego barrier for one who may be resistant to *your* ideas for *her* job.

If you have authority to persist, you may proceed, "Well, I'd like for you to give this particular system a try for a few months and see if it works a little bit better for you and then we'll reevaluate."

If you do not feel comfortable suggesting a different method or solution directly to your peer, consider going through your boss. Suggest a change in procedures and let the boss mention it to the other individual without mentioning the source of the suggestion.

Although it may be your responsibility to see that the entire office runs smoothly, you cannot run your effectiveness slipshod over other people without causing resentment.

Competition and Jealousy

"We all compete," says Harvey Ruben in his book *Competing, Understanding, and Winning the Strategic Games We All Play*, p. 24. Competition is an instinctive part of survival, beginning in our mother's womb for food.

Ruben outlines the benefits of such competition: We compete to understand something about ourselves, and we compete to make us feel good about ourselves. We continue to learn competition throughout life in our families, school, sports, and business.

Companies even encourage competition among their own employees, particularly in the area of sales; they promote contests and foster group competitiveness because studies have shown that production goes up in such situations. Competition within a group often increases the output of individuals belonging to that group, thereby resulting in a better service or product. It develops initiative on the part of different group members and enthusiasm about the product. In fact, we've all read about Pulitzer Prize winners, Nobel Prize winners, and great sports enthusiasts who have competed with colleagues to find the best solution to a problem, to develop a new life-saving drug, or to set a new world sports record. Their competition was a healthy thing.

But competition can be distasteful, depending on what we are competing *for* and whom we're competing *against*. Psychologist Terry Orlick, in writing in *Winning Through Cooperation*, distinguishes between rivalry and competition: Competition is generally straining *for* a certain goal—to attain a certain level or position in the company. There is a possibility for more than one winner.

But when there can only be one winner—only one position to be filled, only one person who walks away with a certain assignment—then stress and anxiety usually go up. In such a situation we may sense *rivalry against* another person rather than simply *competition for* the goal; the goal for which we're competing may become secondary to the behavior against the other person.

This feeling of rivalry, of course, creates problems in dealing with other people. So if you're having problems with a situation in which there is jealousy or rivalry, the situation may not be something you can control. If there can be more than one winner, possibly all you need do to lessen the rivalry and the tension in the situation is to point out the fact that both of you can be winners, that both of you can have your needs met.

Or to lessen the other's sense of rivalry, you may find a way to build the other person's self-esteem so that he or she no longer feels "put down" just because you succeed. In fact, there are several questions to ask yourself when you sense that a competitive situation is turning into rivalry:

1. What is it about my success that is making the other person feel bad about herself or himself?
2. Is there something about my manner that creates a sense of jealously rather than healthy competition?
3. In what way does my winning make the other person feel less of a person?

If by analyzing the situation you can build the other person's self-respect or find a way to help her save face, you can probably lessen the stress for both of you.

For example, if you have been successful with a particular project, don't talk openly about your success: Don't brag about authority you've been delegated. Don't talk about your special assignments that turn out to be more fun than work. Don't brag about the important people you're hosting for a company tour. In fact, bragging about special treatment will probably embarrass your boss and may even result in the loss of these privileges. Try to enjoy your victory without rubbing the other person's nose in her commonplace situation.

Remember, however, that people feel jealous for many reasons other than goals for which they're competing. They may be jealous because you work for a higher-ranking boss, have a better work assignment, have more authority, or get preferential treatment such as flexible hours. Sometimes they feel jealous because you have more education, are younger, are more attractive, dress better, or drive a nicer car.

Finally, if you've done everything possible to build the other's self-esteem and lessen the rivalry and hard feelings still exist, it may help to remember that jealousy is just a part of human nature. If you're a top performer, you may have to learn to live with others' jealousy.

Criticizing Peers

Why is "constructive" criticism almost always destructive? Because what usually matters is how the criticized person feels, not the criticizer's intentions. Therefore, you should be aware of the effects of even your well-intentioned remarks for a co-worker's "own good."

Analyze the situation before you attempt to offer criticism:

- Do you always look for what others do wrong rather than what they do right? What are your own perceptional hang-ups that may be fostering inaccurate judgments? Are your comments meant to merely condemn past actions, or will they really guide the other person's future action?

- Will the criticism improve the other person's outlook, performance, and your working relationship? Will he or she be the kind of person to improve or to merely become depressed or angry and give up all efforts?

- How many times has this person heard a similar criticism before and not made changes? What makes you think your comments will bring improvements where others have failed? Do you have more authority? More insight? More motivational information or rewards to share?

- Can praise be just as effective as criticism in bringing about a change? Many people have a frugal attitude toward praise, thinking that others should do what is expected without having to have someone pat them on the back for the effort. But praise has a powerful ability to make the "should" seem more attractive, workable, and worthwhile. People are generally more motivated to *improve* something good than to *redo* something bad.

- Could you use a problem-solving technique, rather than criticism, to bring about change? For example, if a co-worker has difficulty with a customer within your hearing, can you later help her reflect on the situation in the following way: How did you think it went with that customer? That's not usually the way you handle things, is it? Why do you think his behavior upset you this time? What do you think we should do to prevent this the next time he comes in or calls? In other words, lead the other to assess the situation and plan her own improvements.

If, despite all these screening questions, you decide that it is appropriate to criticize a peer, give great care to your approach:

1. Understand the situation before you give the answer. Some people shoot out criticism as it rolls through their minds, leaving the hearer to sort out what's applicable and what's not. As a writing consultant, I know from experience that consultants who walk in with all the answers walk out very fast. Clients must explain their situations, problems, and needs before they can trust the consultant's answers to be the right ones. Before you begin to tell someone how she can do things faster, make sure you know why she is doing things as she now does and make sure that speed is one of the criteria for judging an effective job.

2. Separate fact from opinion. Did the client say the figures were miscalculated or that the report was misleading? One is a factual statement; the other, opinion. Don't be guilty of passing off your opinion as fact. Perhaps you should check your perception against that of others who observe the same behavior.

3. Criticize yourself first and assume some of the blame. Perhaps public relations is why the editorial "we" has come into use: "We have a problem that needs resolving..." Or, "I must not have explained this procedure well because some of the details are still missing. I need to ask you if you would please..." Even when you are in no way involved with the difficulty, be willing to shoulder some of the blame simply because you have the ego strength to do so.

4. Don't analyze why someone does or feels a certain way: "I think you simply refuse to be on time for these meetings because it really makes you feel important to keep us waiting, doesn't it?" Never assume someone has behaved badly or botched a job on purpose. Perhaps she lacks maturity, knowledge, or needed skills. Analyzing only serves to humiliate, embarrass, anger, or all three. Simply deal with the behavior, and leave motivations to the psychiatrists.

5. Include some credits with your criticisms. Credits not only encourage the other person but also add weight to your criticism. If she admires your good sense in recognizing her

strengths and successes, she will also sense your attempt to be objective about her weaknesses and failures.

6. Don't get personal; criticize only the viewpoint or behavior. Not: "You're being immature about this invitation list. None of the secretaries are invited." But: "I can't include you on the invitation list, because none of the secretaries are invited. But I don't think Ms. Wyatt's leaving your name off was meant to offend you, and I do think you may regret going without an invitation."

7. Use phrases that build, not destroy, goodwill. Not: "Let me tell you something..." But: "We need to discuss something..." Not: "You're doing that backward." But: "I've got an idea for a faster way to do that."

8. Be specific, not general. How can someone properly respond to a criticism such as, "You're not cooperating" or "You're careless"? Try: "I need for you to keep a record of every incoming call for the next two days. This past week three very important messages have been misplaced."

9. Avoid what psychologists call the "halo" and "pitchfork" tendency. That is, avoid the tendency to focus on one good or bad trait or behavior and let that impression overshadow your opinion about everything else. Even contest judges make special effort to guard against this "halo" or "pitchfork" phenomenon by insisting that all contestants make their entries anonymously to ensure objectivity. In other words, simply because Marsha is a poor typist, don't assume that she is also a gossip.

10. *Never* say *always*, *totally*, *completely*. "You never tell me ahead of time when we are going to have to work late to handle these invoices" generally brings the response, "Yes I do; I called you last March when we had that contract with Belton Corporation." The hearer focuses on the absolute word in your statement and immediately supplies the evidence to shoot holes in your blanket comdemnation. Criticisms that begin with absolutes usually revolve around

exceptions and seldom get the desired results in changing the habitual viewpoint or behavior.

11. Criticize to some end, and offer your help with the resolution. One of the prominent characteristics of destructive criticism is that it only applies to the past. To be helpful, turn your comments into a challenge for the future or a mutual goal, if possible. Be willing to help those you criticize see a purpose and find a solution to what you're criticizing. Don't simply berate their negligence.

12. Don't belabor the point. On occasion we all feel the compulsion to explode with, "Okay, okay, I hear you." Translated that means, "You told me already and already and already." Most people are acutely aware of their weaknesses. What they need is someone with solutions and challenges to improvement.

13. Is the time right? Before you pronounce your judgments, make sure you know what the individual's other concerns and problems are at the present, both at home and at work. Are you sure that this comment of yours won't be the proverbial straw that breaks the camel's back? Sometimes we are fooled by an outer facade of strength, ego or pride, when the person may be near to crumbling on the inside. Sensitivity to time and place is never more important than when you're criticizing on the job.

Receiving Criticism

Although many criticizers began their comments with "I hate to say this, but...," most people don't hate giving criticism nearly as much as receiving it.

How do most people respond when they are criticized? The first, almost automatic reaction to criticism is to deny its validity. Usually the comeback is an outright, "That's not true." Or perhaps it begins, "Yes, but..." followed by excuses or reasons the evidence shouldn't be taken at face value. When someone criticizes your ideas, there is a tendency to marshal forces and argue your own position more forcefully instead of holding the ideas up to the light for closer scrutiny. It is to your advantage to squelch the almost instantaneous reaction to deny and to take time to examine what has been said.

Perhaps you need to stall for time to make the appropriate examination: "I haven't considered my views (or behavior) in that light; I would like to have some time to think over what you said. May I phone you later today?"

A second common reaction to criticism both justified and unjustified is to *counterattack.* "Well, sure, I took it upon myself to make that decision without consulting you because you never responded to the phone message I left." Be assured that most of the discussion to follow such counterattacks will center on anything but the real issue. Even if the criticizer has faults that you think contributed to your criticized behavior, it is more effective to listen to the other person's perception of the problem with an open mind. Admit your shortcomings and express interest in finding a solution. And *then* explain how you think the other's behavior contributes to your problem—or better, can contribute to the solution.

A third common reaction to criticism is an *emotional collapse*: humiliation, embarrassment, tears, depression, resignation. This reaction generally comes from people who have trouble separating ego from performance. When someone comments to Sheryl that she has misspelled a word, she takes it to mean that she needs remedial spelling classes. We all have known people like that. Being able to separate behavior from personal worth seems to be more difficult for some people than for others.

A fourth reaction to criticism is to calmly *accept all that is said as "absolute truth."* People have a tendency to apply the same passivity to medicine and exercise. If it tastes bad and hurts, it must be effective. Although we may maturely "take it like a man," the criticism may be inaccurate altogether and hinder your forward progress if you put too much stock in the critical judgment.

So what is the proper response to criticism? Instead of denial, counterattack, emotional collapse, or total acceptance, try to evaluate criticism objectively:

First, *assess the source of the criticism and examine the criticizer's motives*. Second, *gauge the emotional climate of the situation*. Is this something the person was saying at an emotional time when she was extremely angry or in an overwhelming predicament? Or was this criticism made at a time when she was calm and collected in her thinking?

Third, *reevaluate your own perceptions of yourself and try to substantiate the criticizer's claims in light of other opinions.* Have other people offered the same criticism to you? Do you hear similar comments at home? Did you hear them in your school setting? Has your boss mentioned the same criticisms to you? If so, perhaps you should listen and make changes.

Fourth, *react to the criticism only insofar as it applies to your goals.* For example, if someone criticizes the way you have the plants arranged in your office and you are not interested in becoming "Interior Designer of the Year," forget the comment.

And finally, *learn what you can from the criticism and discard the rest.* If you've made a mistake, admit it. Correct the situation for the future, and you will have turned it into a valuable learning experience for your career. Channel any emotional upset and energy generated by the criticism into correcting the problem. Then if you're still upset, use leftover emotional energy to restructure your files, type a new telephone list, reword your form letters—whatever is necessary to channel that energy into productive work.

The next time someone says to you, "I don't mean to be critical, but...," listen and learn.

Office Affairs

This section deals with office dating and office affairs as one general subject because often the repercussions are the same in the work place. Of course, the effects if both of you are unmarried are less consequential than if one or both of you are married. Nevertheless, the political situation around the office is still affected for several reasons.

The problem with dating anyone from work is that secretaries in particular have long been stereotyped as sex objects, and you only feed that stereotype by succumbing to the pressure to date someone from the office.

If, however, you feel that you want to begin or continue a relationship and that you are willing to take the repercussions that may develop in the company, you may try to determine the company's position on office affairs: Do men and women travel together alone on business, or does the manager always send four, five, or six people to a convention or a seminar? What kind of comments are made about males and females traveling together? Does the boss ever talk about company image and "avoiding all appearances of impropriety"? From these comments you can infer the attitude your boss or the company may take concerning an office relationship.

Remember, dating relationships and office affairs are never secret: People—

Notice the longing looks
Overhear the conversations at lunch and over the intercom
Calculate the extra time spent in one another's office
Smile at the pats when you think no one is looking
Resent irregular hours
Scrutinize your coming and leaving together
Wonder about your long conversations over work

You can minimize this public knowledge of the dating relationship to some extent, at least, by not dating people in your department or those you come in contact with regularly. But even if your "interest" works in another department, news travels. Love life in the business world is rarely private.

Also, you'll have to be aware that everyone will have opinions about the affair and who's being used by whom. This is particularly true if the secretary is unmarried and the man married: Others think that the affair is bad for her reputation and that he's "getting away with" more than she is. Consequently, many conclude that the woman is not too bright for letting the relationship continue.

Now to the "side-effects" of an office affair. First, management fears the office affair for several reasons: There's the loss of professional objectivity about any given project. Bosses may fear that confidential information will be passed from one area to the other. Also, they are concerned about productivity when your mind is always on the other person and how much longer until lunch when you can see him. Naturally, your work tends to take a back seat to the love interest.

Additionally, there's always the cry of resentment from peers, particularly if you're dating a superior. And even if you're dating a peer, others in the office may complain that your superiors are allowing you special privileges just to carry on the affair. The affair can also make your peers angry; they realize that when your mind is not on your work, then they are going to have to pick up the slack.

Some will lose respect for you because you have become one of the stereotypes. When you go to watch a star-struck lover in a movie, that's one thing. But when you're assigned to work with a star-struck lover at the next desk, you lose patience.

Of course, when the dating relationship is over, there are even more serious consequences. The couple may find it difficult to be civil enough to each other to work together on a project. If they constantly make snide remarks to the "ex," others around them will feel particularly uncomfortable. Then, when the affair breaks up, there is the uncomfortable situation of dealing with comments of sympathy, advice, and "I told you so's" from others around the office.

And finally, not to be overlooked as a consequence of dating someone in the office is the actual loss of your job. In several situations secretaries report being aware of exactly what cost them their jobs. In one situation where the boss was having an affair with his secretary, the staff was very fond of the wife, who had frequently volunteered her services there in the small business. When the husband and wife split and he married the secretary, everyone else in the office resigned.

Another secretary tells of a situation in which the secretary to the president was having an affair with the owner of a parent company. Consequently, this secretary was allowed to take off Friday afternoons and arrive late on Monday mornings to take long weekends—to fly out of state to be with the president. Of course, the others in the office had to pick up the slack for her and began to resent her special treatment. When they complained to their immediate supervisor, he insisted that his hands were tied about correcting the situation. Finally, the secretary having the affair had to transfer out of the corporate office into a branch away from all other people she knew. Eventually, the relationship ended, and she left the company.

If all these side-effects sound a little too much, keep your social life outside the office. Here are some suggestions for turning down an affair or simply a date invitation:

Mention your spouse frequently or "the person I go out with." This sometimes serves to put off further invitations. If not, you may want to reject the man but save his ego: "I've got so many other interests in my life now that I simply don't have the time to date."

Another way of rejecting an invitation is simply to ignore the remark or advances, to change the subject, or to give the person a cold shoulder. Or, try to make light of the situation; tease or laugh off the invitation. Make the other person think that you don't take him seriously, and many times he will back down rather than risk rejection.

Finally, as a last resort to rejecting a persistent person, refuse an invitation loudly so that others will hear: "No, I'm sorry, I'm not able to go to such-and-such. I do not date anyone from the office." This will, of course, embarrass him and cause him a sense of rejection, so you only want to use this as a last resort to get your message across. And, of course, often you may be able to limit your opportunities for harassment or invitations by avoiding this person. And when you are thrown together, initiate small talk that puts you at a distance.

Particularly with married men in office romances, be wary of all the different lines you hear. If you are unmarried and would be open to dating, you will hear the old "My wife and I are separated" routine. You may hear "My wife is terminally ill. We haven't had any relationship in a year." Or maybe the "I'm old enough to be your father" routine, in which case you can always agree with him and hope that you have wounded his ego enough to leave you alone.

Etiquette When Lunching, Traveling, Treating, and Generally Shuffling Around the Office

Lunching

Much of the confusion today on matters of etiquette centers around the question of the new roles men and women play in the business world.

First on the matter of business lunches, don't assume that when someone of the opposite sex invites you to lunch it's a date invitation. Do consider accepting the lunch invitation for several reasons: 1) to establish or strengthen informal business associations; 2) to cultivate other workers; 3) to learn more about the business in other departments that may affect your work; and 4) to discuss details of a mutual project.

And, of course, there are also lunches to evaluate prospective employees transferring into another department and lunches to celebrate someone's promotion, raise, accomplishment. So for any of these reasons you may find yourself lunching with the opposite sex.

Generally, you can assume that when your boss invites you to lunch it is for a specific purpose—either to celebrate a raise or promotion or to discuss business—and that he or she will pay for that lunch.

On occasions when you want to host lunch to cultivate another employee or to maintain a social contact, you can make sure the other person understands that you intend to host in one of several ways: You initiate the invitation and set the time and place. For example: Not, "Let's have lunch sometime next week"; but, "Could you have lunch with me next Thursday, say about 1:00, at Romera's?" And, of course, as host you should arrive first. If for some reason you are later than your guest, you should apologize and then let your guest precede you into the restaurant or dining area.

A stronger way of suggesting that you plan to host is to make reservations ahead of time. When you walk into the restaurant, you introduce yourself and tell the maitre d' you have reservations for a certain time. If you arrive earlier than your guest, introduce yourself to the maitre d' and explain that you have reservations and are expecting a guest; ask that your guest be shown to your table when he or she arrives.

And, of course, as host you will ask for the check. You can signal to the waiter, lay your napkin on the table, or stand up to let the waiter know that you are ready for the check. Don't be conspicuous about paying for the meal, particularly if you're with a man who may be uncomfortable that a female is hosting. Paying with a credit card is generally the easiest way to handle that situation; most men don't feel too offended when all you do to pay is sign your name. Another way to make the paying less conspicuous is to do so beforehand. Make arrangements for the restaurant to bill your company directly. If you frequently host vendors or out-of-town guests, ask your supervisor for an expense account or direct-billing arrangements.

When you are the guest, you should wait in the lobby for your host to arrive. If you arrive after your host, make sure that your host selects the table. Also, the pace of the meal and what you eat should be set by the host. When the waiter asks if you would prefer drinks, turn to the host. If the host returns the question to you, say, "I will if you will" and leave the decision to the host. Or, if your host orders an alcoholic beverage and you prefer not to, you may order a virgin drink or soda. Again, the same rule is true of an appetizer. When you both order the same courses, the meal tends to be a more equal sharing.

In this day and time men no longer order for women unless an older women prefers that arrangement; therefore, you do not have to feel uncomfortable at all about expressing your order directly to the waiter as a host or a guest.

About smoking, always ask permission and don't smoke before everyone at the table is finished eating. Particularly keep an eye on the direction your smoke is going; move the ashtray and be considerate of the other person.

It is assumed that when a group gets together to go out to eat, each individual pays his or her own way. When the group intends to go "Dutch" and you are making arrangements, suggest several restaurants in varying prices (expensive, moderate, and inexpensive), and ask the rest of the group for opinions.

If for some reason you happen to be with a group of males who seem uncomfortable with your paying your way, continue to volunteer but don't embarrass them by being too insistent. The simplest way to split the check when there are several colleagues is to take turns paying. However, this can be a problem if you don't get together often or if some meals are elaborate while others are fast-food dinners. Then you run into two other problems: Who hosted last time? Is this meal more or less than the previous one? Therefore, a good way to handle most group lunches is simply to split the check.

Traveling

When you're out of town with a group to attend a seminar or a convention, remember that such occasions are business, not social situations. When you go out for an evening on the town, it's an extension of the work day.

Meet the others of your group in the lobby so that all of you travel together. Also, plan to end the function when you are together in a public place, such as the hotel lobby or the restaurant. If a male offers to escort you to your room you can always make the comment, "No, that won't be necessary. I've really had an enjoyable evening." Then change the subject to other topics.

Whatever you do, you want to avoid appearances that suggest

you view the situation as a social encounter. Keep in mind that most executive women who take their career seriously suggest that you politely refuse to turn a business situation into a social one.

Deferring to Status

People have any number of ways to express their status around the office. One of those ways is going through doors and getting on elevators. The higher the status, the first on the elevator and the first through the door. Technically, a male boss should go through the door before a female subordinate, but some men defer that privilege and traditional etiquette wins out. If you are hosting guests, then hold the door for them no matter what. Other than these two general rules, the first person to a door holds it open for the others.

"Pet" Names

When you permit someone in the office to call you "honey," "dearie," "sweetheart," "lover," or any other "affectionate" term, this habit reflects poorly on you as well as the name-caller. Try not to embarrass the other person in front of others, but if pet names are a recurring problem, privately suggest that the terms bring to mind put-downs in your past work experience and that, of course, you wouldn't want to identify him with such.

And, of course, there's nothing wrong with an outright statement: "I prefer that you don't call me 'dear,' 'honey,' 'sweetheart,' or whatever." Or, when someone calls you those names, you may try to make your point with a flippant, "Gee, I didn't know we were on such intimate terms." Chances are that if you smile when you say it, the other person will not be offended.

Telephone Privacy

If you are in someone's office and a personal call comes through, excuse yourself politely with "I'll step outside until you finish the call." If, on the other hand, you have a personal call that comes through while someone is waiting in your office, either ask the caller to phone you again in a few minutes or ask the visitor to excuse himself: "Will you excuse me? I have to take a personal call. Would you mind waiting in the receptionist's area?" Generally, the visitor should be given preference to the caller.

Attending Formal Company Functions

The problem in handling various social functions such as retirement dinners, farewell drinks, award banquets, or gift-giving situations is that relationships cannot always be taken at face value. There are always political repercussions to evaluate. Therefore, people "in the know" will tell you that the best company social "perk" is a day off rather than a business party disguised as a social affair.

If you have occasion and think you should attend these after-hours functions, avoid the following traps:

Don't huddle with cliques, particularly known to be antimanagement or malcontents. When superiors see you with these groups, there tends to be guilt by association. So at company picnics, cocktail parties, or luncheons, circulate rather than fall in with one particular group.

If you happen to get stranded socializing at a cocktail party or luncheon or to be caught with the "wrong" group, you can always glance over your shoulder and comment, "Oh, there's someone I've been wanting to speak with. Would you excuse me please?"

And if you find yourself alone at a cocktail party, simply approach two other people who are talking and begin smiling and listening until they turn to you. When they turn to you, they will introduce themselves or say, "We were just talking about..." You can either introduce yourself in turn or comment on the subject: "I overheard you talking about so-and-so, and I have a particular interest in that subject because...," then join their conversation.

Another precaution about attending business affairs disguised as parties: Be careful about drinking and "telling all." A colleague of mine once broke this rule by getting drunk at a business dinner. As we left the restaurant, she began to compliment me on my work and say that she would like to make me director of the department. But because the salary was not much more than my current one and the details more involved than I wanted to handle in what I considered a dead-end job, I told her I was uninterested in the position. Consequently, she began to lament about her only remaining choice for the job with very derogatory statements. The following morning as she recalled the specifics of our late-night conversation, her embarrassment was apparent.

Another trap is the invitation line: "casual dress." Don't take this too seriously. And remember that "casual" doesn't mean "grubby." When in doubt, dress up rather than down.

Finally, the question arises as to whether to attend company functions alone or to bring a spouse or date. If spouses are invited and they want to attend, feel free to have them do so. But if you would like to attend alone, that also is perfectly acceptable. If you are accompanied, however, you as a woman will tend to be accepted more easily if the function is one at which most males will have their wives along. You may be viewed as less of a "threat" or a "free date"—whichever the case.

Making Arrangements to Acknowledge the Guest of Honor

If you are called upon or think you should take the decision in hand to honor a colleague with a birthday, raise, or promotion celebration, refer to Chapter 6 for specific details. If the prospective honoree (your boss or colleague) says no to a party, you should abide by his or her wishes. However, when a person insists no celebration or no party, he or she does not necessarily mean no recognition.

You can acknowledge an event in one of several ways:

- A small gift and a gathering for presentation of the gift
- A memo sent out, recognizing the accomplishment or the event
- A card, note, or clipping on the bulletin board
- A message from top management to be distributed throughout the office
- Flowers, cake, or candy
- A suggestion such as, "Let's all get together to go out to lunch in honor of so and so's accomplishment."

All of these ways will give peer recognition and still not put the employee on the spot.

Making a Presentation to a Peer

You, as a close friend or associate, may be called upon to make a presentation (comments, certificate/award, or gift) for a group of employees to wish someone well on a retirement or to announce a wedding, job transfer, resignation, or whatever. Please do not feel that your being appointed to act as host in this situation means that you have to assess the person's merits and demerits or begin with "once upon a time" and go through that person's biography until he or she "lived happily ever after." Simply explain what the occasion is and why the presentation is being made. Then single out the person's main qualities or contributions connected with the occasion.

If you are presenting a gift, remember that the gift is a symbol; stress the *reason* for the gift rather than the gift itself. As a presenter, remember that you are not the center of attention; the recipient is. Make sure that most of the time is allotted for that person's remarks. Being too long or lavish embarrasses everyone.

Be careful about assumptions. Not everyone who is retiring is happy to be doing so. Not everyone who is transferring to another department is doing so voluntarily. Not everyone who is going to a *new* job feels that it is the *better* job.

In general, remember to keep the presentation to the point and be specific about the event, honor, and praise. Specific praise and factual statements of accomplishment or contribution sound more sincere than overblown comments, which often come across as phony.

When you have been selected to choose the gift for someone else from your group, remember that your gift should not be personal. Either perfume or cologne is a borderline situation; both may be considered a little too personal for the average office. You may want to consider a high-fashion item such as a scarf or billfold. Another suggestion is to choose utilitarian gifts for home or office: pen-and-pencil sets, picture frames, flowerpots, plants, health-club visits. If you know the group well and want to reflect a light occasion, you may choose a gag gift. Finally, rather than a gift, you may instead consider a gesture of friendliness or camaraderie such as, "Let's all go out for lunch together." Or, arrange to have a cake or flowers delivered to the office in lieu of a specific gift.

As for paying for the gift, never buy a gift and then tell others how much they must contribute to cover the cost. Gather the funds first; then shop. If people ask you how much you need, you may simply relate "average" contributions: "I think everybody has been putting in $2 to $3. Do whatever you like." Make sure that you handle the donations privately or individually in such a way so as not to make anyone who doesn't want to contribute uncomfortable.

If you're on the contributing side and feel you have overspent your gift budget, you do not need to give a reason. Simply say, "I really wish I could afford to contribute, but I can't this time."

Being Guest of Honor

Modesty and sincerity are in order here. Showing your feelings is okay—that you are pleased with the honor—but you should avoid resorting to clichés such as "I'm overwhelmed," "I don't know what to say," "I just can't express what I'm feeling." And your bursting into tears will make your fellow employees even more uncomfortable.

Simply accept any gift and express your appreciation specifically. If you can make some specific comment such as, "I've really been eyeing these pencil-and-pen sets ever since I saw them advertised. I thank you so much. Maybe I'll throw away my word processor and go back to longhand and the legal pad." And then later, of course, you may want to type a thank-you note and post it on the bulletin board or circulate it in the usual manner.

When You Are Promoted Above a Peer

When you are promoted above peers, they will probably sit back and depend on you to establish the new relationship. You'll find it difficult to maintain a close friendship with them. But do show them that you do not plan to "lord it over them."

Communication either verbally or in a memo that now you are in a position to help them is a good approach. Mention your intentions to recommend that secretaries get more training than they've been provided in the past, to improve their work environment or equipment, to help them get the recognition they deserve, or to get them assistance in career guidance. In other words, plan to take on much the same position as a newly elected politician. Promotion above your peers is an accomplishment, but it can also be a matter of responsibility.

In general, though, you must expect the old peer relationship to change. You may want to ease out of a chummy relationship while still maintaining a friendly contact by inviting a group of your old colleagues to lunch with you occasionally. Or, go to lunch with them one-on-one infrequently. But gradually decrease the frequency until you have eased yourself into the new supervisory relationship required for you to be effective, as described in Chapter 3.

When a Peer Is Promoted Above You

Expect the best from her. Demonstrate a positive frame of mind and show her you are willing to cooperate. If you had wanted the promotion, it's natural to be disappointed; but don't sulk and get your relationship off on the wrong track. If it was a "one-winner" situation, acknowledge that you were disappointed because you wanted to assume some of those new responsibilities. But take the lead in congratulating the promoted peer and expressing your optimism that you both will be able to work together.

Don't back yourself into a corner as one executive secretary did. She sulked for so long and had made such a to-do leading up to the promotion that when the colleague was promoted, she left the company out of embarrassment. Don't be phony, however. Specifically, let the other person set the pace for how the new relationship will be.

Remaining Neutral in Peers' Squabbles

Some squabbles you can stay out of by treating them with humor. For example, when you hear an "exchange" escalating into a heated discussion, try something humorous such as, "Hey, are you people going to need a referee? My rates are cheap." Such comments will often embarrass peers into recognizing that they are making the rest of the office uncomfortable.

Occasionally, you can mediate an escalating situation by speaking with arguing peers separately to clarify the situation as you see it, to play down their differences, and finally to concentrate on the facts rather than on their *interpretation of the facts*. For example: One co-worker comments, "I really don't see why they've done away with messenger service. I spend my time going from desk to desk, delivering messages when we used to be able to pick up the phone and call a runner to take these papers to other floors."

The second co-worker responds: "I disagree. The messenger service was a real drain. We were paying those people just to deliver eight, 10, maybe 15 messages a day. I don't understand why any company would hire an in-house messenger service."

You can step in at this point and emphasize that whether they agree on an inner-office runner as the answer to the situation, they do agree on the inconvenience of having to deliver messages themselves.

Often, people who are immediately involved in exchanging views don't really listen to the other's position. Instead, they are planning what they want to say next. Avoiding a break in their relationship may be as simple as your helping both sides to clarify what they are and are not saying.

Second, when you do help people to clarify their positions and to see that they are not in direct disagreement, try to turn the conversation into an "exchange of views" rather than an all-out attempt to prove the other wrong. Interrupt their conversation with a summary of both sides; then tack on some neutral comment of yours: "Well, you both present a good case for such-and-such; however, the problem at the moment is, how we're going to handle Mr. So-and-so when he arrives." The neutral subject provides a transition. The silence that follows will tend to ease the feelings from the previous discussion and make the others walk away thinking they've merely exchanged differing viewpoints rather than "had an argument."

If neither of these first two attempts work, suggest that your two peers table their discussion before something "more serious" develops: "Come on, let's change the subject. You are making us (or me) uncomfortable." Such a statement puts them on the spot and usually will end the open disagreement.

But when a disagreement cannot be turned aside easily and when you find yourself in the position of being go-between, you will need to take more specific steps:

First, keep in mind that you should treat both people with respect and show no favoritism. And when I say treat both peers with respect, that means to treat them as individuals with the right to their feelings and the right to be upset. Many people trying to mediate a conflict between disputing peers act as if both are spoiled children arguing over candy. If the issue is important enough to the other two people to argue about, then you will get nowhere by implying those involved are childish, foolish, stubborn, or closed-minded. Refusing to take sides also means that you will not agree with one position and then try to "talk the opposition over to the other side." This mistake is the reason many mediators get scratched and bleed during the thorny untangling of peer squabbles. If you have agreed with derogatory remarks about the other person; and the two finally are reconciled in their relationship, both may turn against you. They may be be embarrassed by comments they've made to you and drop you out of the relationship altogether. If you are forced to take sides on an issue, make sure it is the issue you endorse—not the person representing that issue. Your taking sides in one disputing person's mind may mean only that you smile and nod approvingly when the other expresses an opinion.

Second, as a mediator, try to work with both sides separately to clarify facts and to formulate solutions that both can live with. Look for areas of agreement and allow both parties to save face. Remember that when mediating, you must deal with facts, not the conflicting peer's interpretations of the facts. Consequently, it may require much digging on your part to get the essentials of what was said and to cut through the innuendos and feelings that have been attached to the facts.

A third principle in mediating a conflict between your peers is to pass on complimentary things each has said or felt about the other in the past; express your confidence that they are willing to work out the situation. Of course, you will not want to be phony or make up complimentary remarks; but if you can remember one peer's showing respect for the other's accomplishments or procedures, pass on those comments.

Finally, in mediating a conflict, remind both people of their common goals for a good reputation, career advancement, and productivity for the department or company as a whole. In other words, let both of them see "what's in it for them" and "what's in it for the company." Both people will feel uncomfortable about thwarting an ongoing project that will have detrimental effects on the department or company. Their situation is much like a relay race on the playground. If one pouts and loses the race, he endures not only the wrath of one angry person but the wrath of the whole team who "loses" with the project or the sale.

If all of these efforts in mediating conflicts between colleagues fail, remember the old adage, "Live and let live." Above all, avoid being drawn into the conflict yourself.

How to Disagree Without Being Disagreeable

Do you recall the "is/is not" arguments of childhood when you and a peer finally had to appeal to a higher authority—a teacher or a parent—to set the situation straight, to mete out punishment, to tell who was right and who was wrong, to determine who won and who lost?

From nursery age onward, kids pick up the idea that those who disagree with them are enemies and those who agree with them are friends. So the name of the game becomes "making more friends than enemies" or "agreeing more and disagreeing less." For some, avoiding disagreement becomes a lifelong pattern. Many people smoulder under the surface and let their anger sabotage work projects, when verbalizing disagreement would bring about solutions to their problems.

First of all, before expressing disagreement, understand that two sides can be right, that two sides may have equal merit. No two people ever perform or carry out a project in the same manner. Some people prefer to send a memo, while others prefer to phone. Some communicate directly one-on-one, while others call a meeting. Both situations or manners may have equal merit, and workers need to get past the idea that there is one right way to do anything.

A second principle to keep in mind when you disagree with someone is to separate ego from your work, your possessions, and your opinions; then allow the other person to do the same.

When conducting business-writing workshops for corporate clients, I always note the close tie between employees' egos and the writing tasks they perform on the job. Workshop participants frequently share with me the bitterness they feel toward supervisors who continually edit their memos or letters for what they consider no reason at all other than "personal preference." To many people, having a memo criticized or edited is no less offensive than being told that the supervisor doubts the subordinate's basic honesty.

Work has become so attached to ego that many conflicts arise over disagreement or criticism of any performance on the job. Understand that when someone tells you that you overbooked the conference room or chose an unexciting luncheon menu, she probably does not consider you an inferior person.

A third principle in dealing with disagreements is to make sure that a specific situation merits your attention. We've just passed through a couple of decades of "let it all hang out" and "tell it like it is." With such encouragement, you need to be careful that you use an acceptable measuring stick for determining what is worth expressing disagreement over and what is best left alone.

The fourth consideration in handling your disagreement is to remember that people don't necessarily like or respect those who always agree with them. In other words, expressing disagreement is not necessarily going to bring down others' wrath upon you. In fact, several studies show that people who tend to disagree at first with a position and then are won over seem to be more highly thought of because they are not considered "yes men." Therefore, your agreement should be to solve a problem and not simply to avoid creating one.

The following guidelines should offer some help in your expressing disagreement when you feel you must:

Reduce or expand the opposing idea to it's ultimate end. That is, in a practical or calm manner lead the other person to see the full implications of what she's saying. Make a statement or ask a question that will cause the other person to rethink the issue: "All right, if we rearrange the office as you have suggested and move all the desks to face this direction, we will need to find a way to coat the front windows to avoid the glare for guests who are sitting on these couches. What would be your suggestions on that?"

This nonthreatening manner will help the other person understand all that's involved in her original idea and may lead her to change her mind. Or, she may at least modify her position to accommodate any objections you have. In fact, this technique can be so innocuous that most people won't realize you are disagreeing.

Examine the sources of both your and the other person's information. Perhaps the basis for disagreement is incorrect data or details. Confirm the basis for your opinion or your objections, thereby suggesting that the other person do the same: "The reason I said that we should lower the budget allocation for this particular expenditure is that I talked with Sue Gibbons last year about the funds contributed to this charity; she said the charity itself had suggested only a $700 donation. How exactly did you arrive at your figure of $2,000?"

The following discussion of the proper budget allocation then should center on getting the most reliable information on which to base a decision. Also, sharing your sources allows the other person a graceful way to save face; her disagreement or error, then, seems natural or logical due to inadequate access to correct up-to-date information: "Perhaps you didn't have access to the most recent figures that came in this month's XYZ report, but one article said..." lets the other person dismiss her previous idea in favor of your more recent or reliable information.

Use analogy when you can. Try something such as: "I think the difference in these two computers is comparable to the difference between a manual mimeograph and a copier that collates." Or, "Attempting a project like this would be like trying to cut my lawn with a pair of scissors. I don't think we would ever make any headway."

Use your own experience or history. Having no facts or sources of information, you can always identify your own experience or that of someone else in your department as your basis of disagreement. Personal experience is difficult to refute. But before you use personal experience, consider the possibility that your experience is not applicable to a particular situation.

Talk "around" the subject rather than through it. Don't force someone to make you disagree. Simply use silence; withhold an opinion. You may have to refuse directly: "I'd rather not express an opinion on that"; "I haven't given it enough thought"; or, "I'm too busy right now to get into that; maybe we can discuss it sometime over lunch."

Often when someone brings up a subject of disagreement, she is not necessarily trying to force you to express your opinions but merely wanting a forum to express hers. To avoid conflict, grant that forum and then withhold your own views.

Use words that emphasize agreement rather then disagreement. Not:

- "I don't agree with you."
- "You are absolutely wrong."
- "You are dead wrong about that."
- "You don't know what you're talking about."
- "Oh yeah? Says who?"
- "Yes, but...,"

- "Yes, but you don't understand..."
- "Someone told you a lie."
- "Someone misinformed you."
- "Listen, people, I'm afraid that you've got the wrong picture."

All of these comments emphasize areas of disagreement and put both of you on the alert to be defensive.

Whatever you say, don't force the other person to lose face. Instead, give the person credit for what he says and then state your opposing view in a positive way:

"It's interesting that you should say that, because I've got just the opposite feeling from reading the same journal. I interpreted the author to mean..."

"I'm glad you brought up that subject and your feelings. I, too, have been giving that a lot of thought, and, while I don't quite see the situation as you do, I think that we can agree to postpone or to change the procedure in that..."

"I understand what you're saying and (not but, which emphasizes contradiction) it also seems to me..."

"You could be right. There is more than one way to look at the situation."

All of these statements and phrases show acceptance of rather than disagreement with the other person's opinion. When disagreeing, you want to sound like a court witness rather than a prosecutor or defender. A matter-of-fact tone and careful wording takes the pressure off the other person to play judge and reach a decision about the issue in question.

Additionally, when you're part of a group decision and you're outvoted, then go along wholeheartedly. If a project fails and you do not meet your deadlines, the others will tend to cite your disagreement and balking as part of the problem. On the other hand, if things do not turn out as the group hopes, others can't blame you for the situation. They will remember only that you were the one who offered an alternative way to handle the problem.

Again, then, disagreeing does not mean that you have to become someone's enemy; making waves doesn't necessarily mean making enemies if you know how to sail through choppy waters. In fact, if you save someone from a costly mistake by expressing opposing views, you may turn disagreement into quite an agreeable situation.

Resolving Your Own Conflicts

Our mothers taught us that ladies do not make scenes; and then to counteract this advice, some assertiveness experts told us *not* to *avoid* making scenes. Somewhere between rolling over and playing dead and standing up for our rights loudly and dramatically, there's a happy medium.

An executive secretary tells of a particularly embarrassing situation: A co-worker, who was frequently absent, scolded her for not leaving important telexes on her desk until her return to work. The secretary responded to the reprimand as follows:

"I would leave them if you were ever here."
"Shut up."
"I'm sick of your big mouth."
"And I'm sick of your whole face."

Several people heard them, the secretary recalls, and "that was not good behavior."

Another secretary mentions a conflict with a woman who had invited her to attend her church; when she refused to accept the invitation, the co-worker gave her the cold shoulder and tried in every way possible to intimidate her. In fact, the co-worker lied about the secretary, saying she had not done certain assigned work and announcing in a meeting that crucial reports weren't ready because the secretary hadn't typed them. This secretary, then, had come to her own rescue by looking through the in-box on her accuser's desk to find a report that had been buried and unfinished.

Another minor conflict a secretary related was the problem with riding the company van. Her boss called her in at the last moment to run an errand, and the driver of the company van left without her. Consequently, she was stranded downtown with no other transportation home. The boss, of course, became angry the next day when he learned of the incident, calling the van-pool driver to reprimand him. The driver, then, continued to take his anger out on the secretary.

Most of our conflicts, thank goodness, are not of this ongoing, vicious, verbally abusive kind. But many smoulder underneath the surface.

So, should you avoid conflict at all costs? Be assertive at all costs? Force yourself to remain in a situation of conflict?

None of the above. Long-term conflict can be injurious to both your physical and mental health. Long-term conflict diverts your time, your energy, and your thoughts away from specific goals and usually results in poor job performance.

So because conflict has potential for both good and bad, the question becomes, how do you resolve conflict while it's ripe for positive benefit and before it becomes detrimental to you and your organization?

Generally, people handle conflict in one of three ways: You can overpower the opponent and force her to accept your solution. You can do this through the boss, having your solution come down from "on high." Or, if you have authority in your department to force your method or your procedure on the other department, you can do so yourself.

The second method involves your withdrawing from the conflict, giving up on your goals, and completely closing down the channels of communication. You choose to have someone else take on a certain project because you simply do not want to reap the consequences of carrying it out.

The third way to deal with conflict is to seek compromise. You find common goals and improve communication channels enough so that you both solve your problems and reduce tension along the way.

What causes conflict?

Conflicts arise on the job from different viewpoints of a problem, loyalties to certain persons in the company, competition for financial resources, competition for power, competition for recognition, access to different facts, or various interpretations of the same facts.

We also have conflict due to age differences. Sometimes older people who are surrounded by younger ones see themselves as "in the way" and feel insecure in their job. They may feel as though others are looking down on them because they have not progressed further. Or, they may feel resentment when another person seems to think that a job or a cause to which they've devoted many years has been a "waste of time" or a "rip-off." And, of course, younger people sometimes think loyalty to a company is ridiculous. Or, they may think that older people are just "putting in their time," reaping undeserved privileges, benefits, and salary.

Another kind of conflict involves a conflict of values. People or procedure. For example, you may work in an office where employees' self-esteem is a high priority—whether the work does or does not get done on time. Or, you may work in an office where the work is paramount, regardless of how people feel about themselves or each other.

Unlike the other causes of conflict, a conflict of values cannot be solved. If you have a conflict of age, methods, procedure, resources, or needs you can restructure situations so that conflicting sides can both be in a winning situation. However, if you have a conflict of values, such as overdeceptive advertising campaigns or expense-account practices, these conflicts usually cannot be solved to the satisfaction of both parties.

The following guidelines should help you confront and resolve all but the "value" conflicts in a manner more conducive to accomplishing your goals:

Confront privately on private issues. When someone attacks you verbally in front of others, try something like: "I see that you are upset. Let's talk things over privately. Why not in my office or yours?" Then immediately direct the person to another area so that you don't have a crowd of witnesses to the difficulty. Direct, angry confrontations make onlookers uncomfortable.

But do let the other person vent any emotions privately. As long as there are pent-up emotions, there is tension; and the other person is thinking of his anger, embarrassment, or whatever rather than the problem at hand and how it can be solved logically.

But if the other person continues to shout and refuses to control his or her emotions in front of others, then rest assured that onlookers will generally side with the person who is the cool underdog—the one who minimizes the conflict.

Researchers Jay Hewett and Morton Goldman reported (*Journal of Social Psychology*) results of a study involving how people receive hostile criticism and how the audience views the way various people handle criticism. These researchers discovered that the person who was under attack was seen in the best light by his audience when he could successfully defend his own position with logic and reason; when he treated his attacker in a courteous, friendly manner; and when he tried to establish and maintain good relations with the criticizer or angry other person.

If the verbal attack is minor, such as a reprimand for a late report, either shrug off the attack or answer with cool logic and kindness.

One real estate secretary mentioned a conflict with one agent who continually called her down in front of clients for not taking what he considered "complete" messages. Rather than reacting to these constant put-downs and belittling remarks at an inopportune time in front of clients, the secretary chose a time when the agent was alone. She went to his desk and asked to speak to him about "something that had been bothering her." She expressed exasperation in not being able to handle his calls as he wanted them handled, asked specifically what directions he had for her in handling future calls, and then explained what limitations she had in taking "complete messages" for 10 agents.

When confronted in a private way, he was very meek, agreeing that she had been handling his calls to the best of her ability within her time limitations. He stopped the put-downs. This, of course, would not have been the case had she yelled back at him in front of others. Instead, the issue would have become a struggle of egos.

Deal with conflict promptly. An unresolved conflict can grow until it cuts off communication and cooperation between people. Conflict spreads much like gossip. Each time a story is told the punchline gets bigger. In the same manner, each time a conflict comes to your mind, the hurt, the tension, and the frustration cut deeper.

Treat the other person with respect. By respect I'm not talking about sugary sarcasm, always accommodating or agreeing with the other person. But I am suggesting that you permit the other person to feel like a free agent, not a trapped insect. Show respect by giving attention to what the other person says, by a tone of voice that is neither patronizing nor antagonistic, and by word choice that is neither derogatory nor threatening.

Listen until you understand the other side of the issue. Many people have what writer David John calls the hit-and-run approach.

These people start a conversation about the conflict, hit the other person with their feelings, and then walk away before the other person has a chance to respond. This method of confrontation tends only to build resentment and prolong the difficulty rather than to work through it. Often you can completely calm your opposition by simply inviting the other person to explain the conflict or problem as he sees it. And then really listen. You may surprise yourself, finding that you agree with his perspective; and then, of course, you no longer have a conflict!

State your own needs, feelings, views, or goals. Occasionally we fail to give others a chance to meet our needs because we never even ask. Don't resort to your "ultimate" resolution, resigning your job, before you ask for the adjustments you want. Rather than referring to a "time-consuming project" or a "meaningless meeting," be specific about your objections. Unless you are willing to be clear about your needs, conflict discussions can be only one-sided. People can't be mind readers.

Define areas of agreement and disagreement. I'm sure you've sat in lengthy meetings in which people kept repeating areas of agreement for fear of upsetting anyone. But they felt compelled to continue the discussion, because the real conflict lurking in the background hadn't been outlined and attacked, much less resolved. Thus, they keep talking in circles saying nothing new. Possibly you too have met with another person on occasion and yet left feeling that nothing had been accomplished. Instead, you tiptoed around each other's sensitive spots. It should not be an embarrassment to you to admit having to settle a conflict.

Limit discussion to the here and now and keep to one issue. You will never resolve the "problems we have with the accounting department." Instead you need to talk specifically—about a problem you have "in processing travel reimbursements," and how to correct the specific situation. Then gradually, on other days, at other times, in other places, you can work out general "problems with the accounting department."

Guard against character attacks. It is very dangerous to play analyst. For example, don't make statements such as, "If you were not basically a lazy person, you would not be overwhelmed and sick and off the job two or three times a month." Simply describe the person rather than calling her lazy. Not: "It seems that you try to make this audit report more difficult to read every month, that you have something to hide." But rather: "I'm still having trouble understanding the audit report in this new format. Would you answer some questions for me?"

Don't back the other person into a corner. Offer the other person options. Ego is a precious thing. Stripped of all reasons and/or excuses, people feel exposed and grasp at straws to cover their responsibility and their viewpoint.

Rather than always looking at conflict as a negative situation, most offices should also look at its positive effects, of which there are many. First, conflict helps us to gain a better understanding of ourselves—our own emotional and physical reactions. Conflict may lead you to analyze, justify, or discard your own methods or beliefs about a situation.

Additionally, conflict may result in better decisions rather than mediocre ones. When we communicate openly and are unafraid to express disagreement over the method, deadline, or type of work, then the company as a whole profits by uncovering minor problems that can be dealt with before they become major ones.

Finally, conflict makes work atmosphere and life in general more interesting. It sparks curiosity; it adds spice to a project or organization that would otherwise be monotonous over a long period of time.

chapter 3

COACHING THE TEAM UNDER YOUR SUPERVISION

Supervising other employees is a new experience for today's secretary. In the past, she has performed personally every task her supervisor assigned—typing, filing, phoning. However, now that companies realize how many more judgments a secretary can handle, they have assigned clerks to help her with the workload.

Unfortunately, companies have often failed to provide secretaries with training in such skills as supervising, delegating, hiring, firing, evaluating, and mediating. The reasoning possibly is that since the secretary will supervise so few—maybe only one or two employees—training costs will not be justified. Nevertheless, this training is essential; as with a manager, a secretary's own effectiveness and career are on the line according to the productivity of those she supervises.

Thus, the following introduction to the skills necessary in making people productive:

Hiring

Before you can coach, you need the players.

With little more than "Ms. Schultz, why don't you find someone to help you with the clerical work on a full-time basis?" from the boss, you may find yourself in the role of interviewer.

Touching first base, of course, is contacting the personnel department for referrals of those who may want to transfer into your department or those applicants who have wandered in off the street for an interview. Other sources for possible job candidates will be employment agencies, local colleges, newspaper ads, and word-of-mouth.

While you're waiting for applicants, prepare yourself for your hiring decision. You'll need skills in four areas:

Social: How much do you know about human nature? Can you "read" people? Are you aware of your own biases and motives that may affect your interviewing skills?

Communicative: How well can you establish rapport with people and get them to give you information about themselves? Can you establish rapport while remaining neutral and objective?

Evaluative: How well do you interpret facts? Does your reasoning lead you to valid, well-supported conclusions?

Decision-making: Can you decide if a person matches your job? Can you determine what a person needs to be successful in a job? Can you act on your decision and work to bring about the desired results of your decision?

If you have time, read the advice of experts such as Felix Lopez, Henry Morgan, John Cogger, Richard Fear, and Richard Irish. Brief guidelines from these interviewing experts follow:

Start the hiring process by requiring an application. Even though the person has handed you a resume or even though you've had a glowing recommendation from a friend, seeing how someone fills out an application at least tells you if she is functionally literate. The resume may have been prepared by someone other than the applicant, and the referring person may certainly have overstated the case. Furthermore, a completed application gives you an idea of writing skills, spelling skills, attention to detail and thoroughness, neatness and pride in work, and reasoning skills in interpreting questions.

Additionally, if your own personnel department or an

employment agency has not given a typing and spelling test, you may wish to screen employees with those tests before wasting time on an interview.

Planning the Interview

Steel yourself against the tendency to do the talking. You should not talk more than 15 to 20 percent of the time—those comments in establishing rapport at the beginning, asking questions, describing the job, and summing up the interview and next actions.

That means for the remaining 75 to 80 percent of the time you will "set your applicant up" for talking about herself. Focus on the following discussion topics in the order listed: work experience, education, personal history and early home background, present goals, and finally how the person thinks she would like or fit into the job under consideration.

The first few times you interview, it will probably be best if you prepare a written set of questions.

Conducting the Interview

Take notes during the interview. Some experts estimate that an interviewer forgets approximately 50 percent of what the applicant says. Note-taking is particularly important if you interview several people and if there will be a lag between interviewing and hiring. If you sense that your note-taking distracts the applicant and makes her feel uncomfortable, the next best thing is to summarize your impressions immediately following the interview.

Before beginning to take notes, explain to the person that you are taking notes so you can remember everything she would like you to consider. Stop taking notes when the applicant begins to say something negative; otherwise, she may have second thoughts and withhold valuable information. You can always make a quick note of the negative when the interviewee resumes talking in more positive areas.

Finally, remember that you are only taking notes, not acting as court reporter. Jot down key ideas but never try to write everything the person says; you'll miss general impressions and nuances about the answers.

Following are guideline questions that will lead you through the basic structure of the interview: establishing rapport, gathering information from the applicant, describing the job, matching applicant to job/self-assessment:

Establishing rapport: While you look over the application, you give the applicant time to look over you and your office and become more at ease. Rather than beginning with questions, start by making observations about things you see on the application form:

"I see you were born in Omaha. I have a cousin there who sure likes the city." Or, "You graduated from Kennedy High in Del Rio? Sounds like a small school much like the one I came from." Or, "I see you worked over in the east part of town? Is the traffic worse there than here?"

In the absence of an application to review, you can make comments and let her elaborate on the following topics:

"How did you find out about the job opening?"

"I understand Bob Jones told you we were looking for someone in our office."

"Did you have an opportunity to walk through the place and see what goes on around here?" Or, "As you may have noticed when you came in, we're adding another wing to the building on the north side."

You may comment on a project you have at hand: "As you can see, we're hard at work on a major project—budget justification."

And, of course, there's always the weather.

Such questions and comments put the applicant at ease and give her a few minutes to understand that this will not be a hostile, stressful situation.

Gathering information from the applicant: Here are several broad and then specific follow-up questions to help you discover more about the person:

1. Tell me about your previous jobs, starting with your first job and concluding with your last or present job. What were your specific duties and responsibilities there? What did you like most about the job? Least? What duties did you perform the best? Were there any special achievements there? What was your beginning and ending salary there? What did you like best about your supervisor there? Least? What kinds of people do

you work with at your present job—what kinds of personalities or work styles? How would you describe the work environment there? Why did you decide to leave that job?

2. Tell me something about your education. What subjects did you do best in? How were your grades? What about special academic or extracurricular achievements or honors? Have you attended any self-development courses since you've been in the work force? Do you have any plans for further education?

3. Tell me a little about yourself personally. (Be careful here because in this category you may be asking questions that are discriminatory and are acceptable only if they are asked of both males and females. Much depends on the implication and intent of your questions.) Tell me a little about your family. What hobbies do you enjoy? Would there be any objection to working overtime occasionally? What do you consider your greatest strengths? Weaknesses? What accomplishments give you the greatest satisfaction? How do you handle crises? How do you handle deadlines? (You may even pose hypothetical situations and ask how she thinks she would react). What are your career goals?

When asking any of the above questions, keep in mind that your manner of asking determines to a large degree the answer you get. For example:

- Keep your voice at a conversational volume and tone. Soften questions with introductory phrases such as, "Is it possible that..., Would you say then that..., Has there been any opportunity to..., How did you happen to..." You don't want to come across as prosecuting attorney. "Tell me about your experience..." sounds less threatening than "What experience do you have?"

- Don't telegraph the answer you want: "The job will require a lot of computation. How are your math skills?" Or, "This is a really laid-back office with little direct supervision from the boss. Would that atmosphere bother you?"

- When asking a sensitive question, explain your reason for asking: "The reason I ask about your having small children is that part of our benefit package is reduced tuition in our company-owned child-care center."

- Asking what is "the *most* or *least* or *one*" anything can make an applicant nervous and pause with indecision. Better to ask: "What are some of the most..."

- Use qualifying words and phrases to help the applicant admit weaknesses: "might, maybe, to some degree, somewhat, would you say a slight problem in..."

- Establish a common evaluation criteria for comparison so that you both understand the answers: Instead of, "Do you like typing long technical reports?" Try: "Do you prefer being assigned major projects such as typing long technical reports or having responsibility for several shorter, nontechnical documents?" "Did you enjoy the accounting job or the receptionist job more?" "Why?"

- When the applicant seems blocked or puzzled about a question, give a multiple choice: "You said you didn't get along with your previous supervisor. What was it about the situation that bothered you—too much or too little supervision? Standards too high or too low? Personality conflicts?"

- Use the calculated pause to get the applicant to elaborate when you'd like a fuller answer. By maintaining eye contact and waiting, you signal the applicant to keep talking.

- Make a habit of commenting after the applicant answers a question: "I know how that goes." "I understand." "Those things sometimes happen." "That sounds interesting (exciting, distressing)." By showing an accepting attitude you help the applicant be more revealing about weaknesses that may show up on the job.

- To stop an applicant from rambling or to close the interview, interrupt with a closed question: "What was the date of that clerk-typist job with the insurance agency?" "Did you say you have your own transportation?" Bringing her to a factual answer stops her and gives you a chance to lead the discussion in another direction.

- Demonstrate your openness with a pleasing facial expression and body language. Don't furrow your brow or cross your arms as if you have closed out the applicant. Instead, lift your eyebrows, smile occasionally, lean forward in your chair as if you're interested in what's being said.

Describing the job: Tell the applicant a little about the job, briefly or elaborately, depending on how interested you are in pursuing this applicant at this point: Mention the overall function of your department or office and how it fits into the organization as a whole. Explain the kind of service or product you provide. Mention specific duties and what percent of her time would be devoted to each duty.

Be honest in your description. If the job is a monotonous, tedious one, say so. The person you're interviewing may have an active social life or an emotionally draining situation at home and welcome the routine, "boring" job as a relief from constant demands and decisions. Also, mention the other personality types she would be working with and to whom she would report, if someone other than you. If she will report to you, be open about your expectations and how she will fit into your productivity plans. Mention the salary for the job.

Match the job to the applicant: The applicant can often help you conduct the final part of the interview, an advantage to both of you. Keep in mind that no matter how talented, educated, personable, or attractive the applicant is, if she doesn't fit the job, she will fail miserably. And that failure reflects badly on your judgment.

Lead in to the self-assessment with these questions: What do you think you could contribute to this job? Is there anything about my explanation of the duties, work atmosphere, or other people that causes you some concern? What things do you think you would enjoy most about this job? Least? What types of people do you get along with best? Least?

Remember that your questions about people skills may be the most important questions of all. Personnel specialists and various studies suggest that more people fail on a job because they can't get along with others rather than for lack of technical job skills.

When you ask about these social skills, put the applicant at ease by explaining that nobody can be expected to get along with everybody. But emphasize that you would like some reading on personality types that cause her the most or least difficulties. (Of course, this line of questioning applies only if the job calls for contact with others.)

Remember that if you help someone formulate a list of strengths, she will more likely be willing to reveal her weaknesses also.

Finally, don't oversell the job. An office manager of an insurance agency says that she makes the situation sound so good that no applicant leaves her office without "drooling" for the job. Such zealousness will eventually work against you. If you say the job has variety when it is in fact monotonous, what have you gained after spending two weeks training someone and having them resign a month later?

Summarizing and closing the interview: If you've determined early in the interview that you are *not* interested in hiring the candidate, you will, of course, be brief in all the above areas. For example, as you describe the job, you may simply tell the duties in broad categories, failing to mention others she will be working with and omitting salary and benefits.

It is a good idea not to tell the person on the spot your decision not to hire. Make notes to yourself about the reasons for your rejection; and then in a follow-up phone call or letter, explain that the job is not right for the person. Always leave the applicant's confidence intact by explaining that you are aware she has valuable skills, and/or experience. In your later call or letter, explain that you feel *this particular job* is not right for her or that you have found someone more qualified for the job. Then thank her for her interest in the position.

Even when you are interested in hiring the applicant, don't promise a job on the spot. Rarely do you have that total responsibility without discussing the situation with your supervisor.

To end the interview: "I will discuss your qualifications and the job further with my supervisor, and we'll let you know of our decision in a few days." Or, perhaps you prefer to suggest a date for the applicant to call back for your answer or to come back for a second interview.

Evaluating the Interview

After the applicant leaves, spend time collecting your general impressions and considering not only what was said but how it was said and what implications the answers may have for the particular job. Did she answer questions in a quiet, intelligent way or with a sarcastic, belligerent tone?

What kinds of things are you looking for? Generally, a pleasant manner and neat appearance. Ability to listen and to talk in an organized way. Good attitudes about responsiblity, supervision, co-workers. Attention to detail. Quickness to learn and general intelligence. Enthusiasm for a better-than-average job. Initiative, ambition, energy. Values. Personal goals. Emotional maturity—does she want a mother? Social skills such as sense of humor, tolerance, even-tempered disposition, friendliness, and communicativeness.

As you consider the presence or absence of these traits, guard against the halo or pitchfork tendency. For example, don't let one strength or weakness overshadow your evaluations on other points. Don't assume that because the person is well-groomed that she will also be self-confident and assertive. On the other hand, if she tells you that she doesn't work well with overbearing people, don't assume that she is necessarily shy, withdrawn, and quiet.

Finally, when you evaluate the information you've gathered, make sure your reasoning leads to valid conclusions. For example, rather than quickly judging someone who has held four jobs in as many years as flighty, consider that the person may have been overqualified for the jobs she held and therefore bored.

If the applicant says she disliked something about a past job, consider these points: Did she dislike the task to the degree that she wouldn't be happy in another job doing that task only 10 percent of the time? Did she not enjoy that task because she had not been trained properly? Or, did she dislike the task for other reasons? In other words, note cause-and-effect relationships.

Hunches are fine. But if you can't follow them up with evidence, give them up. Psychologists are now telling us that whereas intuition used to be looked down upon, there is a logical basis for it. Possibly, when you have a "hunch," that feeling is based on clues you've observed subconsciously from body language, voice tone, or dress. Avoiding the word *intuition*, men, too, are now admitting to acting on hunch or "a gut feeling." Nevertheless, you will feel better about your hiring decision if you gather tangible information to support your hunches or gut feelings.

Finally, verify your evaluations by checking references. Of course, most references will be favorable or the applicant would not have listed the reference. If, however, you can talk with direct supervisors, you may gain further information. Be mindful, however, that many are reluctant to give unfavorable references due to possible legal difficulties and may give you only "name, rank, and serial number" answers.

A phone interview is better than a written request for reference for two reasons: First, some references are reluctant to commit unfavorable comments to paper. (If difficulties arise, they can always deny things said to you on the phone.) Second, you can learn much through how facts or opinions are given. Is there a pregnant pause before the answer? Is there reluctance to give details about attitudes? Does the reference keep talking in general terms?

Remember, however, that an unfavorable reference does not necessarily mean the employee will not work out in your job. Probe to find the whys behind an unpleasant situation. See if the applicant's details of a situation check out.

Decision to Hire

Finally in the hiring process you must compare all applicants and make your choice. The most frequent mistake in this step is that of making apples-to-oranges comparisons.

In other words, you may not have equal information on all applicants: You may have asked different questions to each applicant. You may have forgotten answers. You may make snap judgments with some people and tune out the remainder of the interview. You may interpret your information unevenly with different standards of judgment. You may have interviewed with a different approach or attitude or in a different environment—either more or less stressful than the rest.

Guard against these uneven comparisons when selecting the right person. And remember that the right person for one job is not necessarily the right person for the next job. The key factor should not be "whom do I like best" but "who best fits the job I want done."

Welcoming New Employees

When your new employee reports for work, introduce her to your boss and to others with whom she'll come in contact around the office. Higher-ranking people and older employees are to be honored in the introductions; therefore, you mention their names first. "Mr. Warren, I'd like you to meet Sylvia Waters." Use first or last names—whichever they will likely use for each other later.

When you introduce, make a few explanatory comments to give the new employee and the older worker something to make conversation about: "Mary will be working with me primarily on the word-processing projects. She's had a lot of experience at XYZ Corporation before coming here." Turning to the new employee then: "You'll be in frequent contact with Joanne because she handles all our requisitions for office supplies."

Or, if you're a large office, you may want to handle only a few introductions personally and introduce the new employee to the rest of the office by way of memo. In the memo, mention that Mary Smith is joining your company in such-and-such a position, to do whatever tasks, reporting to so-and-so. Then give a sentence or two about her work experience, previous jobs, or education. Finally, add a personal touch—mention a few personal details such as a hobby or hometown. Be sure, of course, to clear those details with the employee. These introductory comments, then, will serve as a beginning of conversation between the new and older employees.

If you haven't already done so in the job interview, give the new employee the "big picture" of the organization and explain how your department fits into the whole. Then summarize how her job fits into the smooth operation of your department and office.

Show her around the building, pointing out restrooms, cafeteria, snack bars, elevator banks, supply cabinets, and so forth.

Don't overload and confuse the employee with all the information about retirement plans, stock options, time sheets, insurance, vacation, rules and regulations until she has been around for a few days or weeks. Learning about what task she must do immediately is enough for the first few days. These other details will be forthcoming from the personnel department.

It's always a nice gesture, also, either to include her in your plans for lunch on the first day or to arrange for another worker to invite her along.

Finally, put her at ease. Show a tolerant, patient atmosphere and a willingness to help. Don't give her the impression that it's a solo "sink-or-swim" situation. Make sure that she knows you do not expect her to master the job in eight hours and that mistakes are not immediate cause for dismissal.

Giving Clear Instructions

Ideally, you already have a desk manual for the new employee with "everything she ever wanted to know about her job without having to ask you." If you don't have such a manual, while you're training this new employee may be the appropriate time to develop one.

In either case, first outline the various categories of things the new employee needs to know: what supplies are available and where to get them; forms to be used and where to find completed examples; typing tasks to be performed and where to find samples of layout; how to use, maintain, and occasionally repair equipment; how to file and where to find offsite files; how to use the telephone, along with proper screening techniques and greetings; how to find and use reference books such as secretarial books on grammar and writing, company policy manuals, annual reports, and product or service brochures; how to handle the mail; and any other procedures for doing her tasks.

When you begin to move through these various topics of training, avoid these common errors:

Don'ts

Don't give the trainee too much information at once. Information overload can frustrate the new person to the point of paralysis.

Don't get impatient. Just because you think someone who's worked in an office before *should* know thus-and-so, that does not necessarily make it so. When you show impatience—raise a shocked eyebrow when asked a question, sigh when asked to repeat something, smirk when discovering a mistake—you make the learner tense. And when the trainee becomes tense, the learning curve goes down.

Remember that every person learns at a different pace. Some nod readily and accept hasty instructions as if they understand completely—then do everything wrong. Others may ask innumerable questions, write every minute detail down, and want a demonstration from you of how to operate every machine—and then do everything correctly ever after. Don't form snap judgments about how someone will or won't work out and begin to lose your enthusiasm for training her.

Now to the do's. Follow these basic guidelines in teaching most all tasks:

Do's

Tell the trainee what you want her to learn and what the finished goal or product should look like. In other words, tell her the standards by which you will judge a good job. For example: "Eventually, I want you to be able to put a rough draft of this technical report into final form with the appropriate headings and white space, although the engineers don't always give you their drafts set up in the proper format. Finally, you will be responsible for rechecking the addition of all columns of figures."

Break tasks down into steps or stages before you give details. "Basically, the requisition procedure involves four steps: 1) an agent's request to you; 2) your putting that request into the correct typed form; 3) approval from Mr. Smith; 4) submission of justification to Ms. Orvall's office."

Gather for her or tell her where to locate all materials, forms, examples, and equipment necessary to do the job. "Somewhere over there" and "up on the second floor" are inadequate explanations.

Make sure you have the learner's attention before instructing. If she is shuffling papers, taking a phone call, thinking about an embarrassing mistake of mispronouncing the boss's name, wait. Undivided attention is a must.

Write complex instructions down or talk them into a recorder. With many details to the job, you may find that your writing instructions or allowing the trainee to write as you instruct are too time consuming for you. If that's the case, consider dictating your comments onto a cassette tape. Because this method is fast, you will tend to give more complete directions and more elaboration. Also, the trainee has the added advantage of being able to replay the tape as necessary when you've moved on to your other duties.

Mention any safety precautions to be taken before she does the task and repeat them again immediately before the step in which they are involved. For example, should old work sheets always be kept for a certain length of time? What should she do in case of power failure? Where should backup storage disks be located for safekeeping? What should she never do with the only set of keys to the copier room?

Show or demonstrate the procedure. Not: "The files you'll need for this assignment are up on the fourth floor in the north wing; someone up there can show you." But: "Let's walk up to the fourth floor, north wing, so I can show you how these reports are filed." Don't just tell how to make an acetate transparency on the copier; make one.

Give details in some logical order. Use chronological, geographical, most-to-least significant, or whatever arrangement seems most appropriate for the subject.

Have the employee demonstrate or explain a procedure back to you. Don't just ask, "Do you understand?" The new employee may be eager to please and say she understands even if she doesn't. You cannot check misunderstandings until you have the other person repeat back to you or demonstrate understanding.

Explain the whys behind things. People need to understand the whys to be able to cope with things that don't work out just as you or someone else said they would. And when the unusual comes up, that person will need to make a judgment call; "whys" always help.

Stay in the "instructor" mode, not the fault-finder mode. Emphasize the positive. Give compliments on a job well done. Turn errors into learning and coaching situations. Do not expect perfection at the beginning.

Always use the "you" approach. Not: "The reports will need a cover letter before they go out." Who's supposed to prepare the cover letter? Rather: "You will need to type a cover letter for these reports before putting them on Ms. White's desk. You'll find a sample letter entitled 'Budget.Cov' on the computer."

Train properly the first time. Hasty instructions may get you through and onto your own work that first day or two. But you will eventually find that the follow-up questions, the interruptions, the do-overs will amount to much more time than if you had given adequate directions in the beginning.

When, What, Why, and How to Delegate

Some secretaries find that "hiring help" doesn't automatically mean they themselves will have less to do or be able to get more done. Even with clerical or messenger help to perform the routine tasks, some secretaries still operate under the philosophy, "It's easier to do it myself," or, "If you want it done right, do it yourself." These secretaries haven't learned proper delegation.

Why delegate? First, your helper is encouraged to see how she fits into the total picture of a project rather than doing little piecework projects that have little meaning. Second, the employee develops her skills and becomes more versatile. Third, delegation spurs initiative.

And what's in it for you? You have more time to do the more interesting aspects of your job. You can take on more responsibility from your boss, freeing him or her for more important tasks. Finally, you develop your own supervisory skills.

What to delegate? Repetitious, routine tasks. Details that take exorbitant amounts of time. Tasks that require few judgment calls. Tasks that will be an occasional "reward." Tasks that will help the employee learn new skills.

Granted, there are understandable fears and problems in delegating: 1) You may be a super-intelligent and efficient person to whose standards no one else can measure up. 2) You may have grown up thinking there is only one "best way" to do things. 3) You may be afraid you will lose control or credit for the project. 4) You may refuse to allow mistakes. 5) You may lack the organizational skill to balance your and other's workloads. 6) You may lack the organizational skill to oversee and follow up on someone else's project. 7) You may not be able to give clear instructions.

And, of course, because delegation is a two-way affair, you may have difficulty delegating due to an employee who doesn't want to be bothered with thinking for herself, to an employee who doesn't like you or want to do projects in a manner that will please you, to an employee who is overdependent on someone to call every move for her, or to an employee who is already overworked.

Thus, before delegation will work, you may have to change your own frame of mind or that of the employee to whom you wish to delegate.

How to take the fear out of delegating? Set up periodic checkpoints for your approval and direction. Make sure that these checkpoints and deadlines allow you time to correct any errors. For example, if you delegate arrangements for a certain meeting, you may establish these checkpoints and controls: Ask the employee to come back to you after she had composed a list of possibly interested attendees. Suggest that she contact caterers XYZ, ABC, and DEF about price, menus, clean-up service, and report back to you before making her final selection. Then mark your calendar to check with her two weeks before the meeting to make sure invitations have gone out.

In other words, let her know what schedule to follow and then mark your calendar to follow up and confirm that she is on schedule. Then, let her know which decisions and actions she should take on her own and which decisions you'd like her to get your approval on.

Another way to take the fear out of delegating more important tasks is to turn a project over to a subordinate while you are available to supervise and answer questions. Then in your absence or with less supervision, you will feel more comfortable about the pending results.

Remember that people usually have a way of measuring up or measuring down to your expectations of them. And they are as willing or unwilling to make judgment calls and decisions as you are willing or unwilling to tolerate mistakes while they learn.

Improving Productivity

The way your office runs and how you are able to get your team to produce often reflects your supervisory style. In the best-seller *In Search of Excellence*, authors Thomas Peters and Robert Waterman, Jr., found that respect for the individual was a major tenet in the best-run companies of the nation. More and more top executives have modified their management styles to embrace the theory of participative management. In other words, they actively seek collaboration and suggestions from their subordinates about how things should be done. And I think one can assume that the individual supervisor, you in this case, shows respect for those supervised.

Examine the supervisory sketches that follow to see if any changes are in order in your style:

Blaming Bertha: This secretary gets most of the work done by digging out errors, assigning the blame, telling who should correct the problem, threatening about future problems and punishments, and waiting for the next thing that isn't "done right."

As a result, her workers become defensive, feel frustrated and give up easily, show resentment and anger, and never do more than asked for fear of making more mistakes.

Martyr Martha: This secretary does most of the work herself while her clerks sit around and watch. She complains about the heavy workload and how complicated all her tasks are—much too important and complicated to turn them over to someone else.

As a result, her workers are bored and spend most of their day chitchatting to pass the time.

Mother Marian: She spends most of her time thinking about how her subordinates feel about doing this or that. She encourages them to confide about personal problems and offers advice freely. Rather than letting them learn from their mistakes, she always steps in and rescues the situation, either punishing them for being careless or soothing them with "now, now, it's okay."

As a result, employees get little work done because something more interesting is always going on in their lives to discuss and get advice on. And because "Mother" is always willing to "cover" for their mistakes, they never learn attention to detail or stretch their competencies and develop new skills. In fact, sometimes they deliberately do things wrong to get "Mother's" attention. Occasionally, they become angry at "Mother" and rebel, seeing how far they can go—dress, absences, sloppiness—before getting a reprimand.

Nagging Nancy: Every sentence begins with "Haven't I told you..."; "Why did (or didn't) you..."; "What have you done with..." This whiny manner sets a negative tone and makes the nagger always seem irritable and angry. As a result, her clerks become discouraged because they never seem to get praise. They like to stay out of contact as much as possible because the atmosphere is depressing. They take up her time with constant reports of where things are, what they've accomplished, and what their next plans are. All of this information is a before-you-ask-me-let-me-tell-you defense.

By-the-Book Becky: This secretary doesn't care what circumstances may have changed or what problems you may have, the work goes on. The company policy is thus and so. She will get the work out over your dead body—literally. As a result, her workers usually accomplish much. But they as a group continually have "people problems"; they feel isolated, unrewarded, and used—as if they were robots.

Selling Sally: She provides all the information, resources, instructions, and motivation to do the tasks. She turns errors into problems to be solved in cooperation. She rewards with prestige, recognition, approval, and tangible "perks" when possible.

As a result, her employees feel part of a team. Because they join in both the glory or the consequences of the whole effort, they work to the best of their ability due to internal motivation, learn to take on more responsibilities, and take pride in a job well done.

Extensive supervisory studies reveal that competent, high-achievers trust their subordinates, expecting and wanting them to do their best. Low and average achievers usually think less of their subordinates, believing them to be incompetent and unwilling to do a good job (Glasgow, Robert K. "High Achievers..." p. 7).

If you as an office team are not as productive as you would like to be, reexamine your supervisory attitude and style before firing an employee that you've spent time and money training.

Getting Feedback from Subordinates

Many people get transferred or fired—or they resign—for what someone labels "attitude problems," a vague term that usually means no one has identified the real problem in the work relationship.

But competent supervisors value open, two-way communication

that allows subordinates to express their feelings and ideas. Supervisors of low and average competence are preoccupied with their own ideas, methods, and problems and listen only to their bosses. They only talk to, never listen to, their subordinates.

When your office is not running as you or your boss thinks it should, make an effort to get feedback from your subordinates. Perhaps the productivity problem is a matter of insufficient instruction, lack of resources, poor communication, uncomfortable location or atmosphere, or inappropriate deadlines. Or any combination of the above.

Personnel specialists tell us that most people leave a job not for more money or a better job but simply because they have the feeling that they're not listened to or that they don't get the respect they deserve; they don't have a sense of camaraderie with the supervisor or department.

Learn to listen to your subordinates. Do you hear only what you want or expect to hear? Do you ask for their opinions only when it's too late—after you've already made a decision or after you've missed a deadline? Perhaps through certain controls such as weekly desk audits you can spot work-flow problems and go to that worker and turn the situation into a problem-solving situation: "I noticed that typing that BGH report is taking longer than usual. Is there something unusual about it? Are there some difficulties we need to work out?"

Then listen.

Following are some common problems you may discover from their feedback along with tips on solving them:

Why are we changing things? We feel anxiety about changes and the why behind them. Your subordinates may fear economic changes—will her raise be withheld? She may fear changes will disrupt her personal life—will she have to reschedule her transportation or make new child-care arrangements? And possibly, she may fear change simply because habits are difficult and inconvenient to break.

Make sure you explain the whys behind changes and then move slowly.

Nobody asked me: People like to believe that what they think and feel makes a difference. That's why most companies encourage participative management—letting the subordinate have input to the decision-making.

When you can't give the subordinate complete say in a matter involving her work, give limited choices: "Both of these manuals must be copied and collated by 4:00. Would you rather find someone in another department who's not busy to help you, or do you want to call a temporary?" Or, "These petty-cash funds will be your responsibility from now on. Would you rather others tell you the details about the expense and let you enter it yourself on the petty-cash forms, or would you like the others to fill out their own forms and then submit them to you?"

In other words, ask for ideas, opinions, options. Permit choices where you can.

This bores me to death: Some people like a boring job that leaves them free to daydream about their personal affairs or gives them time to dry out emotionally from other problems. But if you have an employee who wilts under monotony, do your best to accommodate her by changing assignments, providing some incentives for superior work, changing the location or environment, giving more frequent breaks, or allowing her to assume more creative tasks as she shows competence.

Effusive praise over an "ordinary" task comes across as patronizing to the intelligent person. But you can, and should, give recognition. Mention that you appreciate the speed, the accuracy, or simply the results of having a monotonous job completed.

Yes, Ma'am, whatever you say: Some employees feel compelled to tell you only what they think you want to hear. If you say that you need a certain report typed by noon, they will nod as if expecting that they can do the job. But when noon strikes, they're hiding out because the task was impossible to accomplish.

Let your subordinates know that it is okay to tell you no. Tell them that you'd rather have a *realistic* answer about when they will finish a project than a positive one.

You don't treat us fairly: Relate the Biblical parable about the workers who reported to the vineyard at different times of the day—6 A.M., 9 A.M., noon, 3 P.M. and 5 P.M.—and all got paid the same price, and you'll soon discover that most people don't want to be treated *equally*. They want to be treated *fairly*. The two terms are not synonymous.

People want to be treated according to merit. But keep in mind that people have to be supervised differently because they have varying personal needs. And, at the same time, you must be careful to appear consistent in your treatment of them in similar circumstances, or you may create bad feelings among the group.

Some subordinates will be jealous of others who have more skills, experience, or knowledge in certain areas. In fact, they will tend to be more jealous of those closest to them in abilities than of those who far exceed them.

To minimize these jealousies that surface, take the "sting" out of a potentially rivalrous situation when one clerk gets a "choice" assignment by pointing out your criteria for deciding—special qualifications in essential areas. Then immediately pinpoint other avenues for the jealous individual to improve skills or take on more responsibility.

A particularly troublesome situation is avoiding feelings of partiality on special events such as birthdays. For some more popular secretaries in the department, friends may organize brief parties and order cakes, while for others, no one recognizes the special event. To avoid the appearance of partiality when you are supervising the group, try having a once-a-month celebration. On the last Friday of each month, order a cake and recognize everyone who's had a birthday or other special event during the month.

To minimize jealousies about special privileges such as leaving the office early or taking a long lunch break, treat individuals the same in the same circumstances. Beyond that, you have to make allowances for differing circumstances.

Well, at your age: Many conflicts develop due to age differences—the at-your-age-how-would-you-know attitude. If you supervise older employees, they may feel resentful that you had "all the breaks"—society's more open attitude about women in the work force, freedom to get more education, and financial resources. If this resentment is the case, you would do well to show the older person respect by deferring to her opinion occasionally, asking advice, and drawing on her broader experience.

Younger employees, too, show resentment toward older

employees. They may think, erroneously, that they are obviously incompetent or that they would be holding a higher position "after all these years." They may erroneously decide that the older worker has little initiative or drive. Make sure that you don't equate satisfaction with a present level of achievement with incompetency. There's no correlation.

I'm waiting on you: You may discover from some subordinates that you are interfering in their work—by constant interruptions and new instructions, by keeping them waiting for assignments, by oversupervising.

All of these kinds of constructive feedback will make you a better supervisor. Turn the feedback comment into a how-can-we-change-the-way-we-do-things discussion.

Countering an Attack by a Subordinate

You can distinguish between honest, helpful feedback and hostile attack in three ways: the emotional tone, the timing, and the logic behind the comments. I don't mean to imply that both kinds of feedback can't be beneficial, but simply that you handle them in different ways.

With the reasoning subordinate, you discuss in an open, orderly manner.

But when a subordinate lambasts you in a frenzied, angry tone at an inappropriate time and place for imagined slights or difficulties, then you must take special care to defuse the situation and keep the problem from escalating.

First, direct the employee to a private place and then let her "get it all out" before you probe, justify, or explain. Second, take time to think over what she has said. If you can't immediately see the cause of the problem or offer an explanation or solution, explain that you'd like to think over what she has said and set up a later time in the day to discuss the matter.

Third, when you've both had a chance to regain composure, begin a problem-solving discussion: Restate your understanding of the problem as the other person sees it. Let the individual know that you understand and accept her feelings, whether they are logical or not. Then give your explanation, criteria, perspective, or solution. Be clear about what behavior or action you expect from her in the future. And don't bring up her past mistakes, problems, or failures unless they have direct bearing on the problem at hand. Be as positive as possible, without embarrassing her further over the previous outburst.

Recognize that sincere praise and recognition go far in soothing an overly sensitive person. Try to stress the benefits for both of you in working out the problem cooperatively. Finally, try to reestablish rapport and a back-to-business-as-usual atmosphere as soon as possible after the discussion.

Giving Negative Feedback to Subordinates

Some secretaries think it's easier to correct errors or redo jobs assigned to their subordinates than to hurt the assistant's feelings. But consider the long-term effect of that approach: You're making it more difficult for the subordinate to please you and to learn to handle more responsibility. How will she ever improve if you don't tell her what changes you expect?

Mistakes due to lack of information, training, or skill are not the subordinate's fault anyway. If any of these are the problem, apologize for not providing the correct training or information and then help her overcome your own error.

If the mistakes are due to her own carelessness or negligence, you are doing her a favor to point that out. The top secretaries I interviewed overwhelmingly insist to their bosses that they point out errors to them so that they can correct and perform their jobs according to expectations. You should do no less for your subordinate. When you ignore the careless or negligent mistake, you convey the idea that it is unimportant and that the assistant can get by with less-than-efficient work.

Of course, errors occurring in one-time-only situations may best be corrected yourself. If the employee could not have recognized the error or will never have to perform the task again, that's another matter. Pointing out this kind of error may only discourage her or make you seem unreasonable in your standards.

Where to Give Negative Feedback

You may find that talking to a subordinate at her own desk stresses informality and an open, noncondemning atmosphere.

Summoning an assistant to your desk tends to make the discussion more formal.

But, wherever you choose to talk, make it a private place without interruptions or clues to those who may be watching that "Barbara is getting chewed out."

When to Give Negative Feedback

Don't give someone negative comments immediately before lunch or some other break. The comments will be fresh on her mind, and she will be likely to discuss the situation with whoever is within hearing—which may create more problems for both her and you.

If your assistant will be surprised at the comments and is alert in the early mornings, that may be the best time for a negative discussion. Then the remainder of the day, she has time to come back to you and add other details or feelings about the situation. She will not be going home immediately to brood over the situation, dredging up all kinds of imaginary implications and options to present in the morning.

On the other hand, if you think the subordinate will be terribly upset and unable to carry on throughout the day, wait until late afternoon for the discussion. She then will have time to think over the matter and work through her emotions overnight.

How to Give Negative Feedback

Plan what you want to say. Know exactly the facts of the problem and what changes in behavior or attitude you want. Otherwise, you may use less than clear directives and your language may be less than tactful.

Be specific. Don't say things such as, "You don't seem to be cooperating with other people." Instead, try, "When Mac Smith phoned our office for figures, he said you told him you didn't have time to look them up in the files. I want you to understand that in the future, requests from that department should always be given top priority over any other work I've assigned you."

Focus on the behavior or action rather than the person. Not: "You seem uninterested, as though you don't care whether we get the work done or not." Rather: "Typing that report yesterday took three hours; usually you can type that many pages in an hour. As a result of missing our deadline, someone will have to come in early in the morning."

Encourage the subordinate's own evaluation of the action, behavior, or performance. Often the subordinate knows when she is not performing up to par and will agree and respect you for expecting her to meet higher standards. And when the subordinate agrees with the difficulty, you can then turn the discussion into a motivational one. Try such guides as: "If you could do this over, what changes would you make?" Or, "How can I offer more help in making these changes?"

Use phrases that build rather than destroy goodwill between you:

Not: "How many times do I have to tell you?"
But: "Did you not understand my earlier instructions?"

Not: "You're doing it the slowest possible way."
But: "Let me suggest a faster way to do that."

Not: "That's not your place to take that kind of action without asking me."
But: "It's my responsibility to see that..."

Not: "I don't want to hear any more about it."
But: "If the situation changes significantly, let me know and I'll reconsider my position."

Make sure the other person understands the criticism. Don't assume she understands simply because she nods that she does. Ask her to verbalize her understanding of the situation now that you have discussed the difficulty.

Don't resort to "I told you so." Such a comment focuses more attention on your correctness and superior wisdom than on the assistant's action or behavior that needs to be corrected.

Voice the negative in a matter-of-fact tone rather than in an angry, spiteful tone. Particularly sift through personal feelings of disappointment and irritation so that the hearer understands you are dealing objectively with the issue.

Don't overcriticize. She can usually change only one behavior at a time. If you're discussing sloppy filing procedures, save your comments on spelling errors until a later discussion.

Never say *never, always, totally, completely*. When you use those words, automatically the other person becomes defensive and focuses on the one time when she can make you a liar. You say,

"You are always late." She comes back with, "I'm not. In fact, last Thursday I was 30 minutes early." Then the discussion revolves around the absolutes rather than the real issue.

Bring the negative around to the positive. In other words, tell the person the point of the discussion. Don't end with, "I'm upset about the typing errors that weren't caught in that report to the board of directors." Lead to the positive future: "Therefore, before any typing goes out of the office, I want you to have two other people proofread it. Correct any errors they find, and then leave the report on my desk for final proofing."

Encourage about the future but don't promise what you can't deliver. Don't allude to the fact that if this behavior changes good things, like raises or new responsibilities, will be forthcoming unless you can deliver. In her own mind, a subordinate often turns a maybe-someday comment into an unkept promise.

Shoulder some of the blame when you can. After all, coaches share the blame with their players when the team loses. "Perhaps I wasn't clear in explaining the necessity for backup copies of all discs. Do you understand now that such copies should be made twice a day regardless of how much work you have typed?"

If the matter is a serious one, let her know what action will follow if the problem is not corrected. Remember, however, that threats may cause an insecure person to become so tense that she gives up rather than improves. And never threaten when you can't carry through; your feedback will not be taken seriously in the future.

Above all, remember the true meaning of criticism. It comes from the Greek word ***kritikos***, meaning to discern or judge. That is, a criticism should be an objective description of ideas, performance, behavior, or action. Think of your role in giving negative feedback as similar to the book or movie reviewer. You judge the good and the bad of the object, situation, or performance. Your purpose is to communicate what your standards are and what should be changed to meet those standards and to motivate to make those improvements. Your negative feedback should ultimately encourage personal and professional growth.

The following special suggestions will give you help with specific, negative-feedback situations frequently facing supervisor-secretaries:

Inappropriate appearance: Subordinates who do not dress

appropriately for the office and who have poor grooming or hygiene habits present especially difficult problems to correct because it is difficult to separate the criticism from the person. Most people consider someone's hairstyle, clothes, makeup, or perfume to be an extension of personality. Therefore, much tact is in order.

Try something like: "Susan, I need to talk to you about an image problem. The company insists that we dress the way our salespeople (or customers) do. You never know when we'll have an important higher-up official or client drop in. So I need to ask you to wear something a little more appropriate for the office. Rather than culottes and sweaters, do you have dresses to wear?"

Or, "Susan, I like the perfume you're wearing, but I'm afraid several of our customers (or co-workers) may be allergic (or bothered) by heavy scents. (Or, I'm afraid our customers will have trouble keeping their mind on business.) Would you mind wearing less or none at all at the office?"

Personal telephone use: Appeal to the subordinate's sense of common courtesy. Explain that you hate to make arbitrary rules about when and how to use the telephone because emergency circumstances alter the situation. But consider these approaches: Explain that a casual conversation in front of customers presents an unprofessional image. A prolonged personal call in front of co-workers seems to indicate that she has a light workload and may create feelings of unfairness. Or, explain that time on the phone in personal calls is time away from what she is paid to do.

Profanity: Again, remind the subordinate of the unprofessional atmosphere or image she creates when using profanity in front of customers or co-workers. Certainly, remind her that she doesn't want to cause your company to lose a client by offensive language.

Housekeeping chores neglected: Explain that an attractive, organized work area is more conducive to efficient work. Also, emphasize that the look of the office often is one of the main criteria clients have for judging your products, service, or expertise in other matters. Finally, point out that her own reputation with higher-ups in the company is affected by a sloppy work place; a disorganized desk suggests a disorganized mind.

Emotional or crying subordinate: Keep your own composure. Suggest that your assistant take a break to regain composure and return to discuss the problem when her emotions are under control. Recognize and accept feelings, but don't let them deter you from making necessary suggestions for action. Be supportive after you have discussed the situation in a calm, reasonable manner.

Poor grammar: Whether evident in her speaking or writing, poor grammar tends to reflect badly on the person and the company. Like dress, comments about language skills make people especially defensive because ego is involved and because improvement does not come quickly or easily. Rather than trying to solve this problem through constant nagging, suggest (or insist) that the assistant attend a basic secretarial course offered through your company or by an outside consultant or university. Also, make available standard grammatical reference books and set an example yourself in checking questionable grammatical structures in the letters leaving your office.

Giving Positive Feedback to Subordinates

Some supervisors have a selfish "stroke style"; that is, they think that when people are performing as they should, it's unnecessary to call good performance to anyone's attention. But because someone *should* do something or is paid to do something is no reason to fail to give positive feedback. Everyone enjoys being recognized for accomplishments and good performance; *should*s are beside the point.

But remember when giving praise, don't do so with ulterior motives—to manipulate that person into even better performance or overtime hours tomorrow. Praise does often have a motivational effect; but when people see that motive, they feel manipulated and resentful.

To praise, be specific, not general: Not: "You did a good job in setting up the meeting." Rather: "I appreciate the trouble you went to in selecting this catering service. I understand that they had six menus to select from. Also, I noticed you were able to negotiate a better price than we got last year." Specific praise sounds more sincere and gives the subordinate time to "enjoy" your comments.

She always knows that you understand the effort involved in doing the job well.

Praise the performance, not the person. Not: "Mary is a superb receptionist." But: "Mary handled that angry client so well that he increased his order rather than canceling, as he had intended to do when he first phoned."

Praise publicly. When criticizing, make it a private affair. But praise is always more enjoyable when shared. If you praise the action rather than the person and you are specific rather than vague, you will not likely create jealousies among those not praised. More likely, they will focus on the performance that pleased you and be motivated to duplicate it.

Praise to make a good thing better. Notice the difference in your own motivation from these two statements: 1) "This newsletter layout is really attractive. If we can think of a better heading on this last item, it will be ready to go to press." 2) "This can't go to press until we think of a different heading on this last item." It's more motivational to "improve" something that already pleases than to "redo" something that's not right.

There are, of course, other ways to give positive feedback to those you supervise other than verbal praise. Try any of the following to show that you recognize and reward good performance: Give them more independence and less direct supervision. Vary their responsibilities to make their job more interesting. Teach them a new skill. Give them extra time off during a lax period. Circulate a thank-you memo for their contribution to a project. Spend extra time chatting with them.

Always be as willing to give positive as negative feedback.

Handling Disputes Between Subordinates

Try to ignore the one-time occurrences—misunderstandings that you feel sure will not be repeated and will not affect the productivity of your office. Only when the dispute escalates so that one or the other is not able to perform her tasks to your satisfaction should you take the conflict upon yourself to settle.

Most often when two of your subordinates involve you in their conflict, you should function as a mediator rather than judge. That is, you will lead *them* to discuss, reason, and problem-solve rather than make a decision about the conflict yourself.

As a mediator, make sure you treat both with respect and insist that they treat each other with respect. Don't nod and agree with charges against one or the other, smile knowingly, or sympathize with the predicament the other has "caused." Basically, you will help both of them sort out the facts in separate discussions. Tell each in advance about the discussion so that you will not take her by surprise and so that she will have time to "cool down" and collect her thoughts. Or, you may prefer to have each write you a memo describing the situation.

Then after you have separated fact from interpretation and helped both individually to see the real issues, discover each person's objective in the situation. If you think they can do so without emotional upset, then get them together to work out a solution that will meet their needs to the greatest degree.

If the resentment is still too strong at this point, you may have to tell them of your decision and how you expect the problem to be worked out. You cannot insist that two people change their attitudes about each other, but you can insist that their behavior not affect productivity and effectiveness.

If you can see that one person is clearly at fault, talk to her privately and tell her exactly what changes you want to take place. Allow her to save face by listening to any excuses she may mention, but make it clear that you expect a change in behavior.

After a trial period in which you see that the dispute will not be worked out and that the two employees will not work together cooperatively, you have three last options: change assignments so as to minimize contact, arrange a transfer, or dismiss one or both.

How to Build Loyalty from Those You Supervise

Management expert Peter Drucker says, in his book *The Effective Executive* (p. 53), the following about loyalty and team work and their effect on productivity:

> The man who focuses on efforts and who stresses his downward authority is a subordinate no matter how exalted his title and rank. But the man who focuses on contribution and who takes responsibility for results, no matter how junior, is in the most literal

sense of the phrase, "top management." He holds himself accountable for the performance of the whole.

With the title of secretary, administrative assistant, or office manager, you may not have power that comes from position (rank and title), or the power that comes from opportunity (access, money, or liberty to take important actions that affect the entire company), or the power that comes from expertise (special skills that others can't replace). But you can have *personal power*—power from a strong relationship and loyalty derived from those you supervise. And with that personal power you can go a long way in making yourself and your subordinates productive for your organization and in enjoying your work.

If you want to develop true loyalty among your subordinates and inspire them to give you their best, keep the following guidelines in mind:

Give everyone information at the same time. People who have always "talked to you first" seem to flaunt the fact that they have such direct access and often imply that you have taken them into your confidence before others, thus suggesting your partiality toward them. When someone reports to her colleagues, "she mentioned to me yesterday that she was thinking of doing that," others in the office assume you have a closer relationship with the confidante or like her best.

When you have big news to tell, call a quick stand-up meeting, send a memo, or amble through the office in some orderly fashion so that all can see they are getting the word at approximately the same time.

Always set the example. Never ask a subordinate to do a task you would not consider doing yourself. Never give all the menial tasks to assistants and take all the interesting assignments yourself.

Treat them with respect. Allow them space to disagree with you. Make it clear that you understand contradictory feelings and can accept their disagreement, as long as they do what you have directed. Respect also involves treating them as persons rather than part of the equipment around the office. Introduce them to guests when the occasion arises. Never say your assistants work *for* you but rather *with* you.

Take the blame for them. When another department calls you to point out an error or a problem, don't pass the buck with "I'll have to talk to Sherry about that. She's not too accurate sometimes." Rather: "I'm sorry we let that get out of the department with an error. We'll see if we can't get it corrected."

Share the credit with them. When a higher-up compliments you for a job well done, pass on the nice remarks to your subordinates and thank them for their part in the project.

Discuss your ideas and plans with them and share your goals. Even if you have already made a decision, discussing with and informing your assistants shows that you value their opinions and feelings about the project or situation. The opportunity to give advice is a form of praise for them.

Never give busywork. Subordinates like to be involved, as does everyone, in meaningful tasks. If someone can't understand the purpose behind the tedious, give her the reasons. Allow shortcuts when you can.

Give feedback about performance. Those who aren't motivated to do their best lose respect for you when you don't demand top performance. Those who are self-motivated always are concerned about your standards and how they are measuring up.

Give opportunities to grow. Show your concern for their own professional and personal growth by giving subordinates new tasks with increased responsibilities; sending them to seminars and conferences; letting them attend meetings with you occasionally; recommending special university courses they may be interested in pursuing; encouraging lateral moves with the organization or department to help them gain more experience.

Admit mistakes. Don't be afraid to show doubt or indecision; these are not signs of weakness but of strength. Only a fool is always positive. Assistants feel loyalty to you when you make mistakes because they see your vulnerability. They can then permit themselves an occasional lapse and feel free to discuss their own weaknesses or lack of skills that need attention.

Ask favors. Asking a favor is an act of humility. You are expressing need for another person and lessening your own self-sufficiency. Of course, when you ask a favor, make sure the subordinate doesn't feel it's a "must" that she comply.

Show your appreciation for work well done with tangible rewards. If you can't grant raises, you can still reward with favors, small gifts, invitations to social functions, training, your personal help with projects, or introductions or contacts with others who can enhance their career growth.

Don't make promises you can't keep. Adults are often like children when it comes to promises. Make a comment such as, "I sure would like to get you a new desk in here" and it often comes back to you later: "What happened to the new desk you promised last fall?" The subordinate may begin to feel that you made the earlier comment to pacify or manipulate. Reward first, talk about it later.

Socializing with Subordinates

Don't. You will often find yourself in the position of having to act like "one of the girls" and may find yourself passing on directives from your boss as if it's a "her-against-us" situation. This position or attitude that you are "on the other side" can jeopardize your own standing with your boss and other higher-level officials.

Another difficulty in socializing with subordinates arises when you must give negative feedback or encourage improved performance. You'll find it much more difficult to tell a *friend* that she will be dismissed if she doesn't start running the "spellchecker" on her typing than to tell an *acquaintance*. Subordinates with whom you socialize will also have difficulty in taking your words at face value and will more likely feel insulted or interpret your negative comments personally.

Of course, you can still go to lunch with a subordinate occasionally and stop to chat about personal matters in the hallway. But let your primary conversation center on business matters. You can be friendly without being personal or intimate. A few tactful turndowns for lunch with explanations such as "no time," "too busy right now," "already have plans to do such and such" will gradually discourage further invitations.

Then, on occasion, just to maintain an open communication channel, you may suggest lunch together.

Conducting the Informal Performance Appraisal

Occasionally, you will be given the responsibility for formally warning your subordinate about deficiencies, evaluating performance, and passing on recommendations for raises, and possibly recommending transfer, promotion, or dismissal.

Basically, this formal kind of interview can be divided into four steps:

1. *Begin by establishing rapport.* Be positive if you can. ("I hear you finished putting together the final draft of Harriet's report two days earlier than she expected. She certainly was pleased.") If you can't be positive, at least be neutral. ("I want us to talk about your performance over the last few months.")

2. *Discuss performance.* Comment on the things she does well. Then move to the areas where improvement is needed. Give her your honest evaluations about the situation and invite her comments about the performance and the standard required.

3. *Develop a plan for action.* If the subordinate agrees with or accepts your observations, get her to "buy into" the improvements you want. Expect and accept defensive feelings. Accept part of the blame if you can. Explore possible explanations for the problem. Then lead her to suggest possible solutions. Help her to see the benefits of change for herself and for the organization as a whole. Give specific suggestions for improvements and tell her at what time and by what standards you will measure her work the next time.

4. *Make notes of what you both have agreed to do.* Later, turn these notes into a memo and have her sign to verify agreement about the plan of action you have discussed.

5. *Summarize and end on a positive note to reestablish rapport.*

Formal reprimands follow the same structure, except that you must be careful to make a formal report of the date of the discussion, dates and details of unacceptable behavior, and warnings about next actions issued.

Occasionally a dismissed employee will insist that the warning was not seriously given or that she had no idea of the serious consequences of such and such a behavior. That's why complete notes, dates, and "next actions" must specifically be put in writing.

Here are some common pitfalls to avoid in evaluating others' performance: One is a tendency to mark everyone the same—whether low, average, or excellent. That makes it difficult for your boss or whoever is administering raises to reward actually outstanding performance. Also, if everybody gets evaluated the same, motivation to improve decreases.

Another pitfall is to distort performance because of your own biases. Be sure you are not rating the person according to how well you like her personality rather than according to how she does her job.

Another common tendency is to evaluate people higher because they "make an effort." In school, such an attitude about performance may be permissible. But in the business world, organizations can afford to pay only for performance and results, not effort and activity.

A final pitfall in evaluating performance is the "halo" or "pitchfork" tendency. You see one strength and you tend to give good ratings in all categories because of one or two outstanding qualities. Or you mark the subordinate low in all categories because of one overshadowing fault. Give proper thought to each topic you evaluate.

Firing

Unfortunately, your assistant's agreeing about substandard performance doesn't necessarily mean she will accept suggestions and make improvements. But do remember that dismissal should be a last resort. You can't fire every unproductive person who has a personality problem; you would be continually understaffed and lose a great deal of money retraining people until they are productive.

But sometimes when you have to dismiss someone, you may do so for the good of the department as a whole. When others notice someone "getting away with murder," they often let their own performance slip, decide their job isn't so important after all, or lose respect for you or your boss when you permit such behavior to continue.

Again, when you are the one to have to dismiss someone, treat her with respect. Wait until the close of the day so she will not have to face others immediately and offer explanations. By all means, give her the news in private. Finally, take care to explain the exact reason for the dismissal and remind her of previous warnings.

Then be positive. Try to emphasize that just because she did not work out in this particular job does not mean she would not work out well somewhere else. Reassure her that you will not give her a bad reference. (In fact, it may be your company's policy to give only dates of employment, duties, and salary as reference information when requested.) Also, assure her that you will not bad-mouth her around the office.

The fired employee's reaction may be anger, hurt, shock, disappointment or tears. You must be prepared to handle any of these reactions by letting the person "get it all out," by repeating your reason for dismissal if asked, and by being firm but positive and reassuring about her success elsewhere. Simply make her realize, "This is not the office or job for you, but you can be successful elsewhere."

chapter 4

HANDLING PROBLEM PERSONALITIES WITHOUT JEOPARDIZING YOUR PRODUCTIVITY

"Hell is—other people!" wrote Jean Paul Sartre. With so many people in the business world subscribing to that sentiment, it's amazing some of them haven't gone over to the other side—becoming part of the solution rather than someone's problem.

An administrative assistant with a large manufacturing company explains her "hell" that lasted over two months:

> This one secretary had a bad childhood and everyone felt sorry for her. The company I worked for, more or less, hired girls who were good-looking and didn't care about skills. This girl decided she didn't like me and became obnoxious. Would cuss me out in an elevator. Would threaten me. She even had her boyfriend call me and threaten rape. She would say she would beat me up. She would say she hated my guts. She'd call me on the phone and make obscene noises and cuss and hang up...
>
> I called her up twice and asked what I'd done to her. And she'd never tell me. She'd go out at lunch and smoke pot. And afterward she would or would not be rational.
>
> My immediate boss felt sorry for her, so he allowed this to go on for two months. I came to work with a knot in my stomach every day,

> and it became unbearable. So I went to the project engineer—over my boss's head—and told him what was going on. I said I'd never dealt in ultimatums, but that it was I go or she goes.
>
> And she went. Then she came back and threatened to kill me in the office. They had to get a peace bond on her. She finally joined the Marine Corps, and I hope I never see her again. I was scared to death of her. She was about five feet eleven inches and a really rough girl. The sad thing about it was that she didn't know how to type or Xerox and I had showed her how to handle her job. And then one day, she turned against me.
>
> My boss was relieved that he didn't have to make the decision. He just didn't have the guts. He felt sorry for both of us; he never held it against me. The big boss said I shouldn't have let it go on so long, that I should have stood up to her immediately.

Though they may not have been threatened with rape or death, many secretaries face coming to the office daily to deal with a personality that puts "knots in their stomach." And as with the administrative assistant just mentioned, many bosses do not know how or are unwilling to deal with these situations. Therefore, secretaries are left on their own to keep their sanity while putting forth the extra effort necessary so as not to let their efficiency on the job slip.

How do you deal with problem personalities—from the isolate to the put-down artist? Understanding is the first step:

Maslow, who has been called the father of humanist psychology, has described five basic needs within all humans that make them act the way they do: physiological (food, air, water, sleep); safety and security (from bodily harm—political, natural); love and social (belonging to someone or to a group); self-esteem (sense of duty, responsibility, contribution to others, feeling of worth); self-actualization (sense of personal power, using your potential to create and get what you want out of life).

One of the more important things that Maslow, as well as later psychologists, has pointed out is that all of these needs vary within each individual and that some motivate and affect behavior more than others. It's only when one need is not being met that it calls attention to itself.

In other words, only when you're lost in a forest at night do you become aware of physical danger and strive to meet your need of safety by locating a way back to civilization. Only when you get locked in an overloaded, cramped elevator do you become aware of your need for fresh air, water, and food.

Others such as McGregor and Herzberg have suggested that at least some of these basic needs can be and are met at work. For example, we can meet our need for self-esteem by being rewarded for a project well done. We can meet our need to belong by feeling camaraderie and friendship with co-workers. We can meet our highest need, self-actualization, if we are allowed to use our talents in a way that brings us inner fulfillment.

For example, many writers spend hours putting together a poem for which their only pay is copies of the magazine containing the published work. If others know of their achievement, their need for self-esteem may be met. Or, if prestige or status is not what motivates them, then the act of writing the poetry may have itself been self-actualization—fulfillment and pleasure within oneself.

On the other hand, when a person is not getting some basic need met at home or in other social circles, he or she frequently brings that need to work. And that unresolved need begins to call attention to itself—and how!

The employee who gets little attention at home may talk incessantly at work, dominating every conversation, afraid to let go of anyone's attention. Another employee who gets little or no attention at home may try to meet her need for belonging by making herself indispensable at work, doing projects no one else wants to do in hopes of getting someone to praise or appreciate her efforts. Or, still another employee who gets no love and attention at home may constantly insult others and reap their rejection; negative attention becomes better than no attention at all.

More recent psychologists such as Eric Berne and Thomas Harris have used descriptions such as game playing, I'm okay-you're-okay positions, and parent-child-adult ego states to describe these same maneuverings to get basic needs met.

All that is to say that we are complex human beings with the same basic needs but with many different ways of revealing those needs. Therefore, it's difficult, if not impossible, for us as amateur psychologists to find out "what makes the other person tick" and more importantly, to find out how to deal with that constant ticking.

But that doesn't mean we should stop trying. Some basic concepts and how-tos of handling others are essential: The first, as mentioned above, is realizing these basic drives of human nature. The two most evident in a work situation, of course, are the need for love and belonging and the need to maintain one's self-esteem.

But remember that employees can express these needs in varying extremes. The employee who has low self-esteem may come across as a quiet, meek, withdrawn individual, who wants you to make every effort to make her feel important. Or, another low-esteem person may come across as a belligerent loudmouth, forcing you to take notice of him.

A second principle in dealing with people, in addition to understanding and recognizing basic needs, is understanding your own tendency to "type" people and transfer your expectations onto them. For example, your father may have been a womanizing flirt whom you despised because he made your mother unhappy. Therefore, when another male at the office compliments you, you may transfer your feelings about your father onto that person and consider him the same "type." Once you label or type someone, you begin to see everything he or she does through your preconceived filter.

A third principle in dealing with people can be summed up: What you "stroke" is what you get. In other words, the behavior that you "reward" with your reaction is the behavior you continue to get from the other person. As transactional-analysis theory goes, you may give out positive or negative strokes; both can motivate. For example, if someone continues to tell you crude jokes that you don't appreciate and you continue to laugh at these jokes, pretending to be amused, you're giving a positive stroke. The joke-teller will continue to unload her stories on you.

On the other hand, if someone tells you crude jokes that you don't appreciate and you get angry, moralize about her vocabulary, or otherwise show disapproval, you're giving a negative stroke. The joke-teller may continue to offend you with her jokes merely because your negative strokes are better than no attention at all, or because those negative strokes reinforce a low opinion of herself.

The only way, then, to stop that behavior may be to give no strokes at all—positive or negative. That, of course, is what you will try to do to stop the "problem" personalities from emotionally upsetting you at work and from making you less productive. Ignore them.

The Complainer

Complainers set themselves up as critics of the weather, falling leaves in the parking lot, office schedule, dress codes, chain-of-command, no cafeteria (or quality of food in the cafeteria if you have one), "incompetent" or "insensitive" top management, terrible people and their idiosyncracies, the boss's inefficiencies and wastes (or her "slave-driving" tendencies and "penny-pinching") no suggestion box (or the stupid things "others" drop in suggestion boxes).

Why do complainers complain? These people play "Ain't It Awful?" sometimes to reinforce a low self-esteem and self-pity. Look at all the bad things around them, and don't they deserve it for sure? Or a constant complainer may be trying to redirect your attention away from his own abilities, performance, or personality by pointing out other terrible things. In other words, he's trying to say, "Can't you see things are tough around here and I'm unhappy? So, leave me alone."

Robert Bramson, in his book *Coping With Difficult People* (p. 48), writes that complainers generally have one of three views of the world: 1) They feel helpless to change anything; all they can do is talk about the awful things. 2) They have a strong sense of "fairness" and of "this is the way things *ought* to be;" and when things aren't that way, they feel compelled to point them out. 3) They have an overactive ego and see themselves and what they do as perfect. When others don't measure up, they feel called upon to point that out.

To stop complainers:

Call them to action. If they're complaining to you about co-worker Dorothy, try: "Have you spoken to Dorothy about how you feel?" This puts them on the spot to "put up or shut up" so to speak. If they're complaining about the lack of sunlight in the lobby, try: "Why don't you write a memo and suggest a solution?"

Offer to take action yourself. If they're complaining about no cafeteria, try: "Would you like me to tell Ms. Smith that you have suggested she investigate the possibility of a company cafeteria?" Or, "Would you like me to pass on your feelings about Katherine to Mr. Sears?" They will usually clam up if you insist on attaching their name to the complaint.

If you know of no action to take, you can ask for their opinion: "What exactly would you like for me to do about the situation?"

They may realize that you have no power to control or that the complaint is ridiculous or without resolution.

Give credit for a job well done. If you sense a complainer only wants recognition for a job well done despite difficult circumstances, give it. What does praise cost you?

Disagree without arguing. Silence, nods, or smiles often give complainers the only feedback they need to continue their complaining; they acknowledge silence or other body language as agreement. You don't have to prove the complainer wrong, but you can offer your contradictory opinion as such: "I am sorry you feel that way, because in my dealings with that department I have always been pleased with..." The complainer may soon come to realize that he is complaining to the wrong person.

Show them you accept what they feel, neither agreeing nor disagreeing. You can repeat back to them what they have said—the facts and their feelings about those facts. You can then end the discussion with "I understand your viewpoint now" and then change the subject.

Turn the criticism into humor. One secretary says she has a poster in her office that can be viewed in two ways; some people see a witch and others see a fair maiden. When someone in the office begins to complain, co-workers chide, "Oh, I guess you're seeing the witch today."

Another secretary tells of a co-worker who constantly complains about the workload. When it's light, she is complaining about boredom; and when it's heavy, she is complaining about the pressure. The others in the office good-naturedly have begun to remind her of her last week's gripes. She has begun to laugh at herself—though still griping.

The Isolate

Isolates are highly effective in discouraging contact. They usually manage to separate themselves physically, pulling their desk or chair around so that they face no one or sit off in a far corner. They manage to go for coffee or lunch whenever everybody else has already left. They answer questions with a word or grunt and avoid eye contact.

An insurance secretary describes the isolate in her office:

> Some days she won't speak at all. She has no patience with others because she's self-taught in her job. If someone else humbles herself and goes to her for advice or information, she belittles and makes them feel ignorant and very small. She wants love, respect, loyalty, but she can't let herself accept it. She doesn't respect anybody; the boss can't even tell her what to do. She doesn't feel she needs to report to anybody. She just walks in and out when she wants to. In fact, I think they're [the bosses] going to let her go in a couple of months.

When dealing with one of these personalities, look for specific details, not general impressions, in understanding the why behind the behavior. Some people isolate themselves because they are boring and bored. They grew up with little enthusiasm about anything. Most activities and life in general seem "too much trouble" to bother.

Others isolate themselves because they distrust people; they feel suspicious of others' overtures and motives toward them and even show that distrust with hostility.

Still other isolates get a kind of perverse pleasure in provoking others and forcing them to beg for information and/or contact. When they then perceive that the other person is "put out" with them, that rejection reinforces their own low self-esteem and feelings of inadequacies.

Finally, some isolates are merely shy on initial contact and with encouragement from others can overcome this tendency and integrate themselves into the office life if others make most of the effort.

What to do if the isolate is slowing down the work flow in your office? If you think shyness is the problem, make her a prime challenge. Help her overcome her fear by providing chances for her to meet and work with others one-on-one. Go to lunch with her alone; she will open up to an audience of one more than to an audience of three or four. Occasionally, suggest an office luncheon where everyone brings a salad and eats together in a conference room or company lounge.

When the problem is more than shyness, try to deal with that person in writing. To get information, write a memo with a series of questions to be answered about the project on which you're working. At least you won't have to deal with the isolate's hostility face-to-face.

If you sense that the isolate is trying to punish or submerge herself in work to lessen some other at-home problem, oblige her by giving her plenty of work to occupy the time!

The Do-It-Myselfer

The do-it-myselfer thinks he's helping you out. While you're away from the desk, rather than leaving a short form for you to "bother with," he sits down at your typewriter or terminal and moves all the margins, the tab stops, and the spacing. And when you return, if he's not finished with the typing, he grins at you and explains how he's saving you time by finishing the work himself; "it'll only take a minute." Unable to get to your desk, you stand and watch him for the next 10 minutes doing a job that would have taken you 30 seconds.

It's difficult to be angry with do-it-myselfers because they are showing initiative and aiming to please. Nevertheless, they can complicate your workload and endanger the results of your efforts.

Try dealing with them impersonally so as not to offend an intended "good deed" or discourage initiative altogether. For example, make sure that everyone in your office knows your feelings about others sitting down at your desk to type or looking through your desk or files for something. If necessary, tape a sign (PLEASE DO NOT USE THIS [WHATEVER] WITHOUT PERMISSION) to the filing or storage cabinets or to the keyboard or the telephone. Then when someone is tempted to "help you out" by going to the files himself, your caution is not taken as a personal put-down.

To keep subordinates from "running off with a project," build in checkpoints for yourself. Ask them specifically to check back with you after certain steps and before proceeding with next steps; don't assign with a general check-with-me-if-you-need-help approach.

The Helpless Imposer

This person always has an excuse for nonproductivity: "I don't know how to turn on the machine." "The equipment was acting up." "Nobody gave me an example of how to do it." "I didn't have the phone number." "I have to catch a ride home."

When your results depend on this person, the damsel-in-distress syndrome can irritate beyond endurance. Most people will try this route if permitted because being self-sufficient takes time and effort. Asking for help is simply easier than finding the answers for oneself.

A few of the helpless really do lack the necessary skills or knowledge to accomplish the task. That, however, does not mean that they should be permitted to persist in their ignorance or ineptitude.

How to cope with a "helpless" co-worker: First, if you think the cry for help is truly based on a lack of confidence in one's abilities, give instructions and a pep talk. Reassure the person that she can do the job and show that you have confidence in her by leaving her alone to do what you've asked. Mention other resources at her disposal—instruction booklets, library information, telephone directories, names of key people, samples from the file.

If she resorts to telling you all the other good things she can do, assure her that you are aware of these but that she must move on to new responsibilities.

If she continues to cry for help, claiming that she doesn't know "heads or tails" about a project, tell her she will have to get specific about the difficulties. In other words, when she says, "I don't know anything about assembling these manuals," don't take on the project yourself or give her the instructions again, A-Z.

Instead, say: "What exactly is it that you don't understand?" If she can't verbalize it, then: "Well, come back to me when you can be more specific about what you need to know." If it's a machine she can't operate, insist that she begin the process while you watch the procedure, waiting for her to ask specific questions as she goes along. Force her to put some effort into figuring out the problem. Often just this simple investigation into other resources or experimentation will result in her answering her own questions.

If all else fails, warn her that if she can't learn to do the job on her own, you will have to relieve her of some responsibilities, implying that you don't know how this will affect salary or later promotions. Then reassign the work to another more capable person with appropriate salary increase or recognition.

If you find the "helpless" problem is with a peer rather than a subordinate and that you are continually having to do her work, go to your supervisor and ask to be assigned the work yourself. You can then use these extra responsibilities as the basis for your own salary increase or promotion.

The Superagreeable

Superagreeables smile a lot, nod enthusiastically, confirm your every word, and promise you the moon. So what's the problem? Often they don't follow through with the action; and worse, they try to manipulate you.

A secretary to a vice-president describes a co-worker: "To this one person, I can say, 'Boy, that sky is yellow' and he'd say, 'You know, you're right—yellow right along the edge there.' I can't stand those people; it's so phony. They're trying to use me."

Another problem with superagreeable people surfaces if you are depending on them for results. One supervisor-secretary insists: "They're just too nice to get things done. You don't have to be a demon, but you have to be decisive, firm, forthright, and honest. Not so wishy-washy that they'll do anything for anybody. There's not much substance to that personality."

Superagreeables can't tell you "no" because they fear losing your approval. They often equate what they can do for you with their personality. If they don't do what you want, perhaps you won't like them anymore. So rather than face the reality of what they can and cannot do, they promise you anything but then can't or don't deliver. Others, of course, have ulterior motives in agreeing with whatever drops from your lips—so they feel freer to ask you to do extra work on a project or to side with them later in a politically sensitive situation.

If you have only to listen to a superagreeable sort and don't have to depend on her for your productivity, reflect her own gooey-sweet tone when you talk with her. Perhaps she'll come to recognize the hypocrisy in your voice as a mirror image of her own.

If you think the person is superagreeable due to fear of winning your disapproval, give her your permission to be honest. That is, do everything you can to get her to face reality, to express objections, to warn you that she doesn't think she can come through with results:

"I need these expense reports completed by Thursday. Is there any chance they won't be finished by then? If you see a problem, let me know so I can make plans accordingly." And don't frown so as to counteract the "permission" you've just given to be honest without fear of disapproval.

Or, "I think this meeting is really a waste of time, and I'm planning to suggest to Mr. Smith next month that we cancel it altogether. However, I may be wrong. There may be some points I haven't considered. I'd like for you to think it over and see if you can offer any other ideas that may help me gain a new perspective on the necessity for continuing to meet regularly."

Let the person know that you would rather have disagreements or warnings about inaction rather than surprise delays, missed deadlines, or bad decisions.

Above all, don't discourage these people from being honest by meeting bad news with a gruff voice, a frown, or other body language that makes them regret having "opposed" you with reality.

The Know-It-All

Some simply take on the tone of authority to let those around them know that they have the final truth. Some know-it-alls simply convey their own intelligence and discount your inferior ideas and efforts by shuffling papers, by smiling condescendingly, or by changing the subject after you speak as if to say, "Forget that; it's stupid."

Others are less subtle and simply tell you that they know it all: "Let me fill you in on how all this got started." Or, "I've talked with Ms. Bonwitt about this before; what she really expects from you is..." Or, "I used to do it your way, too, until I learned that the best way is to..."

Some know-it-alls really do know it all. They are experts but have little tact or regard for how they deliver their knowledge. They leave you feeling humiliated, angry, confused. And when things don't turn out like they said they would, they still do not waiver in their belief that their way is best, instead blaming any bad results on your ineptness in carrying out the project.

Even though these people can be valuable resources for you, you may shy away from them simply because they make you feel incompetent.

Others who come on as know-it-alls aren't. By their very position or title, they are supposed to have definitive answers and instructions. But they don't. Therefore, they have to "fake it" to be able to tell you something or else seem incompetent. Even when know-it-alls don't have a position or title that mandates that they have some specific knowledge, they may pretend to know it all because they seek to win admiration and respect from you.

The situation then for you is to separate, as Robert Branson recommends, the true know-it-alls from the pseudo-know-it-alls and react accordingly. You can't afford to turn a cold shoulder to all those who come across as experts, even when finesse is lacking. A really knowledgeable person may be a great asset to you in teaching valuable skills and helping you move ahead in your career.

To separate the truly knowledgeable from the pretender, try to gather more evidence before taking action. Back in college, I remember being astonished with "knowledgeable people" telling me how a certain professor graded compositions, what kind of easy final exams to expect, or how unnecessary reading the text was. Then I was always perplexed to discover that these same experts, who stood outside the classroom telling the rest of us how things were wound up failing the course.

But upon entering the business world, I again gullibly subscribed to "knowledgeable people" telling me which professional organizations are a "must" to join, how easy it is to make cold calls on prospective clients, and what a mistake it is to advertise through certain media. Not until I learned that some of these "knowledgeable people" had gone out of business, did I learn to ask my variations of the age-old question: "If you're so smart, how come you're not rich?"

If you don't know whether you are getting the "gospel" from certain know-it-alls, stall until you can collect evidence. Are they being promoted or given more authority? Do you hear them constantly recognized for their achievements? Find out how others view their "inside" news and advice.

If things check out and you do discover that this know-it-all usually does, respect and use that knowledge. That doesn't mean that he will always be correct. But rather than disregard what he says altogether, lead him to reexamine his own information or advice with questions such as: "If I take the approach you're suggesting, how do you think that will affect Fred's decision?" Or,

"If I change these procedures now, will they still accomplish what we expect on later orders?"

Tentatively express disagreement or an alternative approach and ask him to "think it over" and get back to you: "This may not work at all, but I was wondering if we could possibly... Would you give that some thought and then tell me what you think tomorrow?" You are not blatantly challenging his knowledge, but merely asking for further consideration and offering to bow to his superior decision or knowledge if there's a conflict.

If, on the other hand, you don't collect some evidence to support the know-it-all's own opinion of her superior wisdom, repeg her into the *pseudo*knowledgeable category.

With these people, you can merely let the "knowledge" and advice fall on your deaf ears and then do what you want. To satisfy their need for admiration or respect, thank them for their "help" or information and proceed with your own plans.

If, however, they push you to follow their advice, try, "I'm comfortable with the way I do things now." Or: "I've got a written set of guidelines here that I've been instructed to follow" [or that "I hate to disregard until my boss tells me differently"] Or: "I'll check that out with my supervisor. Thank you."

The Flirt

Let me distinguish between sexual harassment and the problem personality, "the flirt." Researcher Catherine MacKinnon in her book *Sexual Harassment of Working Women: A case of Sex Discrimination* (p. 1) defines sexual harassment in its broadest sense as "unwanted imposition of sexual requirement in the context of a relationship of unequal power." She goes on to report that from her own experience in talking with women, from testimony given at various agencies, and from one published survey that seven out of 10 women are sexually harassed at some time in their career.

If you are being harassed on the job, you can file charges under Title VII of the Civil Rights Act of 1964. Report the harassment to the Equal Employment Opportunity Commission. If you don't want to take this action, you can keep a log of what was said to you, time, date, circumstances, and any promises or threats. Then place a copy of this record in your personnel file.

But in the less serious situations when no threats are made, the flirt simply becomes an annoyance. He embarrasses you by provocative comments, stares, pats. He lets you and others know he's got interests in you other than work.

The flirt may have low self-esteem and actually be trying to bolster his sagging ego by seeing how many favorable responses he can get. Or, he may be working out his need for love and belonging in the only situation he can—at work. Finally, he may be flirting as an attempt to manipulate you into doing him favors like getting him in to see the boss or typing his engineering report first.

Again, depending on how you perceive his motivation, you may handle him in several ways: If you think he sincerely needs attention or has a serious interest in you, you may discourage him by showing no interest in his flirting comments and looks. But you may want to give him attention in other ways to confirm the fact that you think he is an "okay" person. For example, you may compliment him on a particularly good report you have typed for him or on ideas he has contributed in a staff meeting.

If he asks you out, tell him directly that you're not interested because you don't date people you work with or that you are already interested in someone else. Then take later opportunities to show him that you respect and like him as a person.

On the other hand, the flirt may have no interest in you personally whatsoever; for some males, flirting is simply an empty gesture not to be taken seriously. If a woman takes these men seriously, they are shocked and sometimes frightened.

If the flirt is simply a stand-up comic that embarrasses you, makes other workers uncomfortable, and creates a bad impression before prospective customers or clients, you can try one of several approaches:

1. Use a sardonic smile and facial expression to say that you think he's very immature. Show that you don't take him seriously and make him feel foolish for trying such an act on you.

2. Tell him that his flirting manner isn't "becoming" to him. Most men will be shocked that you are unimpressed and, once they discover that fact, will learn to treat you in a more businesslike, respectful manner.

3. Explain that he is creating a bad impression for himself in front of clients, co-workers, or the boss. Say that you don't want to go into detail, but you just thought you'd pass along that tip.

4. Make no bones about the fact that you are avoiding him. When he comes into the coffee lounge and asks if he may sit down with you, explain that you were just leaving—and do so. Rather than delivering a phone message to him personally, have someone else deliver it. When he approaches you in the hallway, pretend to be deeply involved in conversation with someone else.

Above all, don't talk to others about his flirting with you. First, they begin to notice him and he is rewarded by a bigger audience. Second, if your comments get back to him, he may think that you are talking about the subject because you are interested in his attentions.

The Chauvinist

A chauvinist's viewpoint is this: "If the Good Lord had meant women to be as good as men, He'd have given them the proper equipment." He shakes his head at the irritability of the "dragon lady" who won't let him see the boss but dismisses his own irritability as fatigue due to overwork. He laughs at the typist's "woman's intuition" about the new receptionist, but expects others to understand his "gut feeling" that Max is the wrong person to handle the engineering project. A woman nags, while he only "follows through." She's manipulative, while he "only takes advantage of opportunities."

The chauvinist assumes you wouldn't want to travel in your job, that you frequently will be absent from work if you have small children, that you should take notes for the discussion group because "you write better," that you are flattered to be called "doll," "honey," or "dear."

Much of the chauvinist's manner is a result of cultural training. However, when the media so frequently deal with the issue, pleading ignorance is increasingly difficult for the male who continues to view women in this chauvinistic way.

If you can, give the older chauvinist the benefit of the doubt. Assume he is ignorant about how to treat women in the business place and educate him in subtle ways: First, use questions to cause him to reexamine his thinking: "Why would you think I wouldn't like to attend that seminar in Seattle?"

Second, counter with facts. When he says that "women can't handle the stress" of a certain situation, quote the statistics that reveal that women can handle more stress than men without serious physical and emotional damage.

Third, try "misunderstanding" his remark. He says, "You secretaries spend half the day going for coffee, don't you?" You answer, "Well, yes, it is quite an interruption to have to stop our work to run errands."

Fourth, if nothing else works, you might try sarcasm tempered with humor: If he calls you "hon," you may counter with: "Please, Jack, I didn't know we were getting so involved. Let me remind you that I'm married."

Unless you interpret the chauvinism as an intentional put-down, try to avoid being too sensitive and simply educate: "No, I don't think I'll have to be off work because of the baby's pneumonia. Thank you for asking, but my husband is planning to stay home with her until she feels better."

The Wet Blanket or Cynic

This office personality makes it a pastime to rain on others' parade. He sees your promotion or title change as a "rip-off" of added responsibility that no one else wants. He thinks that the day off management grants instead of holding the annual Christmas party is simply "the cheaper way to go." You plan a surprise party for a favorite retiring employee; he "has heard that Margaret hates retirement parties and is hoping no one will think of such a thing."

Some wet blankets drip all over everything because they feel left out; their need for belonging isn't being met. Others sincerely believe that they are rescuing you from being "taken in" by others who are out to deceive you, use you, and harm you. They sometimes are successful in dampening your spirits because of the basic insecurities in us all about how we perceive circumstances and others' motives.

To find out if their pessimism has a basis in fact, try getting them to be specific: "What makes you think Ms. Borden intentionally overlooked inviting me to the staff meeting?"

Counteract their negativism by stating your own positive position: "I understand your views, but I still am hopeful that Mr. Whitley will be pleased with the changes we have made in the layout."

Finally, counter the wet blanket's effect on you by being alert to your own potential for gloom and doom. When you notice your enthusiasm and energy level dissipating, remind yourself of your association with the wet blanket and make an effort to spend more time with optimists.

The Power Seeker

The power seeker may bombard you with her education, experience, references, once-upon-a-time tales, hoping you will pass the information on to your boss or put it on the grapevine so that others may reward her appropriately.

Remember, particularly, that if you are the boss's secretary, you are seeing co-workers' "best foot forward." They may have ulterior motives for what they do around you.

Others are more direct in their approach. A secretary to a vice-president explains about an accountant in the office who became overbearing: "He would tell everybody that I was his secretary and I had to continually correct that when people called. He would promise information to others that he wasn't authorized to deliver..."

This person may be seeking power to bolster self-esteem and status, or he may simply wish an opportunity to exercise his fullest potential and talents—a goal that management will most probably share with the power seeker.

Therefore, rather than risk thwarting a rising star in the company, perhaps your best approach is simply to observe and keep your boss informed.

If the power seeker is after your own job and is more competent in it than you, all the obstacles you can throw in her way probably won't deter her progress. Instead of concentrating on throwing stumbling blocks in her path, concentrate on making your own footing more sure by improving your skills.

The Satirist

The satirist, or cynic, makes her way through the day at half-mast. Rather than unleashing an all-out attack as the complainer does, she operates through innuendos (raised eyebrows accompanied by: "I wonder whatever in the world he means by that") and "playful" humor ("Don't throw those doughnuts out; we might as well get used to day-olds since things are so desperate that a 5 percent raise will throw us into bankruptcy.").

Another approach the satirist takes is to discount you by saying or doing something that makes you feel insignificant or stupid: "Well, of course, I realize you probably won't be affected by the flextime; secretaries will still need to punch the clock." Or, "Of course, you couldn't be expected to know these figures were wrong. After all, you just type what you're given, right? Mr. Hatfield should have rechecked them himself."

Why do satirists dig and snipe? Many people have a basic habit of putting themselves down; so they do it to others, too, without even thinking of the potentially devastating effects. Additionally, some feel that by putting others down, they make themselves taller. Again, they're working on the need for self-esteem.

To cope with satirical remarks and put-down humor: Let the cynic know you see the underlying intent. For example, "What exactly did you mean by that comment? Were you suggesting that...?" Or, "I sense that under that laughter, you really are upset about the situation. Would you like to discuss it?"

Put her on the spot before others: "What do the rest of you think? Would you all prefer that we cancel plans for the volleyball team?" Let the others call her hand and argue the defense, or at least verify that the others agree with the satirist's view.

If you have the authority to deal with the situation, turn the satiric comments and cynical attitude to a problem-solving mode: "Do you have any suggestions for making this process more foolproof?" Or, "Where do you think we should go for answers or alternatives?"

If the cynicism directed to you is meant for someone else's benefit, ask: "Would you like for me to mention your views to Ms. Melton?" The satirist will usually back down or turn off the cynicism around you.

The Gossip and Perpetual Visitor

Listening to gossip has its benefits. If the talk is about business matters—who's getting what promotion, which division is being transferred to Lafayette, that the latest contract netted $10 million—you probably should be aware of what's being said around you, filter it through your own observations, and possibly help keep your boss informed on matters that concern her.

With business-related gossip, listen but don't repeat. With people gossip, don't listen *or* repeat.

One of the dangers of "innocent" listening, of course, is that many times your nod or even silence is taken as agreement and passed on to the next person: "Mary and I were talking about that yesterday. Frankly, *we* think she has a basic insecurity problem with..." When gossips move to the next listener, you may be surprised to find out what you "just said."

Another danger in listening to gossip is that it takes time away from the job. Observers may conclude that if you always have "visitors" at your desk or you are at theirs, obviously you don't have enough work to stay busy.

So why are many tempted even to listen to gossip? Either they don't want to offend people and don't know how to stop the conversation, or they feel flattered that others want to let them in on something.

The gossiper, of course, may have motives other than simply to inform you. It makes some feel important to always have the "inside story"; it's their way of getting attention. Others pass on damaging gossip because in their own minds to tear someone else down is to lift themselves up. Finally, some gossip out of sheer boredom—no matter who listens.

Following are some stoppers or turnarounds that you may find useful in discouraging a gossip:

"Let's go talk about that to Mary Ann. I think you both need to discuss this objectively. I'll mediate."

"I've heard that, but I don't think I believe it."

"Hmmm."

"I didn't know that."

"That's too bad... What was it you needed from the file?"

"Could be."

"Have you checked that out? Things like that have a way of growing until the real details get so twisted."

"I'm afraid I'm not going to be a good listener. I've got to finish this report by noon."

In addition to or in lieu of these comments, use body language. Don't ever stop working to listen; otherwise, you feel hesitant to start working again. It's like turning off the ignition when you pull into someone's driveway to let him out; you've committed yourself to stay awhile. And if you're trapped in someone else's office when the gossip begins, stand up, walk toward the door, and act impatient to leave.

When you're the subject of gossip, the frustration and the solution can be more illusive. One secretary confided a particularly hurtful situation in her early career: "I was just out of high school and working with three older ladies. I worked the late-night shift and occasionally brought my small baby to work and kept him on a blanket on the floor. One of the firemen came to visit with us, and one of the women started telling that I was sleeping with him (the fireman) because we were both on the blanket with the baby. They started all kinds of rumors; my parents worked at the same place, and I was furious and afraid they would hear. I finally went to my dad and told him. He said, "Those who know you, know better. Those who don't, it doesn't matter." So I ignored these women and it finally stopped. They didn't get a rise out of me, and I think they got bored."

This secretary hit upon one of the primary reasons for gossip—boredom. When you're the victim of gossip, ignore what you can. But if you think your credibility may be on the line, go to the person involved and explain that you have heard that she has said such and such and that you just wanted to set the record straight and assume she won't be saying any more about the situation since she now knows the true details. Most gossipers will deny the talk, but they will stop once they know you are on to them as the source.

If you think your reputation may be damaged with your boss, you may want to go in for a talk "just to set the record straight." Don't assume the posture of tattling on the other person, but simply explain that you want him or her to know the situation as it really occurred. On most occasions truth verifies itself over the long haul.

The Flatterer

Compliments with ulterior motives are difficult to handle because we've been trained to appreciate compliments and say "thank you." Yet we resent the feeling that we've been "had"—that the other person thinks we are unaware of efforts to manipulate.

An appropriate response to a sincere compliment is a modest "thank you" and perhaps an explanation: "Thanks—I do try to empty the in-box before the mail is delivered." Or, "I'm glad you thought the reception went well. I was particularly pleased with the caterer's services."

To distinguish between sincere praise and flattery, you may try putting your praiser on the spot for an explanation. Someone compliments you on the way you handled the meeting details; you respond, "What was it exactly that you thought particularly effective?" You can usually tell by how quick and logical the response what the motive was.

The Staller

Stallers never give you decisions until circumstances have dictated the outcome. They don't give you information until you no longer need it, having resorting to beg, borrow, or steal it elsewhere.

Yet, you find it difficult to hate them because they can be so innocent of ulterior motives. They smile, listen, and nod encouragingly but can't or won't deliver. They may stall because they are incompetent or powerless to deliver what you ask; or if the project or information is "bad news," they may stall so as not to upset you.

With either motivation, the results are the same. Their stalling keeps you from getting your work done.

To cope, pry for underlying problems. Listen for hedge words that may cover the real reason for the stalling. Then try to solve that problem or reassure them about their own solution.

Help the staller to take action. Can you arrange for temporary help to get the typing done? Can you phone some people for her? Make an appointment with her to discuss the options again and point out her only viable decision.

When the stalling is habitual, keep the ball in your court. When she says she'll "get back to you with that information in a few days," counter with, "Okay, why don't I call you Monday for the information?" Or, "I'll send a messenger to pick up the contracts on Thursday. Please have the papers signed by then."

Or, you can put it in writing: "Unless I hear from you by Friday, I'll assume these contracts meet with your approval and will forward them to..."

The Kick-Me Kid

This person's trademark is, "Why not? Everybody else treats me that way, too."

> "Me? Work late again? I guess so. What choice do I have?"
>
> "You want to do those copies in front of me? No problem, go ahead. Everybody in here today has had a rush job, too. Maybe I should get mine done now instead of going to lunch."
>
> "You want me to cover the phones while you all are at the party? He hardly knows me anyway."
>
> "Would you look at this report? It's probably not what you wanted. Everything else I've done this week has been wrong, too."

Sometimes the motivation is genuine. The person thinks so little of herself that she expects doormat treatment from others. When they oblige, it confirms her opinion of her unworthiness.

Dealing with a kick-me personality can be a problem if you accept the guilt she tries to put on you. Additionally, to keep this person's self-esteem intact can be a time-consuming nuisance, as this secretary explains: "My boss has to be reassured all the time. She is a lovely person, so it's not difficult, but just tiresome, to keep reassuring her that she is all right. After all, she has two Ph.D's."

Others use "kick-me" as a power play. A kick-me person may like to be kicked because she is praised for her "selfless" acts. For another, kick-me may be a form of protection; if you feel sorry for her about always doing things wrong, maybe you won't make her do it over. And perhaps next time you won't give her something so "difficult" to do.

If you think the other person genuinely feels like the doormat, don't be so quick to rush ahead and let her perform as a martyr. Insist that she attend the retirement party this time, that you'll ask someone else to cover the phones. Take other opportunities to give her special attention and show that you approve of her work without her being a martyr. Assure her that everyone makes mistakes. Help her develop a plan for improvement.

If, instead, you sense that the kick-me act is a ruse for shirking responsibility, insist on specifics about why she thinks the report "is probably not what you want." Then calmly, without putting her down, answer questions or show her how to correct problems. Then ask her to bring the report back to you when it has been corrected. Insist on your standards and her responsibility, like everyone else's, to meet those standards.

Reassure but don't pity.

The Braggart

Braggarts can type a perfect letter, talk on the phone, and sort mail simultaneously; have talked innumerable clients out of "taking their business elsewhere"; have had experience with just about everything short of negotiating for land in the Middle East—and really don't need the job "for the money."

And when they themselves are not in the limelight, they can't afford to let others be. They always top someone else's story: "I know what you mean. I had a similar situation..." When someone else presents an idea, they contradict: "You don't know what you're talking about." Or "You're wrong about that because..." When someone else does a better "good deed," they question the motive.

Most braggarts have lagging self-esteem and tell tall tales to win admiration. Or, to cement their sense of belonging, they hope you will see how important they are to your success and that of the company. Or possibly they may fear that their work is substandard and that they may be fired; the bragging combats security needs.

If your own ego is healthy and intact, you don't have to bother with "coping" with this personality. What's the problem? Listen and forget.

The benefits of working as a cohesive office or department are, of course, numerous: Everyone requires less supervision. Open communication between the supervised and the supervisors ensures better service and higher-quality products. Peer pressure can correct potential problems. People don't dread coming to work. Individual stress decreases. People get their basic needs met.

Anger, for the short term, may have its rewards. You will gain sympathy and attention for having to work with "such a person." Anger also gives you license to go temporarily insane—that is, make dumb mistakes, tell someone off, or in some other way wreck a project.

But in the long run, the company and your boss look for productivity—whether you work alone, with, or through other people. Therefore, doing your part to deal with the "problem" personalities rather than replacing them is part of your responsibility as a productive employee.

Here are four last suggestions for coping:

First, try to change the other's behavior if you can. Try to understand why she behaves as she does and try to help her get her basic needs met in some more acceptable way. Act friendly, but low key. Develop an appropriate "stroke" style; let her know you consider her important and worthy of your attention and help. Show acceptance, empathy, and genuineness. Be respectful of her work style and demand respect of yours.

Second, know yourself. Be confident within yourself. Make sure you are not acting or reacting out of ego problems similar to the other person's. Be secure in your reputation for integrity and good work, and don't be fearful that others have the power to discredit or destroy you in your boss's or others' eyes.

Third, know when to walk away from a situation. Learn what it is that "sets you off" about the other person and learn to walk away when you see that situation or attitude developing. If you're required to work with the "problem" personality only temporarily, deal with each other through writing or third parties. If it's a continual, long-term working relationship, perhaps a transfer is in order; or you may simply be able to vary your daily routine so as not to come in contact with that other person.

Fourth, learn from the "problem" personality. Observe his reaction to circumstances and others—and their reactions to him. Alter your workstyle and attitudes to avoid duplicating his mistakes.

chapter 5

MAKING MEETINGS WORK

For the second time, the secretary offered the waiting client another cup of coffee and another stale alibi for her boss's tardiness.

When the training director/boss finally appeared, the client greeted him with, "You looked zapped."

"Sorry to keep you waiting. We've been in another one of those marathon meetings around here...I'd rather have the flu."

Overhearing such a conversation and new to the business world, I faulted him for disloyalty to his boss and company; now, with several years' experience in the corporate scene, I know he's expressing an almost universal sentiment. An invitation to a meeting has become a summons to the guillotine.

Should someone call a meeting to discuss "meeting dissatisfaction" (quite likely), you'd hear comments echoing those below:

"They're too long."

"We don't ever accomplish anything. I can chitchat in my own office."

"I never know why we're meeting until I get there; how can I offer anything constructive on the spur of the moment?"

"People don't listen to each other; it's a free-for-all and we keep going over the same things."

"I don't know why I'm asked to attend. This has absolutely nothing to do with my job."

"The person in charge never takes charge."

"My boss says we're supposed to decide on a plan of action, but most of the time he already has his mind made up. Why fuss with a meeting rubber stamp?"

"We can't make decisions when certain people don't show up. So the whole discussion has to be repeated to them the next time."

"Somebody always gets his feelings hurt and pouts."

"There's just so much information any one person can take in one sitting. I simply can't concentrate on or remember it all."

"Some people sound like a broken record."

"Several in our department don't get along, so our meetings resemble a cold war with little or no détente."

To top off all the grumbling and interpersonal problems in the ranks, top management must total up the cost. Consider the hourly salary of each attendee and add those figures together for a total meeting cost. Of course, an additional cost of meetings lies in the time attendees spend complaining to colleagues about what did or did not happen in the meeting.

And often you as secretarial support staff must put projects on hold for lack of direction about problems that surface while the boss is "tied up in a meeting." Additionally, even though you may not be required to participate in the meeting you often must be "on hand" to see that things run smoothly for all involved.

Although costs vary from organization to organization, consultants Michael Doyle and David Straus (*How to Make Meetings Work*, p. 4) estimate that direct meeting costs approximate between 7 and 15 percent of an organization's annual personnel budget.

And the problem gets worse as employees move up the corporate ladder. Xerox Learning Systems of Stamford, Connecticut, says many executives spend 70 percent of their time attending and conducting meetings, when 70 percent of the meetings are unnecessary in the first place.

Therefore, if meetings are expensive, time-consuming, and intimidating to people who attend them, why meet? Why don't supervisors simply hand down decisions and solve problems, and let their employees or colleagues gripe about the decision or the solution rather than the meeting itself?

First, to do one's job without benefit of meeting is a lot like doing a wedding without benefit of clergy or a divorce without benefit of counsel. It can be risky. Few supervisors have such complete command of their job responsibilities that they have answers to all the problems; a wrong solution can be as expensive to reverse as a marriage. And, of course, the higher up the corporate ladder your boss is, the more costly the mistakes.

Second, meetings give critics a chance to work out a compromise beforehand rather than to undercut the plan of action once it is adopted. Third, when others in the office have to be convinced, a group of witnesses to the birthing of an idea carries more weight with nondecision-makers. Finally, when a project or solution calls for intestinal fortitude, a group generally has more guts, creatively speaking, than a single individual.

So despite the time and money involved, meetings are probably here to stay; the question is how to make them pay for themselves. The answer lies in analyzing and controlling the interpersonal dynamics to bring about the desired effect.

Here's where you as secretary come in—you're in charge of scheduling, canceling, hosting, and on occasion leading and participating in these meetings. So how do you turn the free-for-all your department schedules monthly into a productive meeting? Following are some considerations and guidelines you probably never received in a training class but which nevertheless are essential to the modern secretary.

Who Should Attend

Who attends, of course, has direct bearing on your outcome; a group that's too small may be short on ideas and have a very narrow perspective, while a large group may make decision-by-concensus unwieldly. A group of three usually is much too limiting to come up with new ideas but may be fine if you're merely gathering information.

Most experts agree that a group of seven is about right for maximum efficiency—broad perspective and creativity, yet responsiveness to the problem at hand.

When you're making out the "guest list," consider those who may have to approve your final decision and those outside your department who may have to work through, around, or with your decision. Perhaps these people can offer ideas from the ground floor rather than having you rebuild the overhangs on their area of responsibility.

Of course, if your supervisor merely hands you a list of attendees, your job is easier. Do, however, help her refine the list by mentioning those who may have been omitted but have helpful input. Also, discuss with her eliminating those who traditionally come to such meetings but don't have a "need to know" or discuss. Point out that extra attendees often impede results.

Selecting a Location

First decide if the meeting should be on-site or off-site—away from the corporate setting in a hotel, resort, or campus conference room. One advantage of keeping the meeting on-site is that participants have ready access to their own desks and phones for messages and to access help with problems back on the job. Another advantage is less travel time. A third advantage is that you may use your own company personnel or a favorite food service to cater the meeting.

The advantages of scheduling the meeting off-site, of course, are equally worth considering. Attendees can more fully concentrate on the meeting discussion if they are not constantly interrupted by phone messages and back-on-the-job questions and problems. Another advantage is that the catering service may be better than what you can arrange at the office and something out of the ordinary. A final advantage is that a new atmosphere can sometimes spur creative thinking in a more relaxed or unusual setting.

If you do decide to keep the meeting within your company's building, give serious thought to scheduling it somewhere other than in your or your boss's office. Simply moving to another room cuts down on interruptions and also makes it easier to bring the meeting to an end. Your boss may find it difficult to get up and leave her own office to suggest an informal ending to the meeting! Finally, choose a secluded room or one that can be closed off so that every Tom, Dick, and Harriet walking by can't wave in and offer a wisecrack.

If the meeting is to be a long one, consider a site with nearby refreshment areas and restrooms.

Arranging and Furnishing the Room

Whether meeting on-site or off-site, choose a meeting room with care. The room size should fit the group size, because group dynamics begin when attendees take their seats. A room that's too large allows cliques to form, leaving empty chairs between them serving as psychological barriers. Hostile groups sitting eyeball to eyeball around a conference table grow even more hostile. If extra chairs are left sitting outside or away from the intended gathering area, dropouts usually squat there in an attempt to observe and critique the action without full participation.

Round or oval tables often lead to problem-solving or discussion, while rectangular shapes with "Dad or Mom" at the head sometimes stifle opposing views. Also, arrangements that force people to sit facing each other often "set people up" to compete or argue. When attendees sit side by side, they tend to feel more like cooperating. Other possible arrangements include a U, L, panel, T formation, teams, or schoolroom style—with all chairs in rows facing the front.

For maximum participation with the least cause for hostility, meeting consultants Doyle and Straus suggest that members sit in a semicircle facing the person leading the meeting. In addition to more equal involvement of the attendees, this arrangement allows all to see a chart or board on which has been recorded the meeting agenda, time limits, and possibly a list of group ideas developed in the brainstorming process.

In addition to room size and possible seating arrangements, consider other furnishings of the room: Will you need a podium?

Microphone? Audio-visual equipment? Work tables? Easels and stands? Chalkboard? Translation equipment? Computer terminals or typewriters? Copying machines? Transparency makers? Phones? Pens? Pads? Handouts—extra copies for those who may have forgotten to bring with them handouts sent out with the agenda? What about water pitchers and glasses? Ashtrays? Are window coverings arranged appropriately for audio-visual presentations?

Name cards or badges? You may need both. If using name cards at the table, make sure they are large enough to be read several feet away, especially by the leader. Providing smaller lapel name badges also is a good idea if there will be several breaks during which participants will be away from their tables and tent cards.

Also, consider the comfort of the participants. Someone allergic to the smoke snaking into the air beside him may grow hostile before the group even begins to discuss the moratorium on spending. If you've got a flip chart or chalkboard handy, simply scribble "smoking" and a directional arrow for the participants to see as they enter. Make sure the room is properly ventilated.

Setting the Meeting Time

Consider the participants' regular work calendars. If you set the meeting for Monday morning, will that mean attendees' subordinates must wait around to get their instructions until after their boss's meeting? If you schedule too late in the day and the discussion runs longer than expected, will some members have to leave early due to inflexible transportation arrangements? If you schedule on Friday, will there be some out of the office, taking a long weekend? Also, consider that Friday afternoons for many involve finishing up the week's projects.

In addition to considering the "normal" daily or weekly schedule of attendees, you may find it beneficial and time-saving in the long run to phone attendees or their secretaries and ask for major schedule restrictions during a certain three-week period—conflicts such as vacations, seminars, conventions, field trips. Note these major conflicts and then set the exact day and time after knowing that participants at least will be in their offices.

Of course, you'll find it futile to try to schedule your meetings around everyone's work schedules. Simply avoid the "musts" on the calendar. Attendees, then, will have to work around minor conflicts and reschedule their own routine matters after you announce the meeting date and time.

Inviting Attendees

For informal, small-group meetings, you will probably invite attendees by phone. Be careful of your wording when you do, so as to ensure cooperation among higher-ups and colleagues in other departments. "You need to be at a meeting at 3 P.M. in Room 233 to discuss the new supply-requisition requirements" is likely to raise more hackles on a busy day than something like, "We've scheduled a meeting at 3 P.M. in Room 233 to discuss the new supply-acquisition requirements. We'd like you to attend if at all possible." When neither you nor your boss has the authority to command someone to attend, simply inform.

If you're inviting by phone, always inform the attendee about the meeting agenda so that he or she can bring all necessary information and be prepared to offer comments on the topics to be discussed. If the agenda for the meeting is open, ask for any items the attendee may need to bring up at the meeting. Get as many details as possible according to the guidelines under "Preparing the Agenda."

For larger or more formal meetings, you will probably announce the meeting by memo or letter. In the opening "message" sentence, state the what, where, when, and why of the meeting. Second, ask for confirmation of attendance so that if key people will be unable to attend or if necessary information is unavailable, you can reschedule. Third, include the meeting agenda in question form (see "Preparing the Agenda") so that attendees know specifically which direction their thoughts, planning, and comments should take. Also, time limits and order of agenda will allow those whose presence is not required for the entire meeting to come late or leave early. Finally in the announcement memo, give any premeeting assignments to speed the meeting's progress.

Always make it a point to remind participants of the meeting again the day before the meeting with either a phone call or a memo.

Canceling When Appropriate

Make sure that you know all the details about the meeting and what it is supposed to accomplish so that you can alert your boss to developing problems and the possible need for cancellation or postponement.

For instance, what if a key person says she's had a dentist appointment for three months and will not be able to attend? Would it be a waste of time to meet without her? Or an attendee may inform you that key data are still unavailable, that a client has changed the requirements of the project under discussion, that a solution to a difficulty has already been found.

In any of these cases, you should inform your boss and ask about the possible wisdom of canceling or delaying the meeting.

When your boss has said she's taken care of telling the attendees about the cancellation, that's fine. But don't let the matter stop there. Always double-check by phoning each participant's office and leave formal word with the attendee or his or her secretary.

When canceling by memo, the first "message" sentence should announce the cancellation. Include enough detail about the meeting time, date, subject, location, or duration to prevent misunderstandings about exactly which meeting you are referring to.

Give reasons for the cancellation, such as key people who are out of town or missing information necessary for a decision. (Be tactful in wording your reason, particularly if someone will feel "blamed" or lose face about the cancellation. For example, not: "We're having to cancel because Helen Jones has not completed the XYZ report." Rather: "We are canceling due to delays in compiling the XYZ report.")

Second, state any available information about rescheduling.

Third, express regret for any inconvenience the cancellation or postponement has caused.

Fourth, suggest alternatives for handling a particular problem, situation, or decision until the meeting can be rescheduled.

When canceling by memo, following up by phone to see that the memo was received is often a good idea.

Preparing the Agenda

Mystery meetings, although they may promise intrigue, usually deliver disappointment. When you tell participants what you'll be discussing in the meeting, they can come prepared with supporting evidence, opposing documentation, or an open mind—whichever the case. Catching attendees off guard only raises the possibility of a second meeting to quiet the grumbling of a surprise attack or to handle the repercussions of a spur-of-the-moment discussion and decision.

Here are four guidelines to help you formulate an agenda; you will note that you must use your interviewing skills to get enough appropriate information from your boss to make the agenda meaningful.

1. State the issue or topic in question form: "Is the cost of the geological field trip to Nevada justifiable?" Not simply, "Gathering Geological Data in Nevada."

2. State the method the leader will use to cover the issue: Individual presentations by attendees, guest speaker, question-answer, examination of report, etc.

3. Let the attendees know how much authority they have on the issue: For decision? For discussion only? For their information? To formulate a recommendation?

4. List agenda items in priority order and set time limits: Otherwise, you may spend 30 minutes discussing the color of the new telephone system and 10 minutes on how to spend $30,000 for data collection. Listing the items to be covered by priority lets participants know approximately what portion of the meeting they will need to attend. If one person has interest and input for only the first item, why should she sit through the last hour's discussion? This is not to say that agenda items and time limits never need to be shuffled but rather that the leader should do so with reason and care.

Your distributed agenda sheet may look something like this:

Meeting Agenda—June 12

1. Is the cost of the geological field trip to Nevada justifiable?	Examine report Question/Answer	For recommendation only	30 min.
2. If the trip is decided upon, how should we provide orientation?	Discussion	For decision	15 min.
3. Have there been problems with the new insurance forms?	Question/Answer	For information only	5 min.

Hosting

Serving Refreshments

You have several options when serving coffee or more elaborate refreshments. You can ask each attendee for preferences and serve each individually as he or she arrives for the meeting. You can wait until all have arrived and serve them as a group. (Always serve your boss last because you are acting as his or her representative.) Or you can arrange to have the beverages and food on a serving table and let attendees serve themselves either as they arrive or during the meeting.

You and your boss must consider the pros and cons of each arrangement. Certainly, serving each guest personally is the more cordial manner, but this means that you must be on hand for a long time at the beginning of the meeting and reappear frequently for refills. Also, your coming in and out of the meeting can be distracting.

If you can't devote the time to being on hand or must be elsewhere to cover phones or supervise other work, letting guests serve themselves may be the best answer. In our fast-food, do-it-yourself restaurants and shops, people are comfortable with this arrangement. Let the importance of your guests, the political climate, and time and place constraints be your guide.

In the case of more elaborate refreshments, you will need to make arrangements with a caterer. Don't think, however, that your hosting responsibilities are over once you have contacted the caterer and selected the menu. Take responsibility to make serving decisions and supervise the affair, including making sure the number of servers can handle the function, watching to see that food selections are adequate and serving dishes replenished, and detailing stipulations about delivery and clean-up service.

Delivering Messages

Get instructions beforehand from your boss as to whether you are to interrupt the meeting with messages for him and his subordinates. If he'd prefer that you not deliver messages into the meeting or put calls through, be available when the meeting breaks up to deliver the messages to participants so that none leaves without the information. A message may alter an attendee's plans for the day and where he goes after the meeting.

If the meeting participants are your boss's peers or superiors, you will probably be instructed to ask the attendees if they wish to be interrupted during the meeting with a call or message rather than leave that decision solely to your boss.

When you take messages into the meeting, type them for ease in reading. Then wait to see if there's a reply or instruction for you to take care of the situation.

The Extras

Here's where you make your boss look really good. You become a superior host when you can greet attendees by name, remember their preference for beverages, and offer to take care of travel or other accommodations for them or their spouses. You may need to reconfirm airline reservations, make alternate flight arrangements if the meeting runs longer than expected, call taxis or limos, offer to phone their offices or waiting spouses if the schedule is rearranged, locate additional information about an important situation. When someone has forgotten something needed in the meeting, your challenge should be to locate the information as quickly as possible.

Minutes

If you are asked to take minutes at a meeting and you don't know the names of attendees, make a seating chart and fill in names as people arrive or have your boss fill in the chart for you. This will enable you to get names with the appropriate discussion, recommendations, and assignments without interrupting.

When recording minutes, briefly state the major topics of discussion or meeting conclusions up front. However, delay mentioning specific assignments until after you have recorded the essence of each topic discussion.

Use headings to help readers focus on agenda items of individual interest. On occasion, you may want to use your discussion questions as headings and then record key points, conclusions, and decisions in list form.

Remember that space given to recording a topic discussion suggests its importance; don't get carried away with minutiae. You'll have to avoid the once-upon-a-time detail that always surrounds each discussion topic and focus on the major problems identified or solved, the major questions raised or answered, the results and/or related follow-up action.

Arrange topics in most-to-least significant format rather than in order of discussion. (This, of course, should agree with the order of discussion if the agenda has been prepared properly.)

Include specific follow-up assignments—who should do what by when.

Last, include names of attendees.

Helping Your Boss Prepare for a Meeting

If you receive a meeting announcement by phone, make sure that you probe for detailed information about the meeting topics so that your boss can be prepared to attend. When you hand your boss a copy of the meeting agenda—write things down for him even if you have received the meeting announcement by phone—attach a note asking what information you need to gather for him. Perhaps you should list specific topics such as "correspondence," "files," "reports," and "data" to prompt his thinking.

And don't give him the necessary information in hodge-podge fashion. If there is much information, separate it into separate folders in some logical fashion—by project, agenda item, or correspondence/report/statistics.

When You're the Leader

When some emergency arises such as sudden illness or an out-of-town trip, you may find yourself leading a meeting as your boss's representative. Or you may have scheduled the meeting yourself to coordinate various projects assigned to you.

First in becoming a good meeting leader you must recognize a good meeting when you see one—one from which solutions evolve and participants leave in a positive frame of mind. Is the leader totally responsible for the group's success? Must all members contribute opinions on all issues? Does courtesy spell productivity?

No, on all accounts. A good meeting can be characterized by the following:

1. Atmosphere: The physical arrangement looks informal, comfortable, workable. In other words, despite the coffee cups or crumbs on the table, the group looks as though it has rolled up its collective sleeves and gone to work.

2. Members: They are trusting, supportive, caring. Although all may not contribute ideas on all issues, they feel free to do so without fear of attack or put-down. No one member dominates the discussion. They listen to each other. They recognize and deal with personality conflicts. Members do not defer, necessarily, to those who have more rank. They have a clear understanding of their resources, their limits of authority, and their basic goals with regard to the issues at hand. In short, they feel collectively responsible for the group's actions and decisions and commit themselves to carry out group decisions.

3. Leader: The leader does not filter all the ideas through her biases, nor do others defer due to her rank. The leader does not feel challenged when someone of more expertise in one area expresses an opposing view. She does not demand that all members contribute to the group, but she does take responsibility to see that all feel free to do so. Finally, she assumes responsibility for group dynamics and channels the meeting toward its goals.

4. Accomplishments: The group accomplishes clear-cut

objectives, whether to offer suggestions, make recommendations, get information, or solve problems. Members do not leave a meeting feeling that their time has been wasted.

So how do you turn the meeting into a productive one like the one characterized above? After considering all the guidelines for scheduling a site, arranging and furnishing a room, setting a time, and announcing the meeting, you'll need to decide on the purposes for your meeting and prepare an agenda to suit those purposes.

Defining Your Purposes

Basically, you will be conducting one of four types of meetings: to give information to the group; to have the group share information with each other; to elicit feedback or generate suggestions for goals, programs, or problems; to make a decision. Although this may seem like a basic assumption, many who call meetings have not considered their real purpose and consequently anger participants.

You as meeting leader may want to tell, sell, consult, or abdicate your authority to the group, but you'd better know which before the meeting begins. Any of these leadership modes fit on occasion: You may simply *tell* your subordinates about a new policy on computer use whereby they will now be required to reserve computer time on special log-in sheets.

Or you may wish to inform the group that scheduling computer time has become a problem, causing work delays, and, therefore, you have come up with a tentative solution for scheduling that you want to *persuade* the group to support enthusiastically.

Or you may want to *consult* the group for their suggestions as to how to cut down on computer scheduling conflicts and work stoppages. In the end, you may be willing to go along with the group's best solution so long as it falls within your own basic objectives.

Finally, you may *abdicate* your authority altogether and let the group make the final decision about computer use and policy.

Any of these roles, on occasion, accomplishes a purpose; resentment surfaces only when you as leader don't clarify the group's role in the beginning and when you make attendees feel used. When you permit a group to spend time discussing options you know you and your boss will never go along with in the final round, attendees smell manipulation.

That is not to say it is improper for a leader simply to "tell" the group how a certain problem will be solved but rather that the leader should not call a meeting for rubber-stamping a decision that's already been made.

Considering the above, you may decide your regular meetings are detrimental, or at best, useless. Fine, forget about having them. Even true decision-making meetings have a tendency to have a "leveling" effect, as some have referred to it. The group decision leads to conformity, whereby the more conservative thinkers shoot down ideas of high potential and high risk and where mediocrity, the safer course, reigns.

Furthermore, some meetings should never be held because the subject is too trivial for the cost involved. You may decide that it's not worth $80 in collective salary to pull six peers off the job to explain a policy change that can be easily described in a memo costing three minutes' reading time.

And, of course, some issues can be communicated better by phone one-on-one. Where hostility is expected, some matters may best be handled in a confidential, less threatening manner rather than announced to the entire group in a winner/loser situation.

But once you have decided what you actually want to accomplish with the group and that a meeting is definitely in order, then be careful to prevent all the hang-ups along the way.

Open-agenda meetings are probably the most notorious for time-wasting and disgruntled feelings. If you must lead an open-agenda meeting, use the first few minutes to lead your participants to set up their agenda as described earlier in "Preparing the Agenda." Your conversation may follow these lines:

Participant: We need to talk about the underbudgeting of seminars for next year.

You: What exactly? Do you mean which seminars to cancel or that we should consider petitioning for more money?

Participant: No, I don't think that's a possibility now. (If there seems to be disagreement about whether the budget decision is final, send someone to make a phone call to verify; don't spend time arguing a moot point. If this is fact, continue.) What we need to decide is which of the four seminars has the lowest priority this year.

You: Okay. (Record this question-format item on the agenda list for all to see.) Do you want us to make the decision today or just offer input?

Participant: Suggestions, really. I don't have exact tuition costs for each seminar. I'd really just like opinions on which are priorities for each department.

You: (You record "for suggestions only" beside the agenda item.) I think 10 minutes will give us each time to state an opinion by department, don't you? (You've named method for discussion and set a time limit.)

Proceed to next suggestion for item to be discussed. After all have been listed, go back and determine the order of discussion, ranking the most important first in case some items run longer than expected and must be postponed until the next meeting.

Some people use meetings to ask every question they have ever been meaning to get around to. You, as leader, be the judge of topics important enough to take group time. To minor issues raised, you can always say: "Can we hold off on that and I'll get with you personally later?" and then don't wait for an answer.

When you fail to set an agenda, even in an open-agenda meeting, you are in effect conducting a "chat." This kind of nonproductive meeting is what causes members to wring their hands in frustration. After you've established the format, members will learn to arrive with agenda items in proper form and ready for discussion, recommendation, or whatever.

Agenda items requiring decisions rather than only suggestions or information will tend to cause the most interpersonal problems for the simple reason that more ego seems to be at stake. To arrive at definite decisions within a certain time period creates anxiety. For some, it's the difference between the atmosphere of seventh inning stretch and final out.

Coming to Decisions

Basically, you as leader have the responsibility for guiding the group through the four steps of decision-making below:

1. *Define the problem*: Don't go for the quick fix to the wrong problem. Spend time analyzing the real issues; see that you are not treating symptoms rather than causes. Are you asking the right questions? Make sure you are defining the problem in

terms of needs, not assumed solutions. For example, not "How can we coordinate trips across town to the warehouse for supplies?" but "How can we get supplies here more quickly and less expensively?" In other words, you don't want to limit your discussion to coordinating schedules when the best answer could be having a messenger service deliver the supplies.

2. *Develop alternatives that meet your criteria*: If there are specific constraints, state them at the outset—only X dollars available, company policy prohibits Y, and Mr. So-and-So is dead set against Z and therefore would never give final approval.

   After an admission of the constraints and establishment of the desirable criteria, members should brainstorm possible solutions without stopping to evaluate alternatives. Ideally, someone who has no interest in the outcome of a particular issue should list all ideas on a large sheet of newsprint for all the group to see, as a "group memory." Members may want to modify each other's ideas, refining them as they move along. At this stage, no evaluation should take place—no comments like, "That will never work because..." or, "We tried that last year when..." The idea is to generate as many creative solutions as possible. You're developing the Christmas list from which you'll shop later.

3. *Evaluate the alternatives and select the best one*: Now that the group has a recorded list of possibilities, knock out the least viable ones by asking if any in the group could definitely not go along with certain options. That process will probably cut the alternative list to a manageable size. Then proceed with discussion about how each of the remaining options falls within the boundaries or rises to the desirable criteria established earlier. You may find it helpful to develop a matrix something like the one below for deciding what software package to buy:

	User Ease	**Support**	**Applications**	**Cost**
Brand A				
Brand B				
Brand C				

*1 = lowest favorable rating; 4 = highest favorable rating

Fill in the blanks with numerical ratings and total the scores to arrive at a group decision about the best alternative. Perhaps by group consent, you have eliminated Brands D and E because the initial cost exceeds your approved budget.

In some cases, of course, this detailed matrix method is unnecessary; you can orally rule out alternatives and narrow your choices by asking for consensus one by one. If this is the method you choose, be sure to ask opinions of the more hesitant and lesser-ranking people before asking a higher-status boss, or you will likely not get their true feelings on the matter. As you work your way toward consensus by eliminating alternatives and piggybacking ideas, continually test for agreement so as not to belabor a compromise already reached.

When you stop moving forward, you're backtracking. If consensus cannot be reached, you may have to refer the decision to a superior or go for a majority vote. In either case, the group usually feels better for having had some input.

4. *Plan how to put the solution into action*: Make assignments. Who does what—when, where, and why. Remember that few decisions are irreversible. So monitor your decision to see that it continues to meet your objectives. Decisions, like love, are seldom forever. If you discover you've made a poor one, return to Point 1 and start the brainstorming process again.

If the above plan does not run as smoothly as outlined here, perhaps you've overlooked one or more of these bumps in the road: The problem hasn't been defined appropriately; members are not prepared or knowledgeable enough to offer creative solutions; members are unaware of meeting processes; members have unsettled personal conflicts.

If you suspect one of the first two hitches in the process, lead the group to redefine the problem and/or dismiss the meeting for members to gather further information. If lack of consensus involves lack of knowledge about group processes try to emphasize your facilitator role and educate participants on the group interaction stages and happenings. In other words, give them some of the information in this chapter about how to make meetings more productive.

Traffic Cop: Signals the conversational flow—who speaks and when; tries to see that monopolizers are ticketed and that hesitant speakers are signaled into participation; on technical points, stops regular traffic to ask experts to pull onto the freeway with an opinion.

Investigative Reporter: Repeats ideas from several members and then elaborates, clarifies, and formulates them into a cohesive whole for the entire group.

Chemist: Asks questions of members to probe for significance, to redirect their thinking, to test for suitability, to test for consensus.

Diplomat: Modifies suggestions and works to bring members together by pointing out areas of agreement and by suggesting points of possible compromise.

Therapist: Acknowledges and praises superior ideas, participation, and cooperation; recaps ground covered and prods on to new heights.

Entertainer: Reduces tension by pausing for a joke, keeps reminding group that "it's only a job."

Finally, if the problem that's bogging down the meeting is members' unresolved personal conflicts, you as leader must manage to work around obstacles either by helping members eliminate individual problems of which they may or may not be aware or by helping them interact with other attendees in such a way as to cause the least disruption.

Problem Participants

Nonparticipant: This person may be present in body but not in spirit. She arrives late, leaves early, and brings paperwork to shuffle the rest of the time. If possible, she sits in a chair in the back or away from the others. If forced to join the group physically, she often singles out a kindred soul and carries on a whispering commentary on the proceedings. The less-offensive nonparticipant keeps quiet merely because she feels intimidated to speak rather than for lack of interest or as an act of defiance.

To cope: Before the group gathers, arrange the chairs to thwart the dropout who wants to isolate herself. For the late arriver, let her know that you notice that the act is habitual, and don't waste group time by recapping everything she's missed. For the early leaver, ask why she must leave and suggest that maybe you should cancel the remainder of the meeting since her presence is vitally important. For the whispering nonparticipants, make eye contact with them rather than trying to ignore them. If necessary, stop and ask if they have something they'd like to share with the rest of the group.

Windbag: This individual talks just to fill up time; her comments "cover all the bases" past, present, and future. The talker often misguidedly thinks that she is doing the leader a favor by talking when no one else speaks up. A case in point: A small company was considering changing its name. When the group leader brought up the issue in a meeting, most nodded agreement and there was little discussion. Finally, one salesman took the floor and proceeded to give background for name changes of larger companies in the past decade, concluding 15 minutes later with the comment: "Well, I guess that about wraps it up. You seemed to be hurting for an opinion; that should open things up." For some with less noble motives, to hold the floor is power. Still others keep the chatter going to avoid going back to work.

To cope: When the speaker begins to ramble in the abstract, stop her by asking for specific illustrations, figures, dates. Cut her off at the pass when she pauses for breath by commenting, "Okay, who else has an opinion on that?" "We agree; now then..." "Wait a minute, Kerrie. We don't want to make you do all the thinking for us; let's hear from someone else about..."

Interrupter: This person is like a trap waiting to be sprung; every time someone's words flip a switch, she lights up with a show-and-tell. Interrupters of the not-so-innocent variety cut others off as a power play.

To cope: To the innocent interrupter, ask her to write down her ideas so that she won't forget and promise to call on her in a moment "when Martha finishes"; perhaps the urge to elaborate will have subsided by the time you get back to her. For the power-seeking interrupter, comment with a smile, "Just a moment, Charlene, I don't think Jean was finished. Okay, go ahead, Jean."

Pessimist: This is the individual that in the face of irrefutable evidence comments in a slow, deliberate voice reminiscent of the late Everett Dirkson, "But...I...still...think..." A pessimist doesn't necessarily take the negative tack out of spite but rather often sees herself as the last restraining force before the group plunges forth into disaster. Resistant to any change, out of excessive fear of the unknown, she always feels more comfortable with the status quo. Others who have given up voicing their negativism convey their displeasure by eye-rolling, headshaking, snickering, or pencil-tossing.

To cope: If the rest of the group is in agreement, you can remind the vociferous pessimist that you will keep her disapproval in mind and assure her, not sarcastically, that you will remember "she told you so," should the proposed decision backfire. If the disagreement is displayed only through body language, try to ignore it. If it becomes disruptive to the others, ask the pessimist point-blank if she'd like to voice what's bothering her, and then proceed as above.

Attention Seeker: She seeks recognition in one of two ways. If accomplishments merit it, she can sing, "See This Week's Miracles." Continually, she adds asides and irrelevant illustrations to the topics at hand or relates how she has miraculously slayed dragons with a dull sword and a single blow. Accomplishments lacking, she will seek attention by offering off-the-wall opinions or solutions. After all, negative attention is better than no attention at all.

To cope: If possible to do so quickly, acknowledge her accomplishments briefly, letting her know you sense the ulterior motive for the contributed ideas, and then revert to the issues at hand. For way-out suggestions, try to avoid showing shock (the payoff) and record the idea along with the more viable as though it were of equal status. Do not reward the person by teasing, laughter, or comments about how she "always comes up with these ideas." (Be careful here that you're not overlooking really creative, serious suggestions.)

Guru: She is the expert who frequently prefaces her comments with: "What Gery was really trying to say is that..." and "The facts are these—number one..." Then she rattles on in technical jargon that tends to humiliate, anger, or confuse others. She feels a strong mission to enlighten the rest of the world. She believes that with enough facts all problems will stabilize and the plans of action will become clear-cut. Although she can indeed be valuable in getting necessary input for the group, she often oversteps her bounds and refuses to consider other perspectives. She must be right, as a matter of professional pride. The pseudoguru, having noticed the respect often given to true experts, often speaks beyond her knowledge and passes on her judgments as facts.

To cope: With the true guru, consultant Robert Bramson recommends that you listen fully and carefully to her presentation and then repeat back her main points. Only when she's sure you understand her will she stop re-explaining to you. When disagreeing, avoid dogmatic statements that you may have to eat later. Defer to her expertise and work around her with comments such as, "This may not work, but let's just consider the option of..." To force her to rethink her position, ask questions such as, "How will this system affect our processing the invoices?" Further, to call attention to her habitual rephrasing and "clarifying" of everybody else's comments, refrain from adopting her phraseology and stick with the words of the originator of the idea. Or, turn to the one "clarified," and ask if she has been interpreted correctly.

To handle the pseudoguru, state the facts more accurately as you see them and then allow her opportunity to save face with comments like: "Perhaps you didn't have access to these latest charts, but..." She will usually take your cover.

Put-down Artist: She insults, criticizes, argues, and accuses others under cover of humor. She can deliver a real zinger that leaves the victim humiliated, or she can mouth "innocent" double-entendres and roll her eyes at the rest of the group.

To cope: Let the artist know you see through the humor and call the comments for what they are: "I take it that you think Margaret's idea is unworkable. Would you like to be more specific about your opposition?" This puts her on the spot and encourages her to refrain from further aggression in disguise.

Time Bomb: Each time this individual expresses an opinion, he increases in volume and intensity. His voice shows a grave effort at restraint right up until the last moment when he finally detonates with an emotional outburst: "That's the stupidest suggestion I've ever heard, and if that's what you want to do, go ahead without me," followed by a hasty exit. Some stick around physically but break after their "final" pronouncement: "Listen, people, there's only one sure way to handle this, and it's thus." Then his elaborative comments taper from the first loud explosion to the dribbling, quivering, tension-relieved close. The group holds on to its life raft in the wake.

To cope: Don't try to interrupt the tirade; let the person gradually run down. Show that you have listened to what he said and that you understand the issue is important to him. If possible, break to let the group recover and, most importantly, to let the speaker regain composure and objectivity.

Clown: Often the clown romps in from another department looking for "what's happening" as a means of avoiding her own work. She has all the time in the world to tell stories about what happened over the weekend when she ran into the CEO at a favorite bar or to express cynical opinions about company policy. She's nonchalant about the budget expenditures—after all, "it's not her money." If the rest of the group is serious about the task at hand, the clown is a nuisance. If the group is tension-filled, she is the welcomed comic relief.

To cope: Do nothing if she is serving the later function. If she becomes a nuisance, try to ignore her. If her antics become too time-consuming, try: "Marilyn, we really do need to get to a decision in the next 10 minutes; otherwise, we'll be staying during lunch. Do you mind?" Usually, when the audience stops applauding, she will bow off stage.

Yes-woman: Her favorite response line is "It's all right by me." On the surface, you hardly recognize this as a problem participant, but habitual, total agreement often is the cover for later sabotage of projects and lack of cooperation. Because this person feels too insecure to offer conflicting opinions, she lets solutions slide by her without lifting a finger and then conducts a "grump" session afterward. Occasionally, she fails to speak up simply because she doesn't want to appear ignorant or doesn't want to "insult" someone else by disagreeing. Finally, her agreeableness may be dictated by a "teacher's pet" role with the boss.

To cope: Make sure your meeting atmosphere is supportive rather than intimidating. If you anticipate underlying dissension that may go unexpressed, take a one-by-one opinion poll, recording responses. Later when you hear the yes-woman's grumbling, remind them of her verbal support at the meeting. Ask if facts have surfaced that have caused her to withdraw support for the plan of action.

This person usually has a strong need to be liked, so you have to give her "permission" to disagree. In short, be sure that your tone reassures her that opposing views are welcome and, one-on-one, if necessary, let her know that you want honest feedback. Don't forget to publicly praise those who ask penetrating questions that force you to rethink your position.

Caution: Don't look for trouble when there is none. The silent or superagreeable person may simply be uninterested or may be easily persuaded. In that case, she's not a problem participant; pray that her tribe will multiply.

Meeting Games You May Have to Mediate

Consider some of the games that go on in meetings that turn out not to be so much fun:

Power, Power, Who's Got the Power: Although a little more complicated than the similar childhood game, Power becomes more visible as the game moves along match after match throughout working relationships. The object of the game is to be caught holding the power the most times by the most people.

Although intangible itself, the signs of power are usually apparent to all, as Michael Korda, in *Power! How to Get It, How to Use It*, points out the use of bad manners in meetings. For example, only those with true power can introduce profanity into the discussion, interrupt at will, pause in a serious discussion to tell a joke, or laugh at an expert's presentation.

Another move in Power strategy is seating arrangement. Those with power sit nearest the boss, so as to appear on the "inside track." Players manage this by arriving extra early or by having others switch seats with them "so they can see the flip chart" or "to get out of a draft." If forced to sit away from the boss, players can nullify the effect to some extent by alluding to inside matters, mentioning the conversation they had earlier, or by nodding when the boss speaks to indicate prior knowledge of his pronouncements. Or, if the player really wants to call attention to her power, she can take potshots at her rival by suggesting that the opponent do the "menial" chores such as getting coffee for everyone, ordering the lunch, bringing in the file, or typing up the minutes.

A final strategy for Power, Power, Who's Got the Power is to see who can be busiest. Players arrive late because of a last-minute call about the "big contract," have a typist come to her with problems or messages, or if nothing else works, walk out of the meeting early because she "has things to do for the CEO."

The winner of Power is the individual who elicits the most deference from the most players most of the time.

Prosecutor: This game is generally played on teams; however, the teams are seldom equal in number, and it's not unusual to have a team of five against one or seven against two. The way this game is played is that the group, feeling frustrated about lack of progress toward a goal or simply oozing with tension caused by personality conflicts, chooses a victim or two and lines them up as the opposition. If the opponent turns in a good report that she has solicited 10 executives to serve on the Mentor Council, the prosecutors focus on the fact that she hasn't yet designed a system for matching mentors and proteges. The victim can't feel good about getting the executives to participate in the mentoring plan because the opposition keeps focusing on the minor details that she has not yet worked out.

Frequently, this game is so enjoyable for the prosecutors that they prolong it into overtime for the sheer exhilaration of watching the other team writhe in embarrassment over the misspelling in a report's title page.

A final version of Prosecutor involves discounting the opposition simply through neglect. Much of this game can be played without the teams speaking to each other at all. The prosecutors arrange themselves so they sit with their backs to the opposition and have to crane their necks if he or she speaks. All utterances can be met with a slight smile or stark silence.

If the opposition dares to offer ideas anyway, the prosecutors can discount effectively with comments such as: "Your timing isn't exactly right on that"; "I don't think many would take that solution too seriously"; "Let us think about it and we'll get back to you"; "We've always done it this way before"; "Is it really that big a deal with you?" The winner in this game is the team who is able to keep attention focused on the weaknesses in the other's ideas or results rather than the merits. If the game is played long enough, the small opposition team disappears through embarrassment and becomes absorbed into the larger team. When this happens, the group must focus on one or two new players among its own membership and begin the process again.

Poor Me: This meeting game, unlike Prosecutor, is an individual sport. Whatever the payoffs—and Eric Berne outlines several in his best seller *Games People Play*—the Poor-Me player's strategy is to elicit as much sympathy as possible from the group and in the process excuse herself from blame.

Famous lines of the Poor-Me player include these: "Why do I always get stuck with all the typing assignments?" "If it weren't for the accounting department, I could have finished this work months ago." "I have small children to think about." "I told you I couldn't handle this, that it would never work, but you wouldn't listen."

If the group decides to play along, they withdraw blame and take the player off the hook; the Poor-Me player can then keep plugging along at her ineffective game plan. However, if the group passes judgment anyway, the player has a grudge and self-pity as consolation prizes.

If you've ever been a participant in or had to mediate any of these meeting games, you know that the score can run high in terms of time and damage to the group and individual psyches.

In general, handling any of these problem participants or refereeing games involves accepting the disruptive behavior rather than trying to sweep it under the rug and muddle through. Also, mediating involves giving the participant permission to see things from others' perspective and to feel the emotions they have. Finally, the leader establishes the boundaries within which this person and the group must operate.

Inexperienced meeting leaders often feel uneasy about conflict. And it is true that unrequited conflict, like unrequited love, saps energy. Productivity, on the other hand, increases when conflicts are allowed to surface and are then resolved to permit full cooperation.

Therefore, mediate, but don't stifle, conflict. Ask permission to summarize opposing viewpoints and then ask if you have summarized correctly. Then ask if others would like to comment on the two views. Your acknowledging the conflict relieves pressure and opens up further discussion.

This is not to say that all opposition will disappear, or even that that is desirable, but rather that you have a better chance for success when all players stay out in the open. When consensus about the situation at hand simply cannot be reached, you have the option of making the decision for the group, deferring it to your superior, or postponing it until later information develops or the situation changes.

Be careful in mediating conflict and summarizing opposing views, however, that you don't zero in on one side and show your partiality unless you intend to make the decision yourself. When you have called a meeting simply to inform, inform and then answer conflicting concerns yourself. Don't give the impression of having "teacher's pets" by deferring to some people who are more cordial and cooperative and overlooking those who seem negative or at least unenthusiastic about the issues.

Above all, don't leave the impression that you have consulted others in private or will consult them after the meeting before making your final decision. Remember, again, if you are calling a meeting simply to inform, inform. Don't create a false impression that you are leading toward a group decision when only the opinions of a few in the group really count with you. If that is the case, consult these people privately, make your decision, and simply announce it to the others.

Finally, as the leader, you have the responsibility to blow the whistle and dismiss the meeting.

Evaluating Your Results and Following Up

Practice makes perfect, they say; I don't agree. Practicing the wrong methods only perfects errors. Don't neglect to evaluate the meetings you lead: What went right? What went wrong? How did the "wrong" begin? Then what happened? How could you have altered the course? How did it all end when the dust settled? What can you do next time to avoid switching to that meeting track?

Your final responsibility as meeting leader—after arranging the logistics, developing the agenda, guiding the problem-solving process, and mediating the personal conflicts—involves follow-up activities. See that the meeting minutes get typed and distributed, so there's no chance for misunderstanding about what was decided or who was supposed to take what actions before the next meeting or the close of the project or event. Monitor task progress until you call the next meeting or turn the finished project over to your boss.

Being an Effective Meeting Participant

As far as meetings go, following carries almost as much responsibility as leading. If you are attending a meeting as your boss's representative, you may not feel that you have complete authority to participate. When you participate in a meeting in your own right, you may feel more leeway in expressing your ideas.

But in either role—representing yourself or your boss—you create an impression that will either help or hinder your boss's and your own career or projects. Therefore take every opportunity to be an involved participant.

As a meeting participant, be aware of group interactions such as those mentioned above—traffic cop, investigative reporter, chemist, diplomat, therapist, and entertainer. Assume those roles from time to time to carry the group to an effective conclusion—if for no other reason than the selfish one that you can't spend all your corporate life in time-wasting meetings. Encourage participation by asking reticent members' opinions. Summarize accomplishments, periodically evaluate the group's progress, and remind them of the time constraints.

For example, if you are recording minutes, you may help bring the group to a conclusion by a comment such as: "Pardon me, but before we go on to the next point, would someone clarify what we have just decided to do about the campaign?" Or, "I'm having a difficult time in following what this has to do with the decision we're making." Or, "Are we still on agenda item 2?"

And certainly never interrupt or slow down progress by carrying on your own personal conversation on the side.

During discussions, stay alert as the group moves through the four problem-solving tasks: Define the problem. Develop alternatives that meet your criteria. Evaluate the alternatives and select the best one. Plan how to put the solution into action. Remind members which step you're on and where you're going. If the group stalls over missing information about the exact sales percentages, offer to go check them out immediately or to find out before the next meeting.

In handling problem participants, refuse to give the standard "payoff" that keeps encouraging the same disruptive behavior. Instead, exercise control by using phrases that minimize the disruption. Don't try to outclown the clown, outanalyze the guru, or outtalk the windbag. Learn to stop putting others down, and develop trust and self-confidence so that you can express your own opinions and feelings.

That last suggestion—learning to develop self-confidence and to voice your own position—warrants elaboration. Subtle forms of ego attack on others indicate insecurities of your own.

Consider your own comments in a group and what impressions they convey to others: Do you always have the last word—"You think that's something; wait until you hear what we did." "You think you had trouble; we even had to..." Do your questions about others' data tend to make them feel cross-examined? Do you use dogmatic statements like: "You're dead-wrong about those questionnaires"? Do you have a let-me-tell-you-something-folks attitude when you speak? Many of these phrases and manners of speech can be eradicated by raising your own confidence/competence level.

If your boss is supposed to be the group leader for future meetings, you may need to take some of the responsibility upon yourself by suggesting privately how "*we* perhaps can improve *our* meetings." When there's no agenda, offer to prepare and distribute one "to keep *us* from getting bogged down." Or, you can use the regularly scheduled open-agenda meetings to set an example; circulate through the department to gather topics people intend to introduce and put them into the correct format and distribute copies. Let your actions and format serve as a model for your boss for future meetings.

Pitching Your Ideas to the Group

If at all possible, prepare ahead of time to get your ideas accepted. People known for thinking on their feet rarely do.

If you're a newcomer, lay low and observe for a while. Ask questions about practices you consider ineffectual; get the whys and wherefores about the old procedures. Is your "new idea" really old hat that didn't work?

If you are not yet comfortable in participating in a meeting, a low-risk start is to begin by asking questions rather than offering suggestions. Make sure, however, that your questions are thought-provoking ones that will move the meeting discussion forward rather than foolish ones that will halt the discussion while someone fills you in.

If you are still convinced that your ideas are viable, raise your confidence level by preparing ahead of time how you will articulate them to the group. Make notes; anxiety and/or excitement does strange things to memory. Generally, in putting your thoughts together for presentation, plan how you will begin or lead into your suggestion, summarize your key points in about one to five sentences, consider an example of how the idea would work, and plan a recap or lead-out of your idea.

Be brief in your explanation without rambling on about how you were just standing in the elevator and Martha Mecklenut said thus-and-so to you and you got to thinking that...But do give enough background so that the group knows how you arrived at your conclusion. In other words, involve them in your thinking process enough so that they accept your reasoning and solution.

If you can, show how your ideas complement opinions expressed earlier or expand concerns offered beforehand. When possible, recap a series of facts or ideas mentioned earlier that "naturally" point to your idea and make it seem like the logical conclusion. Or, perhaps you can pose a question, the answer to which is your idea for resolution.

Don't make your idea a make-or-break presentation. Avoid letting your emotions ride so heavily on acceptance that you are visibly shaken if all do not agree that your idea is equivalent in importance to the invention of the wheel.

Somewhere between an excuse-me-for-speaking-I-know-this-probably-won't-work-but tone and an if-you-don't-like-this-I'm-going-to-cut-my-throat-and-bleed-all-over-everybody tone, offer your ideas in all their relevant glory and then listen open-mindedly for honest feedback.

When you offer your ideas, don't talk to one person who seems interested and agreeable; that special attention will alienate the others or make it appear as if you two have already discussed the situation beforehand. Speak to the group as a whole.

Should they go for your idea, be prepared with specific data you've put together for just such an occasion. Don't, however, appear to have everything worked out single-handedly. Show deference with comments such as, "One way this might work is that..."

And should the group like your ideas to the extent that they decide to implement them, latch onto the assignment to see them through the birthing process. This will ensure that you and your boss retain credit; always volunteer to be the one to see the ideas into action. Most important, you don't want your idea to fail simply because someone else responsible for putting things into action didn't follow through.

Above all, when you offer ideas, don't make them sound self-serving. In emergency situations such as fire or physical attack, authorities suggest that victims yell "fire" rather than "help" to appeal to bystanders' emotional self-interest; that advice holds here. Don't yell an emotional "help" for yourself, but rather try to make a logical presentation of "fire" from the others' perspective.

What to do when they don't like your ideas? Analyze the situation and your idea. Never forget that it's okay to change your mind when someone proves you wrong. Everybody is entitled to be wrong at least three times a day. Nod your head or shrug to acknowledge the error of your ways and let weak ideas be bygones. The sooner they fade from group memory, the better.

Or perhaps rather than a faulty idea, you have an oversold one—maybe you have some generalizations that can't be supported with facts and thus have weakened the entire idea. Understatement is always more effective than overstatement.

Should you be convinced that your data is more accurate than your critic's, be gracious with statements such as "Maybe I had access to some information you didn't have opportunity to see." Stand your ground and present your case and let the rest of the group judge accuracy and sift through the issues of the situation with pertinent questions and alternatives.

You may want to get further feedback before you give up your idea altogether. Try questions such as "Well, do you all think we should just forget my suggestion?" Or, "Anybody have a benefit I haven't thought of?" Or, "I don't think I did an adequate job of explaining the idea. Somebody want to help me out?"

If you and your major critic come to an impasse, listen courteously; then say, "It was interesting to hear your thoughts and to consider the other side of the coin."

If the group is divided in support of you and "the other side," avoid making it a win/lose situation for either of you. Point out areas of agreement and any of her contributions to your thinking. And don't react to negatives too soon.

As negotiator Herb Cohen says, in *You Can Negotiate Anything*, "no" is a reaction, not a position. Individuals who react negatively at first mention of your ideas may simply need time to evaluate them and rethink the situation. There's always inherent resistance to change. Give others time to come around to "yes" without putting them off by your attitude.

If the group resists your opinions, you've got three ways to go: *Surrender*—with various displays of denial, emotional hype, or resentment to the point of dropout. *Sabotage*—with counterorganization of forces to see that the enemy's plan isn't successful. *Acceptance*—with evidence of good spirit that you're a team player.

The danger in the surrender stance is that others will see by your hurt feelings that you have a difficult time separating ego from work. In the future this will rob you of valuable feedback and suggestions on yours and your boss's projects. Surrender with hurt feelings also creates the impression that you are not acting the role of a professional.

The second stance, sabotage, only alerts the opposition to your quills and elicits caution about any role you'll assume in the project. You may find yourself getting much of the blame when things go wrong with which you had nothing to do; the group simply remembers your sullen opposition, and all your motives and actions become suspect.

Gracious acceptance of defeat usually gets you the next best grade to acceptance of your ideas.

When You Can't Buy Someone Else's Ideas

When you feel opposing views welling up within, offer them early in the meeting. It's much more likely that your disagreement will get a fair hearing early in the evaluative process. Once the group has worked through the problem definition, the brainstorming of options, and the evaluation of the alternatives, a hint of opposition just when they see the goal line ahead will get you little but blank, hostile stares.

Generally, it's not a good idea to disagree when you know nothing can be accomplished—that a decision has already been carved in stone. Disagreement at this point only labels you a disgruntled player. Swallow your opposition and go along in the spirit of compromise. Otherwise, if the project fails, you'll be accused of tampering with the locks. If on the other hand, despite your enthusiastic support, their decision fails, they will remember that you were the sane one who originally warned of impending dangers and you'll wind up a heroine anyway.

On the other hand, compromise isn't always the answer. Before you bite your tongue for good, ask yourself whether you can honestly live with the decision over the long haul. Will your productivity suffer? Will the matter likely surface again in other situations? If it is not an isolated issue that will pass away, voice your opposition to the better, not bitter, end.

The *how* of disagreement is of utmost importance. First, remember that attacking another's ego will only backfire on you and cause any dyed-in-the-wool American group to root for the underdog. Second, let the opponent save face by giving her "outs" to change her mind, offer excuses for her, or permit her a compromise that she can live with. Finally, respect her right to be your opposition. Don't insist that she enjoy munching bitter chocolate, even if you have tried to add whipped topping.

In general, be your own best meeting critic. When setting up and hosting meetings for your boss, you have one of the very best opportunities available to make your boss look good and cement your relationship as a team. Plan well, check, double-check, then go the second mile with the extras.

When leading your own meeting or participating on your own or your boss's behalf, take that responsibility for the visibility it affords to both of you. You are on stage—plan your entrance (agenda), your performance (group facilitating), and your exit (follow-up assignments and resulting rapport) with great care.

And on those rare occasions when you feel a meeting has no specific purpose, at least you can make it suit your own purpose. Use the time to get to know the other attendees. Question them about what's happening in their departments. Allow others, particularly more influential people, the opportunity to get to know you and your work.

chapter 6

COMMUNICATION BY THE BOOK—A, B, C...

Check yourself the next time you go into a bookstore to select a novel. Chances are that if you open the novel and skim through it, the parts you'll read will be snatches of dialogue, not the long narrative passages. Why? Because most scenes that move the story along involve dialogue. Dialogue is at the heart of all relationships, whether the characters are in love or in conflict.

So it is in the corporate world. Communication is what moves our projects and relationships forward or backward. Yet for all its importance, communication doesn't get much "formal" attention other than a few one- or two-day seminars for supervisors.

Perhaps this neglect is due to the fact that everybody talks, and so we assume that communication comes as naturally as breathing. It's not until we get communication hiccups that we decide to pay a little attention to the specifics. Straightening out some of our corporate communication capers is definitely more complicated than holding one's breath and taking 10 swallows of water.

Communication is a two-way process, a shared experience, no matter how much skill you have developed in communicating. Your effectiveness, therefore, can be diminished to some extent by the other person's ineptness.

In other words, communication involves several steps: Your

forming the thought, turning the thought into words, saying the words aloud with the proper verbal and nonverbal signals—and the other person's receiving the words, decoding them, and finally feeding back an appropriate response to show that the original thought was received.

Communication is a fifty-fifty proposition when it's done well. That means that if the other person is a poor communicator, you have to make an extra effort in order for you to understand each other. Communication with some people may be a fifty-fifty effort; while with others, it's a ninety-ten task on your part.

After talking to a ninety-ten communicator, you often think to yourself: "He didn't hear a word I said," or "What you say is what you get."

A boss hears his secretary say, "I finally got in touch with all but one of the sales managers about the meeting cancellation," but he doesn't understand her exasperation about his last-minute cancellation, the inconvenience it has caused, or the effort required to reschedule. As a result, she gets his response to what she said:

"Good. Keep trying."

Psychologists have been busy for years describing the communication phenomenon in hopes that once we all understand where the other person is coming from, perhaps we can meet him halfway. And though their theories go far in helping us understand our own and others' motivations and reactions, most of us need more help with what goes in between—the ABC's of sending and receiving accurate messages. What we say is one of the easiest behavioral changes to make. Have tongue, can control. The following suggestions should help you make improvements in technique so that you communicate in an accurate, positive, and supportive manner.

A—Accepting Attitude

To keep communication lines open—upward, downward, and laterally through the organization—people must have an accepting attitude, one that shows respect and support for others' feelings and behavior even when they don't agree. It's much like the attitude we have about First Amendment rights—I may not agree with what you say, but I believe in your right to say it.

Recognizing your own feelings and foibles tends to make you more accepting of others' weaknesses. But an accepting attitude does not mean that we can't work to influence or change others' ideas or feelings but rather that we don't try to shut them up inside or become insensitive to them.

Some people are unaware of the effect they have on others with their "Oh, really," "That's interesting," "How nice," and "Hmmmm" responses to what others share. In order for people to communicate with us, we must accept what they say, when they say it, for what it's worth—to them, not us. And what it's worth to them is encouragement to keep on trying to communicate.

B—Bloopers

Brace yourself; bloopers are bound to happen. As a secretary, you may have found yourself in a situation similar to one of the following:

"A lady and her new husband came into the office and I introduced them to my boss by her ex's name. When my boss looked at their application, he asked them to explain why the name was different on their paperwork."

"My supervisor said to me on Friday afternoon, 'It looks like you'll have to come in Saturday to work.' And then when he walked out the door, he said, 'I'm going home now.' And I said, 'Okay, I'll see you tomorrow.' He turned and looked at me funny. He thought I was being flippant with him, telling him that he should come in if I had to come in."

"I was making copies of a letter not dictated by my boss and I noticed typos. Without thinking, I just walked into the writer's office—whom I didn't even know—and blurted out, 'There are mistakes in this letter.' He said, 'Well we can't have that.' He took it in stride and laughed at my reaction."

Bloopers like this, yours and others', certainly can create bad feelings if not handled properly. But since no one is goof proof, try to handle your own mistakes with either humor or a sincere apology.

If it's not a serious blooper, you may try something like: "I'm known in this part of the country for my quick tongue and slow mind." Or, if the goof is something more offensive, give an honest apology: "It was a thoughtless statement and, in fact, shows my ignorance on the subject. Will you please forgive me?" Most people are generous with forgiveness when your intentions weren't to offend and when the apology is sincere.

When someone else blunders at your expense, she will be eternally grateful if you will take the initiative in putting her at ease. Again, humor is appropriate: "That's okay. I can play deaf on demand." Or, "Score one; the next insult's on me." Be sure to smile genuinely so that the other person knows you hold no grudge and have not taken the blunder as an intentional injury.

In dealing with a few people who make a goof at your expense, the ball will be entirely in your court to be gracious. Being unsure of themselves and defensive, they may expect, and even read into future situations, your attempt to "get even." That's when you'll have to go 90 percent of the way to maintain a cordial relationship and show them that you're not keeping score.

C—Calling Names

A person's name is music to his ears. Note the big tips service people—waiters, hair stylists, bellhops—get when they call patrons by name. If you still don't believe in the importance of using names, see how fast someone corrects you when you mispronounce his or her name.

And when you can't even remember the name, you certainly erect a communication barrier. Pay particular attention when entering a group; calling everyone's name at least once during the conversation lets each person know that you especially notice his or her presence.

Using names is also important when you give credit. Throwing out group praise ("Thanks go to the personnel department for...") is not nearly so meaningful as specific compliments for a job well done.

Particularly, using names helps in communicating instructions. Statements such as, "Expenses should be kept in line with our austere budgeting directive" get about as much attention as announcing that the streets should be kept free of crime or that the azaleas should be in bloom next month.

When giving instructions to co-workers or subordinates, use names if you want action: "The *authorized person* verifying the transaction should also *make sure* that..." Not: "All transactions should be verified for..."

Finally, make sure that you call people by the names they prefer. Because our society is informal in so many ways, many people make the mistake of assuming that everybody prefers being addressed by first name; however, some, especially older people, may be offended by the use of their first name. A secretary in Houston says that she's worked closely for four years with an older woman who has never once referred to her husband by his first name. When in doubt about first names, ask for a preference or use the last name until asked to do otherwise.

D—Details

Be careful to get the details along with the big picture. Much of communication is expectation; we hear what we expect to hear. We catch a general idea and assume the details to match.

But when someone gives directions, relates a problem, presents a decision, or rejects a proposal, improve your understanding by getting all the details. Ask: Specifically, what do you mean? Like what? For instance? Are there any exceptions? How much? How often? When? Where? Why? How? Who? So what does this mean exactly for you? For me? For the rest of our department? Don't assume; dig.

E—Expectations

Many times we fail even to get to first base in communicating with someone, because we never fully open our minds to what the other is trying to say. We see a frown and we expect to hear a complaint or problem. Examine the following attitudes to see if you recognize them in your own listening habits:

I-don't-understand listening: You don't pay attention because you think the subject is over your head, and you're not interested enough to put forth the effort to listen and learn.

I-know-what-you-mean listening: You assume you know what the other person thinks or feels, based on one thing he's said or on your own experience in a similar situation.

I've-got-my-mind-made-up listening: You already know what you want to believe and don't want her to confuse you with more, possibly contradictory, details.

That's-off-the-wall listening: You make a snap judgment, refusing to listen to unusual ideas, plans, opinions, feelings.

I-don't-want-to-get-involved listening: You mean, don't tell me your problems; I've got my own. You want to hear only the facts and get on with the practical things that directly affect you and your specific project.

Let-me-explain listening: You can't concentrate on listening to the other person because you're thinking about how to make your own rebuttal.

I-don't-like-you listening: You don't like the way someone dresses, walks, looks, chews gum, comes in late, or slumps in meetings, so you're closed to everything she says.

It takes a good force of will to erase your slate of preconceived ideas and habits and to give the other person's message a fair hearing.

F—Feedback

Actively solicit feedback from people to verify that they heard what you intended to communicate. You've read the sign, "I know you think you heard what you thought I said, but I'm not sure you understand that what you thought I said was not what I meant."

Instructors in active listening train students to repeat back to the speaker what was said until the speaker verifies that the hearer got the message right. Obviously, if we practiced this technique, we'd have a lot more conversations that lasted far into the wee hours. So we generally ignore the idea until we're trying to convey important details like telephone numbers, addresses, or the spelling of names, which we repeat to make sure we have them right.

But often in far more meaningful conversations, we fail to solicit any feedback at all, thereby risking serious misunderstandings. People may exaggerate what we say or "water down" what we say and so not hear our message at all.

We can hear the uncertainty with which many of us communicate with use of tag phrases and questions at the end of our statements: "Do you know what I mean?" "Do you understand?" "Get what I'm driving at?" And, of course, to all these, the listener usually nods her head and says yes—whether she understands or doesn't.

This is *not* true feedback.

A listener will usually say that she understands because she had been trained to say so all her life. From elementary school, we hear the teacher say, "Now I want you to do your best on this assignment; do you understand?" Everyone nods. When a speaker asks a listener if she understands, the listener thinks, *"Of course I understand; I'm no dummy."* She's anxious to please.

Therefore, it's up to you, the speaker, to seek feedback actively and to be positive the other person gets your message. Be careful that you don't ask for feedback from only those people who you know understand you and are willing to cooperate with you, ignoring unpleasant feedback altogether. If you do, you're sabotaging yourself.

When you give instructions for doing a task, don't ask a general, "Do you understand?" Instead, ask specifically: "Do you understand why we are setting June 15 as the deadline?" In the case of elaborate instructions, ask the listener to repeat them back to you so that you can verify accuracy step by step. And when you uncover something that the person did not receive correctly, assume the blame: "No, that's not exactly right; I didn't make myself clear." Not: "No, *you* don't understand. *You* didn't hear me correctly."

Plan time for formal feedback with an entire work group. Ask both individuals and the group as a whole how you're coming across. But don't expect much response from general solicitations such as, "Am I coming across?" They will answer yes and you're still no closer to knowing if they really understand or agree with you. Again, get specific: "Am I giving enough background?" "Are we on target with these time arrangements?" "Is everybody satisfied with the design of this form?"

Also, be alert to nonverbal feedback that people can't or won't put into words. Tardiness to a meeting may indicate that the person is not eager to be present, that all is not going to suit her. Downcast eyes may be her way of expressing disagreement with what you've just said.

Finally, to ensure that you keep on getting valuable feedback, reward people when they say what they think. Often, we do just the opposite—get angry with a "wrong" answer: "I just told you why we need three copies of that contract!"

Let others feed back so you can straighten out. In other words, don't imitate the potentates of old who killed messengers bearing bad news. If the feedback reveals a misinterpretation of what you said, be glad for the chance to reexplain and correct.

G—Gossip

Some people have trouble deciding the difference between passing on "facts" and gossip. To help you draw that line, try these questions: Did I get this information *directly* from the source? Will anybody or any situation be helped by my passing on this information? Will any person, project, or relationship be jeopardized by my passing on this information? If this gets outside the company, could I be blamed for a leak? What is my motive for telling?

If you are a gossiper, do a little self-analysis: Does passing on "inside" information make you feel important? What happens when others learn that information is only half true or false altogether? Do you think gossip wins friends? Think again; most people will be afraid to tell you about themselves if they know you gossip to them about others.

Additionally, you should be careful about your responses to others' gossip to you. Watch statements such as, "I can certainly see why you're upset" or "I don't blame you in the least for..." Such responses are often "assimilated" by the gossiper, and then you are cited in the next telling as part of the gossip.

As to the fate of gossipers, an office manager, formerly a secretary, explains: "I've been gossiped about and accused of everything from sleeping with the boss to I don't know what else. I don't worry about it. People will talk. If you make a big deal about it and counter it, it only lends credibility. My proof is that I'm still here and people who say those things are soon gone."

Even people who think they are passing on necessary, helpful "facts," often get them wrong:

In 1982, the Gulf Oil Chemical Company located in Baytown, near Houston, was the victim of bomb threats and attempted extortion of $15 million. During the investigation by company and FBI officials, rumors were rampant among workers about the contents of extortion letters mailed to Gulf:

- The money was to be parachuted from a company plane.
- The plant was selected because of its isolation from a populated area.
- The extortionists warned that another plant—one closer to a residential area—would be a likely target for bombs if the demands were not met.
- The extortionists included three people or groups—someone who masterminded the plan, someone who built the devices, someone who planted them. Corporate headquarters might also be a target.
- The extortionists told the Gulf officials that they would easily find the first five devices but would have difficulty with the last four. (*Houston Chronicle*, October 3, 1982.)

Can you imagine the unrest, the activity, and the cost involved in containing those various rumors until the FBI finished investigations and the matters came under closer examination in the much-later court proceedings?

Make sure you have things right; and even when you do, consider why you should or should not pass the information on.

H—Humor

Humor can lift people up or knock them down, ease tension or create apprehension, display cleverness or reveal hostility, make a heavy disagreement lighter or turn a serious situation into a farce.

Not all of us can have a quick wit, but we can develop a sense of humor in our communication. Wit is an intellectual sharpness; the ability to turn a phrase, play a word, crack a punch line. But humor has much more to do with the emotion and personality. Although it can mean cracking jokes, a sense of humor involves seeing the amusing side of life, laughing at yourself, relaxing in others' presence, putting mistakes and your job in proper perspective. But be careful about making light of others' problems. Often, the intention is to ease the situation for them and help them see the brighter side, but your humor may be seen as your refusal to understand their real predicament or offer sympathy.

Often humor helps in solving a problem; a secretary for a large school district explains: "We had one student who was selling drugs on campus. My boss lightened the situation by telling the parents that if the kid was a born salesman, why didn't we arrange to send him to sales school and get him to sell a better product. The parents laughed and became more relaxed. We then tried to be philosophical about the problem and work for a solution."

Humor based on sarcasm, however, can become a destructive tool to get even with others, to tear them down in an effort to raise oneself, to send someone a hostile message one wouldn't dare say openly. Wit and humor, however, never fully cover hostility; the barbs still stick through and others become uncomfortable in their presence.

If you find yourself in the company of someone who employs humor as a weapon, it is a good idea to confront him with a comment that unveils the anger. "I get the idea from your last comment that you don't agree with the deadline we just set? Do you want to talk about that?" Or, "Under a bit of humor, I feel a note of seriousness. Have I offended you in some way? Would you like to talk about it?" Even if the person doesn't admit his hostility and take up your effort to discuss the issue, you have let him and others observing the scene know that you see through the disguise.

Finally, remember that one man's humor is another man's grief. Jokes on race, religion, or politics often offend others. Always be careful that you never tease someone unless you are positive you have not chosen a sensitive spot. Some bald men crack jokes about their "dome," while others may smile but inwardly cringe when you do so. Learn to recognize a nervous laugh that springs from insecurity.

Finally, be wary of using humor with people from other cultures. A foreign born and reared secretary explains the difficulty in laughing at inappropriate things across cultural lines: "We had this chair in my boss's office with a plastic sheet under it that would make the chair roll around, and sometimes visitors would fall getting into or out of the chair. We had a very important visitor here to see my boss one day, and he fell trying to sit down. My reaction was to burst out laughing, which my boss resented very much. I tried to explain that it's just my culture. We go to help the person, but we laugh. We don't mean to be rude...Americans consider that very rude; they show concern on their face instead."

When in doubt, don't. Let your humor be an asset, not a liability.

I—Inferences

Be aware of subtleties you imply and inferences you make.

Even the subjunctive-mood sentence construction (subjunctive mood—contrary to fact: "If Mr. Martin *were* going to be in today, I'm sure he would like to talk with you.") has dropped out of our everyday spoken language. Instead, we make declarative sentences carry both fact and inference.

For example: "I saw Mr. Wyatt in Mr. Appleby's office earlier today." That's a factual statement that allows for many inferences. Did Mr. Wyatt just get back from his overseas trip? Is Mr. Wyatt upset about Mr. Appleby's latest proposal? Does the speaker mean to convey she has inside information about certain proceedings?

When you hear a message, watch your own inferences. Did the boss actually *say* that you couldn't use temporary help, or did he merely comment that he hadn't realized the report was so lengthy? Did the boss actually *say* that your work was inferior, or that one letter should be rewritten? When your co-worker remarked that she didn't see you come in this morning, did she *really* mean that your tardiness created her present difficulty?

Problems also surface when people make inferences from things they see or hear and then pass them on to you as fact. Be sure to ask for specifics; distinguish between the two.

Before sending your message, think in terms of interpretation and results: How will the other person take what I'm going to say? Is he or she particularly sensitive about this matter? What will he think I mean by the statement? Be careful to word your message so that what you imply is what the other person infers, and listen carefully to see that what you infer is what the person actually means. Confusing? Ignore inferences altogether and see just how confusing things can get!

J—Judging

Refrain from putting a stopper on communication by being too quick to judge another's problem, idea, or behavior and too quick to "fix it" with solutions. Particularly troublesome are statements that begin as the following: "You know what you should do?" "You really ought to..." "That happened to me once, and I can tell you right now that..." "You know what your problem *really* is?" "Let me tell you how to..."

Talking with someone who's ready to offer solutions before you've fully expressed the situation and your feelings is like having the doctor tell you to take two aspirins and go to bed before you even describe your symptoms.

When you are in a position to judge—after you've heard all the facts and feelings—try to describe the situation as you see it and then focus on the solution. An office manager explains how she handles "judgment" situations in her staff meetings: "'I understand we had a problem yesterday with customer Bill White. Could you explain from your perspective what happened?' [Then] 'What could we have done differently there?' Or, I'll say, 'This is not your normal way to handle things. Is something else bothering you about the situation? Can I help with a problem?'"

Mistakes, after the fact, can best be dealt with by simple acknowledgment of the error and statements about the solution. Example:

"The standard enrollment procedures for our June 6 seminar were not followed. As a result, the participants came with false expectations about the course content. In order to prevent a recurrence of this situation, I'd like you to do two things: Find and review a copy of the approved procedures before the next class and then let me proof the announcement memo before it goes out."

Note that the passive-voice verb construction plays down blame: "The procedures were not followed...," not, "You didn't follow the procedures..."

Blaming statements and attitudes tend to make others so nervous that they make even more mistakes than what you at first intend to correct. Further, this nervousness motivates them to cover up errors rather than call them to your attention so you can correct them.

Judging and blaming focuses only on who caused the problem, not on the solution.

K—Keeping Proper Distance

Have you ever noticed that when talking with certain people, you find that you've inched your way back and forth across the office? Chances are that one of you has made the other feel uncomfortable by not keeping proper spatial distance.

Edward T. Hall (*The Hidden Dimension*) describes four zones we use in communicating with others:

Patting someone on the back, letting a friend cry on your shoulder and kissing your spouse represent *intimate* distance—touching range. *Personal* distance is from one to four feet apart, when most conversations are private and not meant to be overheard. *Social* distance, about four to twelve feet apart, is comfortable for conversing with others when we don't mind if others overhear our small talk—greeting each other in the company cafeteria or waiting your turn at the copier. *Public* distance, farther than 12 feet apart, is appropriate for addressing a large group during a seminar or meeting. We use public distance to establish formality and control.

Keeping an inappropriate spatial distance creates tension between people. Someone who stands too far away to inquire about a personal matter may offend by seeming insensitive to the fact that others may overhear the conversation. Once you recognize that someone lacks discretion in these situations or subjects, you'll tend to guard what you say to him next time for fear of his bringing up the subject again at an indiscreet distance.

The reverse is also true; standing too close creates tension. You know the slight uneasiness and breathless quiet that you experience in a crowded elevator, even standing beside a close friend. And those who strike up a private conversation on such an occasion usually make others uncomfortable.

Some people feel "violated" when you take the liberty to sit on their desk or lean over their shoulder. Not only may you infringe upon someone's sense of space, you may spray them with saliva or offend with halitosis.

For others, the offense is touching and patting, when the other person feels that the relationship is not so intimate. The freedom to touch another person—a pat on the back, a touch on the hand—clearly rests with rank. Never make the mistake of touching a superior, who may be offended by your assuming equality with such a gesture.

Be aware of making others feel uncomfortable when you try to converse from too far away; if they walk toward you or seem embarrassed to respond to your comments, save the conversation until you're within private distance. Likewise, don't stand too close, or touch inappropriately; if others inch or lean away, don't follow them.

L—Limp Language

Watch your language for fuzzy words—the abstractions, dazzlers, and weasels: "*Similar* divisions have tried this procedure." What's similar? In size? In location? In production potential? In personnel functions?

Meaning comes from people, not necessarily from the words they use. If you ask someone to do something "in a few days" and you have no deadline in mind, there's no problem. On the other hand, if you ask for a decision "in a few days" and actually have in mind Friday, you're setting yourself up for disappointment or anger if the other person doesn't operate on the same timetable as you do.

In your own communication, aim for simplicity, specificity, and clarity. Say "I want," not "We want." Don't hide behind "We're not getting the support we need," when you mean, "We need for you to attend this meeting." Rather than saying, "This letter was reviewed by our office," say, "Ms. Melton, our legal adviser, reviewed the letter."

And a word about jargon: Jargon tends to irritate people rather than impress them. Some use jargon out of ignorance; they don't realize they're not communicating: "I'm sorry, Mr. Customer, but our *control numbers* do not correspond to your *economic index.*"

Others use jargon to cover for a lack of something to say. A geologist was asked to summarize the findings of a colleague's nine-page technical report written in jargon and gobbledygook. A portion of the report's formal executive summary read as follows: "The efficiency with which an operation utilizes its available equipment is an influental factor in productivity." The geologist's verbal summary? "If we use our equipment better, we can do more."

Say or write what you mean. Strive to express rather than to impress. Use short, clear, unambiguous words. Finally, avoid timid phrases such as "kind of," "sort of," "I guess"—they cause some people not to take you seriously. And that can be a big handicap for both you and your boss.

M—Memory

Good secretaries remember things. They remember names, dates, times, details that need to be rechecked, unfinished tasks, unreturned phone calls, clients' preferences for products and services. And to back up their short-term memory for long-term recall, they make lists and notes to themselves and others.

Memory experts assure us that there's no such thing as absentmindedness—the case is that we simply don't pay attention to routine things. For example, if you can't remember a visitor's name when you get to the boss's door to make the introduction, it's probably because you didn't listen carefully to the name when you heard it.

Only when we pay attention and make an association do we remember. For example, if your boss asks if you made a copy of the letter from Mr. Gomer, you may hesitate for a moment, unsure. Until—until you go over the incident in your mind and associate it with something else, such as finding that the letter had coffee stains on it and trying to blot it dry before making the copy. Then you reassure yourself: "Yes, I did make the copy, because I remember..."

Therefore, to improve your memory learn to be observant about routine things and make associations for the nonroutine. To make associations, you may use mental visuals or create either logical or nonsensical "pegs" on which to hang the information you want to remember. For example, you may visualize Mr. Forester's name by mentally visualizing his bushy eyebrows and beard. Or, you may make up a jingle: "Mr. Forester sounds like he ate a raw oyster." Or, you may make an acrostic out of your daily "to-do" list:

C—check on Hite project
H—help Susan Glover find the budget figures for first quarter
O—open the mail
R—run the newsletter to the printer

E—eat lunch with job applicant
S—service contract—call XYZ, Inc.

Some memory devices require more effort than others; most people will realize a great improvement if they simply learn to be more observant.

One more thing—people who have good memories don't trust them.

The next time someone introduces himself, ask for a business card and really look at the name. Spell it phonetically if that will help you with pronunciation later. Note follow-up reminders on your calendar and in your files. Write questions to your boss in the margin of his or her correspondence. Circle details that you need to recheck or question. Don't clutter your mind with the unnecessary—write it down!

N—Neutral Statements

Neutral statements can be dangerous:

"This proposal has numerous typos in it."
"Well, I didn't type it."

"The staff meeting didn't begin until 9:40."
"Nobody was there on time. We couldn't start without the accounting people, could we?"

In his book *How to Manage Your Boss*, Christopher Hegarty recommends that one make positive statements or give the reasons first, then follow with the neutral to avoid the preceding defensiveness and miscommunications. Examine the rephrased earlier comments:

"Mr. Femmer from Sales had to use a temporary yesterday to get his work typed. This proposal has numerous errors in it."

"I missed my train this morning. But I was able to hear what Mr. Smith had to say. The staff meeting didn't begin until 9:40."

Arrangement makes all the difference in the world, doesn't it?

O—Organization

I recently had the following conversation on the telephone with a training director at a client organization:

Me: May I help you?
Caller: Yes, I have a check here from Barry Davis and I will just mail it to you.
Me: A check for what?
Caller: The memo book.
Me: Does he want to buy one?
Caller: No, he already has one.
Me: I see...I don't recall that name...
Caller: That's where the missing book went.
Me: (Silence.)
Caller: At your last seminar. You remember that we came up with only 14 books rather than 15 after the class? Well, I checked around and found out that Barry had taken it, intending to pay me for it the next day.
Me: So you need me to send you a replacement book for the class set?
Caller: Right...I wasn't making myself too clear, was I? What I wanted was to tell you that I located our missing book—one of our employees wanted a personal copy. I'm going to forward his check to you and would like you to send a replacement book to me for the next class.

Before you begin to communicate anything lengthy—more than a statement or two—organize your thoughts to the hearer's best advantage. For most messages meant only to convey information (apologies, "no" replies, and persuasive messages sometimes follow a different pattern), arrange your ideas in this manner:

"Big-picture" message: "Tomorrow's meeting to review our proposed budget requests has been postponed."

So what action next—either yours or the receiver's?: "I need you to phone the last four people on this list to tell them about the cancellation."

Details—who, when, where, why, how, or how much: Include any elaboration on or explanation of details. "Mr. Benham was supposed to have completed his estimates for training costs, but he hasn't received a response from two major consulting firms about price increases. Therefore, we're going to have to reschedule the meeting sometime next week."

Before you begin the next conversation with once-upon-a-time details, think and organize for clarity.

P—Proper Place and Time

Be sufficiently sensitive to involve others in serious communication only at the proper place and time; meeting someone in the lobby and striking up a conversation about her runaway daughter or the "chewing out" she got from her boss is insensitive. Neither can you expect to get sincere, honest answers. Check for privacy and choose a time that you will not be interrupted for such conversation.

Q—Questions

Use them appropriately. Some people can ask about your weight, will, or wisdom teeth and you answer without hesitancy; while others can ask if you ride or walk to work and you begrudge them the information. Why?

People offend when they don't recognize what questions and information are appropriate for what levels of a work relationship. Learn to distinguish between acquaintances, casual friends, close friends, and intimate friends in the work setting. Some people who work together for 20 years are still only acquaintances; others become close friends in a matter of weeks.

Being unaware of these levels of relationships, people often make the mistake of asking questions that others consider prying and personal.

And perhaps more dangerous to your job, peers may ask questions about confidential business matters such as: "Tell me, did the Board discuss the freeze on wages?" Or, "How are the merger proceedings coming?"

If others invade your privacy or ask you to discuss confidential information, don't hesitate to use silence to avoid answering their question. Or, simply give them a no: "I'm sorry, I can't give out that information." On matters that are not absolutely confidential but simply private such as salary or a relationship difficulty, simply say something like:

"Pardon me for not answering, but I don't really feel like talking about that. Would you mind if we changed the subject?"

"Why do you ask that?"

"Why do you need this information?"

"I haven't given that much thought; what about you?"

"I don't feel comfortable talking about that; perhaps you can ask George directly."

"Pardon?" (with a shocked look) "What did you say?" And if they repeat the question, "I thought that's what you said, but I wasn't sure you were asking something so personal." (They'll usually be embarrassed and back down with, "I guess that was a little personal, wasn't it?" and you're off the hook.)

Or, simply answer a question not asked: "Where is your boss?" Answer: "Oh, she'll be back in a few minutes."

Don't be afraid to answer, "I don't know." Such an admission shows confidence in your own expertise and knowledge, not necessarily ignorance.

On the other side of the coin—when you are the questioner—be aware of invading someone else's privacy by asking about things that she may seem reluctant to share.

Pay particular attention to tone here; when you ask rapid-fire questions and those that call for one word or phrase answers, you come across as a courtroom interrogator. Always question in a courteous, supportive tone.

Other inappropriate questions fall into the category of showcase questions; they are designed to get a short response from the other person and to allow the initiator the opportunity to showcase his or her own expertise. Most people see through this dishonest way of approaching a subject. If you'd like to contribute your superior insight on occasion, do so simply and honestly: "You know, I once made a study of—and found some really valuable ideas. One thing I learned was..."

Another question type to avoid is the one that makes hidden

statements: "Did you say that you were going to keep us here all day for this one project?" meaning, "I think that's too long (or ridiculous)." Don't be surprised that the hearer takes offense, even with your disclaimer: "Well, I was only asking." Most people know *why* you are "only asking" and what you mean to convey with the question.

Finally, watch questions that make the other person feel trapped. "You do want me to finish typing this report so you can take it with you tomorrow to Los Angeles, don't you?" If the boss says yes, then it follows that he should not interrupt you for a short urgent letter.

Also, you make the other person feel trapped when you ask questions to which you already know the answer. To your clerk/typist: "Sarah, did you deliver all the mail upstairs?" When she answers yes, you come back with: "Well, here is a letter to Mr. Snell still on my desk." If you're asking only to verify that you've got the situation straight, say so. Don't hesitate, however, to ask questions that encourage further thought or reflection on a neutral subject.

The idea is not to avoid questions altogether. Simply avoid questions on subjects inappropriate to your particular relationship or work responsibilities—or questions that brag, insult, blame, or trap.

R—Reflecting Feelings

Reflect feelings, not just facts. Some, who for years have heard about reflective listening, feel awkward when they actually do it, feeling that they sound silly. But usually that's the case only when the person reflects facts:

> "I tried to call you earlier to tell you that there was no use in coming by my office for the contracts because Ms. Heather phoned to say she was staying another day in Atlanta and wouldn't be in to sign them."

> "You tried to call me earlier to tell me not to stop by your office for the contracts. Ms. Heather is staying another day in Atlanta and won't be in to sign them?"

This kind of parroting and reflection is valuable in checking factual details, but little else. Deeper, more accurate communication takes place when you reflect *feelings*:

> "I tried to tell you earlier that I didn't know how to figure these percentages. And when I walked in to deliver the report, Mr. Biggers saw immediately that the columns didn't add up."
>
> "You were embarrassed, huh?"
>
> "Yes, but I was also upset. Mr. White, this is what I mean about your taking for granted that I understand these computation formulas."
>
> "I've been a little too busy lately, huh?"
>
> "Well, I simply need more of your time to ask questions when you assign projects such as this."
>
> "You're right. I have a habit of throwing something at you and disappearing. I'll try to be more helpful in the future."

You can see from this dialogue that the facts about the incorrect percentages were not the true, complete message the secretary wanted to send. But you also note that her boss's reflecting feelings rather than merely the facts helped to clarify and correct assumptions. Such a reflection of feelings also enables the other person to discover and reflect on her own feelings and feel understood and released—as if she and her boss have communicated rather than simply talked.

S—Silence

It is a myth that women speak more and longer than men. In study after study of all kinds of groups—social and business—men speak more often and at greater length than women. They also tend to interrupt others more than women do. Yet, males frequently complain that women "talk too much."

Even if that old saw isn't true, secretaries can increase their effectiveness if they learn to use silence. Silence is one of your best weapons for negotiation:

If someone has made an unreasonable request of you, simply say nothing. That person has no idea if you plan to comply and will have to explain or modify his position to approach the topic again. Silence, or at least a delay in response while you gather your thoughts or facts, makes your answer—when you finally get around to giving one—seem more objective, more assertive, and less blunt. And when dealing with an angry or excited person, silence allows him eventually to "run down" and/or modify his position.

Silence can give another person a chance to collect her thoughts, to see where a conversation has been, and to consider where she'd like it to go next. If you have to do something while you wait, nod your head or smile. Give the other person time to reflect and then continue.

Use a probe question if you think it necessary to show the speaker you're still interested: "Why do you think you feel that way?" "What plans do you have now?" "How can you improve the situation?"

Or, if you have asked an honest question for necessary information to do a task and someone hasn't given you sufficient answer or reason, wait. Silence can make the other person uncomfortable and motivate her to initiate a conversation about difficulties or solicit your opinions or feelings on a matter.

The old cliché "silence is golden" is true not only because its opposite is irritating but also because, in a positive way, silence gives you a golden opportunity to enhance your bargaining position.

T—Total Meaning

Words, like gifts, don't stand alone; their meaning always hinges on the spirit in which they're given. For example: "I see you finally got to work" can mean "I'm sorry you were ill earlier." Or, "I haven't got any of my work done for having to take your calls."

Look for the total meaning in someone's message. Frequently we answer the intent of someone's words rather than only the content. Two secretaries accidentally encounter each other in the company library. One says, "You didn't go to the safety meeting?" If the first secretary were to answer the question literally, she'd say: "No, I'm standing here talking to you."

But the intent of the message is, "I'm surprised to see you didn't go to the safety meeting. Don't we all have to attend one of those sessions?" Or, "Is something wrong?" Or, perhaps, "I thought you were scheduled to attend that safety meeting. Did Ms. Walters keep you at work on compiling her Board speech?"

Social researchers estimate that no more than 15 to 35 percent of the real meaning of our oral communication comes from the words themselves; 65 to 85 percent of our message is conveyed by nonverbal signals. Some people think that they communicate only when they're conscious of doing so. But, as I mentioned earlier, it's a big mistake to assume that people mean only what they say or say only what they mean. Many conversations about how a boss wants a letter revised have little to do with clarity or grammar but a lot to do with ego and hurt feelings.

Always examine the total meaning of someone's words so that you can communicate fully. What details did she choose to give? To omit? Why did she repeat a certain idea several times? In what context did she say it? What did her facial expression say? When words and body language conflict, trust the body language; it's harder to fake.

U—Undivided Attention

Give it liberally. When a customer, client, co-worker, or boss initiates a conversation with you, attend with your whole body.

Do you remember sitting in a classroom when the teacher said to the class, "Pay attention now," as she explained something on the chalkboard? Her comment was probably prompted by the class's body language; they slumped away from her and let their eyes drift around the room.

When someone talks to you—even if he doesn't have the financial clout of E. F. Hutton—listen. I'm not referring to a fake display of attention, but rather genuine concentration on what the other person is saying—no interruptions, no topic switches to suit your own interests, no perfunctory comments.

And make sure the other person pays you the same courtesy. When you're talking to someone who keeps looking over your shoulder at what you're typing or watching your boss's door, shuffles her feet as if to make an escape, or makes ho-hum responses, communication has stopped and only the words continue. When you sense you don't have someone's full attention, stop talking until you do.

V—Voice Tones and Volume

Voice tones and volume reveal much about personality, problems, and your enthusiasm for the conversation at hand. A loud voice can express anger or excitement and a soft voice can convey resignation or joy. But volume coupled with tone leaves no doubt in your listener's mind as to how you feel about what you're saying.

How important are volume and tone? Your voice determines the first impression you make on the phone and is second only to appearance in a face-to-face encounter. Some secretaries' voices are about as pleasant as a chain saw—harsh, loud, brash, demanding attention. Others speak up with the volume of a mouse, and, unfortunately, they are often judged to be timid or even boring or incompetent. As a result, they get little attention—unless, like their furry counterparts, they happen to step on somebody's foot.

In addition to volume, vary your speed and inflection. Particularly, this is important when you speak on the phone; the company pays you to answer calls as though you are a person, not a machine.

And if you want respect, attention, and authority, speak slowly, distinctly, and audibly.

W—Weighing Your Words

Some people pride themselves on "saying what they think" as if that were a virtue. *Always* saying what you think is as much a weakness as *never* saying what you think. One is usually caused by timidity; the other, stupidity. Being "honest" does not mean telling everything you think or feel; honesty means that what you say can be verified.

Therefore, think before you speak. Is it true? Is it necessary? Is it expedient? Is there another way to say it that would be more tactful? Will I regret it tomorrow?

X—Exaggeration

Exaggeration has no place in true communication. When you exaggerate to make a point, the point often gets lost in the listener's exasperation over your method. You remember the fable about the shepherd boy who cried "wolf" so many times that he could arouse no ally in his time of need. When you continually exaggerate wants to needs, needs to crises, or simple tasks to daring accomplishments, you run out of words and emotions to convey your true feelings or facts.

Exaggeration may work for the stand-up comic, but it undercuts a secretary on the job by making her appear emotional, irrational, or simply dishonest.

Y—Yielding

Yield to speaking signals of the other person. Mary Parlee Brown, writing in *Psychology Today* (May 1979, p. 48), has outlined some of the general rules of conversation that apply to our American culture. One rule is that the speaker signals his intention to yield the floor. He may do this by stopping at the end of a sentence, by dropping his pitch or volume level, or by using such body language as turning his eyes away or shrugging his shoulders as if to say "I give up."

Another unwritten rule is that the speaker indicates that he wants a response by addressing the other person by name, by asking a direct question, or by making eye contact.

Someone who doesn't learn these rules unconsciously has a hard time conversing with others. The listener never knows when the speaker is finished or if he wants a response at all.

You've had the same experience if you've ever told the punch line to a joke that no one caught. You feel as though you are dangling in midair waiting for the other's brain to compute. The same is true of the person who doesn't yield the floor effectively. When the listener misses a cue to respond, the speaker often feels that what he said was uninteresting or that the other person did not wish to continue the conversation. Either way, they both lose out on what might have been a worthwhile exchange.

Z—Zeroing in on Goals

Many communication difficulties arise when people get caught up in peripheral issues rather than key issues. When others focus on peripherals such as who failed to make a backup copy of your data files rather than on key issues such as what records have been saved in the off-site copy, here are several tactics to get them to zero in on goals—yours and theirs.

First, repetition. Simply keep repeating what you want until the other person does it:

"I wasn't the last one logged onto the system."
"Please finish these letters by five."
"I'm supposed to be typing John's proposal."
"Yes, also please finish these letters by five."
"I can cover the phones if you'd rather type them."
"No, I prefer that you type them. I need them by five."

Second, agree with the other person's comments and needs, then move into a problem-solving mode:

"I agree with everything you're saying. I shouldn't have left these files out on my desk during lunch. But since I did and they're missing, I think we should call Security immediately."

Third, offer to compromise in such a way that will permit both of you to accomplish your goals and will allow the other person to save face. You shouldn't be concerned with what excuses the other person makes for "giving in," as long as she does what you need.

Regardless of how much you take these ABC's to heart, you cannot master the whole game of communication in one lesson. And even if you were to practice all the techniques and attitudes described here, all your communication efforts still may not be successful or pleasant.

Perhaps like bridge signs saying "Cross at your own risk," business offices should remind employees of the importance of good communication skills with posted signs: "Talk at your own risk."

part two

COOPERATING WITH CLIENTS AND CUSTOMERS

chapter 7

CALLERS

Some employers tend to think that anybody can "cover the phone." What a mistake! If your boss thinks so, then get an answering machine. But if he or she wants someone who can deal with people effectively, save time, and build goodwill, then a skillful secretary is a must.

A telephone voice is usually the first impression a caller gets of your boss, department, and company. The way you answer the call gives an impression about company size, expertise, volume of business, quality of product or service, dependability of personnel, as well as attitude toward customers or clients.

And even if people are familiar with your company and plan to do business with somebody there, that "somebody" may not necessarily be you or your boss. In fact, I've had several brokers from different branches of the same company call me about opening an account. And although I already have an account with that company, I switched to a new broker at a new location simply because I got such rude service from the first broker's secretary whenever I phoned for simple information.

And I don't think I'm "abnormal" in my reaction to telephone manners; many others verify the fact that even though they have decided to buy a product or a service from a particular company, they have refused to deal with a certain salesperson or staffer due to some uncooperative, nonhelpful attitude perceived on the telephone with the secretary.

Telephone contact, by its very nature, is dangerous. You must depend on the voice alone to create a good impression. Phone conversations are usually limited, quick, and impersonal. And the method itself involves certain distractions such as bad connections, other ringing lines, accidental disconnections, and "telephone tag" routines.

Therefore, before you answer each call, be alert to both the dangers of a bad impression and the opportunities for a favorable reaction.

Above all, don't look upon a ringing telephone as an "interruption." After all, for most secretaries, handling the phone is one of their primary responsibilities—in other words, it's not an interruption of your work; it *is* your work. And important PR work it is.

A good habit to get into is to put a smile on your face before answering. Answering in a grumpy or hostile tone while smiling is impossible for most. And the caller can hear the smile because the voice takes on a lilt and the tone gets friendlier.

Also, don't answer as though you've just taken the sixtieth call in as many minutes. "Oh, no, not another one" or "Make it quick, will ya?" comes across in your voice. Particularly, be careful not to garble your words due to overfamiliarity with your opening line. It is possible, also, to speak too slowly and make your opener so long that the caller grows impatient waiting for his or her chance to speak.

To find out how you really sound to others—irritability, volume, speed, modulation—try talking your opening "identification line" and an imaginary conversation into a tape recorder or dictaphone. Modify accordingly. To practice projecting your voice on the phone, pretend you are talking to someone at least 20 feet away.

When answering your boss's calls, use the following identifications: "Ms. Comston's office, Mary Smith speaking." Don't just answer, "Ms. Comston's office." If the caller is wanting information from you or readily available information from anyone in the office, he or she will have to go through the greeting part again, finding out specifically who you are and if you can help.

Also, when you fail to identify yourself personally, you convey the impression either that you are a very insignificant person or that you're hiding. If you have responsibility for some duties on your own, you should identify yourself personally rather than answering as impersonally as an answering machine.

And when someone asks for you by name, don't say, "This is she." (Too stilted). And not: "Speaking." (Too blunt). Instead say: "This is Susan Smith." And never take a chance, thinking you know who the caller will be, and answer with a "cutesy" line. Secretaries have lost their jobs for such!

Other do's and don'ts: Do answer calls promptly—and that doesn't simply mean picking up the receiver! Many secretaries are in the habit of grabbing a ringing phone off the hook but then holding the receiver in hand while finishing a conversation or other task. Never, of course, give a caller preference over a visitor standing at your desk. But if you get a call when you're talking with someone else, excuse yourself from that conversation, answer the phone and ask the caller to wait a moment, then finish your earlier conversation. Don't merely leave a caller dangling without any answer or request to hold at all.

Do keep paper and pen handy for notes. Nothing is more irritating to a caller than to give you details about his or her situations, thinking you are noting them, and then hear you say, "Okay, now I've got a pen and paper; would you repeat that, please?"

Do wait for an answer when you ask someone to hold the line. And do explain why you're leaving the line, don't merely "click off" until you say, "Yes, Ms. Caine is in. I'll ring her." Do stay with a caller long enough to see if the called person answers. Otherwise, the caller who doesn't get to speak to his or her party must hang up and dial you again to ask to leave a message. Stay with a call until it's completed.

And when someone asks for Ms. Caine when she's out, don't simply give that information and listen to the caller say he'll call back, and then "click off" the line without an answer. Acknowledge that you heard his closing statement and say good-bye: "All right, I'll tell her you called. Or, "Okay." Or, "That will be fine." Or, "Good-bye."

Do keep food, cigarettes, or pens out of your mouth so as not to garble your words.

Finally, don't keep callers waiting too long. Go back on the line every 30 seconds to ask if they'll continue to hold. Some callers say they'll hold; but when the wait drags on, they change their mind and want to leave a message. When the secretary fails to come back on the line, the caller has no choice but to hang up, redial, and ask you to take the message. When you return to a waiting caller, thank him or her for waiting.

Taking Messages and Keeping Track of Callers

Be sure you add more to the messages you take than most callers give freely. When they give only a name, ask for the organization they represent also. When you ask for a number for your boss to return the call and the caller says, "He has it," don't take his word. Look up the number yourself later and add it to the message before giving it to your boss. His having the number handy will save time.

Also, don't be cryptic in your notes. If the message is lengthy and you wrote in your own shorthand form to get the details down, translate the message to plain English and type it neatly.

Also, be clear about whether your boss is to return the call or if the caller will call again. Some callers merely want your boss to know that they called, and do not expect a return call. Returning the call may be a waste of time because the caller is leaving the office for two days. If the caller suggests a better or best time to return the call, make a note of that.

Feel free to add your impressions about the urgency and nature of the call: "He said he was not in a hurry for the decision." Or, "He'll be out of the office for the next three days and would appreciate an answer before he leaves today." Or, "She seemed annoyed with the figures we sent—has about 10 'perplexing' questions she needs immediate answers to."

If the name is unfamiliar, spell it phonetically for your boss so he can pronounce it correctly when returning the call. In fact, some names are so difficult to pronounce from their spelling that when the boss returns the call, the operator may not even sufficiently recognize the name to give the correct extension.

Finally, keep some kind of record of incoming calls. You can either note the calls on a telephone log sheet, listing date, time, name, phone number or keep a carbon paper between message slips.

This record accomplishes two purposes. First, when the boss happens to misplace a message you've handed him on his way out the door, you have another record of the call. Second, you can more easily help your boss follow up on the calls. When two weeks later you get a second call from Ms. Tittle saying that your boss returned her first call and promised information that has never arrived, you don't have to be caught unaware: "Oh, I'm sorry. I thought he got back to you." You can use your telephone log or message copy to remind the boss about follow-ups or to check on them yourself.

Finally, if you have taken calls for your boss and later find that he will not be coming into the office, return those calls yourself, offering to help and explaining the delay in an expected return call.

How to Screen

Callers should always give their name, company name, and purpose of the call. When they don't, it's up to you to elicit this information as inoffensively as possible.

That means you *don't* routinely ask who is calling *before* you say that your boss can't take the call. "Who's calling, please?" followed by an excuse or reason the boss can't take the call always leaves the impression that the caller is being screened, even when that's not the case. But when you say the boss is unavailable to take the call *before* finding out the caller's name, the caller takes the turndown impersonally and is more likely to believe what you say about the boss's unavailability.

When you get the caller's name, always say, "May I *ask* who's calling?" rather than "May I *say* who is calling?" The latter response implies that the boss is in the office.

When screening, avoid saying any of the following:

"He hasn't come in yet." (Implies that he's late)

"He hasn't come back from lunch (or coffee) yet." (Implies that he's taken an extra long lunch or break)

"He took the day off." (Too personal)

"He's out of town." (May be confidential)

"He's ill." (Too personal)

Do tell the truth:

"She's in a meeting."

"She has someone in her office."

"She can't be interrupted at the moment. She'll be available tomorrow if you'd like her to return your call or if you'd like to call again." (If someone argues that you should interrupt, simply explain that your boss has asked that she not be interrupted and repeat your offer to take a message.)
"She's talking on the other line."
"I expect her back in a few minutes."
"She's out of the office on business. She'll be in at 2:00 (or on Tuesday)."
"She stepped away from her desk for a few moments."
"She's unavailable at the moment."
"She's not at her desk right now." (In fact, some bosses have a "work area" or credenza or table at which they work when they don't want to be disturbed. Therefore, their secretaries, without lying, can say that "she's not at her desk," meaning she's unavailable at the desk where the phone is.)
"I'm sorry, but would you please give me a little more information about the nature of the call? My boss doesn't return calls unless she recognizes the name or knows what the call is in reference to."

Telling the truth when screening does several things: First, your boss gets known as a courteous, conscientious person who returns phone calls and doesn't stoop to hide-and-seek with callers. Second, the truth decreases your chances of using the same "excuse" on the same caller too frequently and antagonizing to the point of having him argue with you: "Has he been in a meeting for the last three days?"

Third, telling the truth cuts down on repeat phone calls from those who believe you don't give the boss messages and who believe their best chance is to "catch him" answering his own phone.

Fourth, the truth is a courtesy to the caller in that it allows her not to waste time calling again and again or waiting for a call to be returned "any moment." Most callers are mature enough to take "no" or "wait" for an answer and adjust their schedules accordingly. It's the frequent lying that goes on in telephone screening that annoys callers and actually creates more follow-up calls for you to answer and record.

Finally, never promise that your boss will return a call; only promise that you will give him or her the message.

Who to Screen

As you probably are aware, you have a big part in whether your boss returns calls. Often the decision to take the call immediately, return the call later, or never return the call at all depends on whether you say one of the following:

"Mr. White is on the line; it sounds important. Shall I put him through?"
"Mr. White is on the line. You look busy—shall I tell him you'll call him back later?"
"A Mr. White is on the line. I think he's wanting the same information somebody called about last week. Shall I tell him you'll get back to him if you have anything new?"

Don't abuse that power your boss has delegated to you. It's probably better to err on the side of putting someone through who shouldn't have had the opportunity than to chance your boss's missing an important call. As soon as possible in a new job, learn to recognize important names of those within the company, as well as frequent client/customer callers. It can be quite a mark on your record to commit the following *faux pas*:

"This is Clyde Coppell. Is Frank in?"

"And who are you with?"

"I'm your CEO!"

And if your boss likes to talk to people—some bosses will talk to anyone who calls—you are wasting your time to answer at all. Why force the caller to talk to two people? Let the boss answer his or her own calls the first time.

Or some bosses prefer to answer their own calls only during a certain hour of the day, say from 11 to 12. When callers ask for a specific time to get in touch, give them this specific time.

If your boss does in fact want and need you to screen, find out his list of priorities and in what situations he wants to take the call. Most callers can be divided into categories such as superiors in the company, clients or customers, subordinates, colleagues from other departments, professional organization representatives, vendors/consultants, personal friends, or personal business callers.

But be careful in categorizing callers that you don't automatically screen out some groups altogether. Unsolicited phone calls can bring your boss beneficial information about new products or services, newly developed procedures or newly available research, or simply the opportunity for a contact that he might find useful at a later date. If you're in doubt about the call and don't want to bother the boss at the moment, take the pertinent information and pass it along to the boss for his final decision.

Remember that your screen is not always for a negative purpose. Not only do you screen to prevent unwanted callers from taking your boss's time or to prevent necessary callers from interrupting your boss's planned schedule, but also you screen in order to take care of some situations yourself.

If you can get enough information from the caller about his or her purpose, perhaps you can provide the necessary information and save time for everyone concerned. If the topic sounds like something you can easily handle, try: "Mr. Brown, if you can be a little more specific, I may be able to provide you with that information now and you won't have to wait until Mr. Smith can get back to you."

When you are asked to screen certain calls or certain callers, be wary of common tactics to get through your screen:

- The caller who uses a gruff voice with a belligerent don't-mess-with-me-lady-this-is-important tone. (Don't be intimidated; continue to get all the information your boss has asked you to get.)

- The caller who says the name quickly and acts impatient that you are delaying an obviously important or emergency call. (Again, don't be rushed. Get the appropriate information and determine for yourself if this is an urgent call.)

- The caller who won't tell you the purpose of the call. (If he's vague or illusive, simply put him on the spot with: "Is this a personal call?" Faced with a yes or no choice, he will usually confess that it is "not exactly personal." If he says yes, and your boss takes the call and the ruse is found out, the caller will have ruined his chances for an amiable conversation.) Or suggest to a vague caller, "If this is a personal call, perhaps you'd like to write Ms. So-and-So and mark your letter 'personal' so she'll be able to deal with you individually herself."

- The caller who is extremely personable and personal with you, trying to "win you over" so you will do her the favor of letting her speak to the boss. (Don't be manipulated; your boss is still unavailable.)

- The caller who asks for your boss by first name, as if they are long-lost friends. (Some of these callers you will recognize immediately because they mispronounce the boss's name, or you know that your boss goes by a nickname with friends. If you're uncertain, ask, "Is this a personal call?" and proceed as above.)

- The caller says the call is "long distance," thinking you'd rather put her through than pay for returning the call. (Usually the caller is a salesperson. Ask for the number to return the call anyway—usually the caller will give you an 800 number.)

Some callers find your screening less offensive if you can give a "reason," such as "May I tell him what this is in reference to so I can pull a file as I put you through?" Of course, at this point, you may also learn that you, not your boss, has the information the caller needs or that the caller needs to be transferred elsewhere.

Transferring Calls

Wild-goose chase calls irritate. When someone calls your office by mistake, take time to be helpful. Rather than an abrupt, "You have the wrong office" or "I don't know, we don't handle that here," spend a few minutes in building goodwill for your boss and your organization. Keeping a customer or client happy while you've got him is much easier than wooing him back after bad treatment.

In your spare moments, study organizational charts or job descriptions in your department to learn who does what so you can transfer calls properly. Keep an organizational directory near the telephone.

And if your caller wants products or services your organization doesn't provide, don't hesitate to offer suggestions about where he may find them. Although he may buy from the competitor this time, he will remember your helpfulness and attitude when he is in the market for something your company *does* provide.

Here are three ways to handle a caller who needs information you don't have:

1. Tell the caller that you don't handle such and such and that he'll need to speak with so-and-so. Tell him that you'll pass the message along to the correct person and that person will get back to him. (Problem: If the correct person doesn't get back to the caller as you promised, the caller may assume you didn't pass on the message.)

2. Tell the caller the correct person or number and make the connection yourself. (Always give the caller the number before you make the transfer in case you get disconnected accidentally.)

3. Tell the caller the correct person or number, and get the operator back on the line, passing on the information to her so the caller himself doesn't have to repeat all the details a second time.

Never, never simply "click off the line" when you need to transfer a call to your boss or another department. Always give a response: "Thank you. I'll connect you." Or, "Just a moment, please." Or, "I'll ring the training office."

Crank Callers

Most people think of receiving crank calls only on residence lines. But, unfortunately, secretaries get their share of such callers at work. If the caller is obscene, the best approach is simply to hang up. If you do something to anger the caller, he will likely continue to annoy you.

AT&T cautions against 1) crank callers soliciting contributions for causes or organizations that don't exist; 2) callers selling ads for publications that don't exist or have limited circulation; 3) callers insisting on payment for bills for services or products never delivered; 4) callers offering to "make you a good deal" on specialty merchandise that they shipped to your address "by mistake" or that they have "an overrun on and are selling at cost" or "deals" that simply don't measure up to the way the product or service is represented on the phone.

In all cases, don't make spur-of-the-moment decisions. Take the name and number and offer to call back if you decide to do business with the caller. When a caller refuses to leave the number, you know you have discovered a shady deal.

But neither should you believe callers' comments simply because callers give you a legitimate organizational name and number that you can verify with a call-back. Do further checking; ask to speak with several customers whose organizations you can locate in the phone directory. Ask to see the merchandise. Ask that the caller mail you some printed material.

Other cranks are more dangerous—threatening a bomb or a kidnapping or such. Be aware of your company's policy about such situations, but generally you should try to keep the caller on the phone as long as possible and signal someone else to get on another line and trace the call.

If that is not possible, at least keep the caller talking and get as much information from the conversation as you can. For example, is it an adult's or child's voice? Female or male voice? Is the caller nervous or calm? Does the caller seem rational and calculating or confused as if drunk or drugged? Try to record exactly what is said. All these details will help your supervisor or police in trying to decide how to respond to the call.

Handling Complaints

As a high-ranking secretary, one of your primary functions may be to handle complaints yourself rather than to pass them on to your boss. And even if you aren't responsible for the resolution of a problem, because you are the first to deal with the caller, you may still bear the brunt of any anger. Also you set the tone for the caller's being either easily satisfied or more difficult to deal with later.

First, listen to him to see if he has a legitimate complaint. Second, write down any names, dates, statements of claims, and major points and let the caller know you are doing so. He will appreciate the fact that you are concerned and want to get the details right. Also, the very act of your writing down the information will slow him down and often help to relax and calm him.

Third, express your regret for his dissatisfaction and any

inconvenience he may have experienced, but be careful not to assume blame for your company until you verify the situation.

Fourth, tell the caller you will check on the problem and call him back by a certain time.

Fifth, verify that the information the caller has given you is correct and then work out the solution yourself or find someone who can. If you turn the matter over to someone else, follow up to see that that person resolves the problem.

Sixth, call the complainant back when you said you would—regardless of whether you have an answer. Your getting back to him even to say that you're "still checking" and will call again tomorrow lets him know you haven't abandoned the situation. Also, this call-back prevents his assuming you have failed to do anything and his calling someone else about the problem with the result that both of you duplicate work toward a resolution.

If you must call back to say that you can't make the adjustment the complainant wants, follow these guidelines:

- Express your regret over the matter; explain how the situation happened.
- Give your reasons for deciding against an adjustment or a full adjustment. ("Company policy" isn't a reason; give the reason behind the policy.)
- State that you appreciate the customer's business and want to please him or her.
- Offer a substitute product, service, or any other adjustment you can make.
- Never assume responsibility for the error for your company without first fully checking the facts.
- Never make light of the problem, inconvenience, or error.
- Never offer an adjustment begrudgingly. (Not: "All I'm going to allow is a 10-percent discount on this, and that is really more than I think it's worth." But: "I'd like to give you a 10-percent discount simply to express our regret over the fact that you were inconvenienced with the product.")

The Long-Winded Caller

Keeping in mind that talking on the phone and building or cementing good public relations with a customer or client is part of your job, be ready to listen. However, when you get a caller on the phone who acts as though she has nothing better to do than chat and you get the feeling that the conversation may be heading in the direction of discussing everything from the stock market to a new diet, it's time to find a way to wrap things up tactfully.

One tactic to close a conversation is to interrupt a long spiel with a specific question:

> **Caller:** ...and so I couldn't very well turn him down about chairing the committee again this year, and—
> **You:** How many years have you been chairperson?
> **Caller:** Six.
> **You:** That's quite a contribution. And I'm sure it will be a success again... Thank you for calling to keep us informed."

Also, you may successfully end an unnecessarily long conversation with various standard "closers":

> "That's all the information I have. I hope that it will be all you need. Feel free to call again if I can help you further."

> "So, you will send the price and brochure in today's mail. Fine. Thank you for your call."

> "If you'll just note all that in your letter to Ms. Davis, I'll be sure that she sees it. Thanks for your time."

Another way to discourage long-winded callers is to put them on hold several times while you take other calls or pull files so you can continue some other detail work. Of course, as you put the caller on hold, explain that you may be awhile and that if she doesn't want to wait longer, she should feel free to hang up and call back later.

If you can't afford to offend a customer by not listening to comments about his vacation or his grandchildren, at least you can put the caller on hold and get something else at hand to work on while listening passively.

Avoiding Security Leaks on the Phone

Some topics are off limits within all organizations with all unidentified and/or unauthorized callers. In general, you should never discuss salaries; individuals' work schedules, absences, routes to and from work, or home phone numbers; contracts; names of stockholders and shares held; litigation; merger proceedings; labor relations; or credit-reference information.

And, of course, in specific situations other, more mundane matters may be off limits. For example, a caller who wants to know "if Mr. Granger has arrived for his appointment with Mr. Brown" may simply want you to verify that indeed the two did have an appointment. That information may tip a competitor off about any number of things.

Or, if a "wife" calls, asking if her husband has "come in yet" or "is at work today," the caller may be trying to find out someone's personal schedule for all kinds of reasons—from kidnapping children to learning if a pending contract has been signed.

On these kinds of "borderline" confidential calls, you will have to use sound judgment. Learn names and voices of frequent callers as soon as possible, and if in doubt about a situation, take a number and offer to "check on the situation" and call back. Then get permission from the person in question to give the information. Or, if that's not possible, at least verify the caller's name and phone number in the phone directory.

Also, be wary of "by-the-way" requests. For example, a caller may phone you to ask for information that is readily available to the public, such as information from the annual report. And when you find and provide that information to him, he, thinking you are busy and maybe careless, may ask a follow-up, "Oh, by the way" question about a matter that is strictly confidential.

When your boss is on vacation or away on business, ask her before she leaves about any emergency calls that may come through. Also ask for names of "the only" people who should be given her whereabouts and/or a phone number where she can be reached.

If you work for a top executive, you may frequently be called by the media for statements on various happenings. Don't feel that you must answer any questions at all. Beware of any off-the-record information you may give out—some reporters are not known for their ethical behavior. And never think that when you or your boss ask not to be identified that no one will know the source of information you give. When a reporter writes "according to a high-ranking company official," the comment can often be traced to you or your boss simply because of the topic or limited access to the information.

Placing Calls for Your Boss

Before you place a call for your boss, make sure he or she is available to take the call; keeping the one called waiting while you chase down your boss is extremely rude.

When you place a call to Mr. Smith and Mr. Smith's secretary answers, say, "This is Marian Jones in Mr. Finch's office. Mr. Finch would like to speak with Mr. Smith, please." Then as soon as the secretary tells you that Mr. Smith is available to take the call, put your boss on the line to wait for Mr. Smith to pick up his phone. If Mr. Smith is unavailable, leave the appropriate message—either that you will call again or that you'd like the other person to return the call.

Make sure, too, that your boss has at hand any necessary information for the call he or she initiates.

Returning Calls You May Not Want to Return

Some people can play hide-and-seek on the phone indefinitely. They return your calls before eight, while you're out to lunch, after five, or late Friday afternoon. They are satisfied simply to leave a message, hoping this leaves the impression "I tried."

Most people aren't convinced. Both you and your boss get a bad reputation for failure to return phone calls. That's why you should never tell a salesperson, for example, that someone will return her call—only that you will "leave a message with your boss and if he's interested, he'll get back to you." Most callers would rather you be honest about your intention to return or not to return a call rather than wasting their time in follow-ups.

Dreading to return calls when you have to say "no" or when the situation is otherwise unpleasant or difficult is, of course, natural. But hiding is cowardly and unacceptable. Once you make the unpleasant call, you'll find a great relief and renewed sense of confidence in your ability to handle your job.

Of course, never should you feel obligated to return a "mystery" call—one where the caller will not leave a name or purpose.

Getting Through to the "Right" Person

Whether placing calls for your boss or calling on your own behalf, you can waste much time by leaving messages with the wrong people or departments or by playing "telephone tag" with people who are always "unavailable."

If you have a complaint to make or need only to collect information from someone, give the screener enough information (name, company, purpose and details of call) so that she can tell you immediately that you've got the right department and the right person. Otherwise, you may waste two days waiting for someone to return the call when he or she doesn't have the information you need.

When you know you have the right department or person and have trouble getting the screener to put you through, try to be more authoritative. Rather than, "Would it be possible for me to speak with Ms. Culpepper about this?" try, "I'd like to speak to Ms. Culpepper, please." Once you know that Ms. Culpepper is the only one who can help you get results, don't waste time giving details to others: "I need to speak to Ms. Culpepper about those details. Would you please put her on the line?"

Other ways for getting through to the "right" person include cultivating service people and suppliers so that they recognize your name when you call; they want to help because they like you and want to give good service. Many secretaries suggest occasional "goodwill" contacts with such people—phoning to say "thank you" for good service, small gifts, lunches, or commendation letters to their supervisors.

Another tactic is to talk with the first person about the situation or decision to be made and ask him with whom you should follow up. Then when you call the second person, say: "I spoke with Mr. Jackson yesterday about this situation, and he suggested that I call you about..."

A third tactic—if you know the person needs and wants to talk with you but just hasn't gotten around to returning your call—is to phone and tell the screener you are *returning* her boss's call. If the person was supposed to be getting some information for you and has called you several times on the matter, he often forgets who originated the calls and will get back to you, thinking you have news for him.

A final tactic—perhaps a little shady—to avoid a screener is to call someone else in the organization and, when he answers, explain that you have the wrong number. Then ask that he transfer your call or give you the correct extension. Often, the one transferring the call will put you through directly to the person you want rather than dialing the secretary who has been told to "hold all calls."

When your call is to complain about a problem, make sure you speak with someone who has the authority to correct the situation. If you have to deal with a go-between on the first try, don't be put off the second time when you don't get results. On the second call, ask to speak to the first person's supervisor.

Be polite in your request for adjustment or information. Indicate your readiness to find a solution or get information rather than convey an attitude of "see-how-irritated-and-nitpicking-I-can-be."

State your objectives—exactly what information you need or what adjustment or service you expect. Don't leave the decision or resolution up to the other person.

Thank the other person, no matter how begrudging the information has been given or the adjustment has been made.

What You Can and Cannot Accomplish on the Phone

Using the phone is a great timesaver, but you should be aware of its limitations for specific situations.

Remember that the phone is considered an impersonal way to do business. Calling customers or clients rather than making a personal appointment may convey their relative unimportance to you. On the other hand, others may appreciate a call rather than a personal visit as a matter for their own convenience and because of their hectic schedule. Know your customers or clients and their preference.

Other occasions when the telephone may be *inappropriate* include reprimands, dismissals, confidential information, bad news, or negotiations. On the first four, the other person may feel that if you cared more for his or her predicament or really regretted the bad situation, you would at least have "the guts" or sensitivity to talk in person.

On occasions when you will need to negotiate your position, you run additional risks: There's more room for misunderstandings because of the lack of body language to suggest how things should be taken. Callers may feel under more pressure to end the conversation quickly rather than to "iron out the details," thus letting necessary information go undiscussed. Finally, it's much easier for the other person to say no or be hard-nosed on the phone than in person. So if you feel that you have something to gain in the negotiations, don't risk the discussion on the phone; talk face to face.

Last, using the phone can be a drawback rather than a timesaver when you have to communicate the same message to numerous people; when you should have a written record to verify the facts of the situation; when the other will need the information as a later reference and reminder; when the details are complex and lengthy. When any of these is the case, write rather than phone.

When you do have a simple task that can be handled by phone, such as:

- requesting or supplying routine information
- offering a yes or no decision,
- expressing interest in a topic
- following up problems or resolutions
- building goodwill

...take the time to plan your call.

Have your objective in mind and outline your key points. Collect and have at hand any files or other sources of information you may need for the discussion. If the situation is one where tact is particularly important, plan the actual wording of your opening and closing lines, as well as phrasing of key issues or requests.

A business phone should rarely be used for chitchat. Make your conversations count.

chapter 8

VISITORS

A few secretaries convey the impression that others will get in to see their boss only if their business involves global ramifications. They believe that their supervisor is quite possibly the busiest person in the English-speaking world and that his or her exalted rank precludes being bothered with lesser mortals.

And, unfortunately, because some secretaries take their role in managing their boss's time to such extremes, some visitors treat all secretaries as if they have to be bribed to let them slip through the pearly gates. Then, as a reaction to that visitor attitude, other secretaries act cold and impersonal as a defense mechanism against manipulation.

Thus, the "reaction to the reaction" puts distance between bosses and the people they need or want to serve. Particularly, this is a disastrous impression to give clients and customers. In fact, authors Peters and Waterman in *In Search of Excellence* identify closeness to the customer as one of the common tenets of the excellent companies across the nation. Of course, this does not mean simply frequent contact but receptiveness—whether in person, by phone, or with a quick response to a problem. And receptiveness is most assuredly conveyed by the "little things" such as secretarial attitudes toward visitors.

This chapter, therefore, will help you to take time to create goodwill rather than distance between your boss and those who visit him.

Scheduling Appointments

Learn your boss's priorities about whom she wants to see. And the key here is *priorities*, not outright refusals. On occasion, she will probably want to see or need to see virtually all visitors. But on the low-priority visitor, you will need to learn as much as you can about his purpose and your boss's interest and make a judgment to give or deny access—not closemindedly deny appointments to all vendors, all job applicants, or all stockbrokers. Remember, at one point she had to interview you for your job, and occasionally she will want to make a purchase for business or personal use.

In other words, keep in mind that your role is not to keep *everyone* from seeing your boss, only to screen the unimportant-at-the-moment visitors and try to help them yourself.

When vendors, suppliers, or job applicants request appointments, you may find it necessary to encourage your boss to see them for his own benefit. The presentation may be educational in that it presents state-of-the-art equipment, techniques, or research in an area where your boss is uninformed.

Therefore, don't "tune out" to any one group of visitors; simply find out the boss's priorities among these categories: family and personal friends, close business friends, higher-ups, subordinates, peers from other departments, customers or clients, vendors and suppliers, job applicants, solicitors for charity or civic groups, unknowns.

When someone calls for an appointment, do your best to find out as much about the purpose of the appointment as possible. When callers are vague about the purpose, put them on the spot: "Is this a personal rather than a business appointment?" Most will back down and admit that it is business; then you can proceed with your other screening questions. If, however, they insist that it is a personal matter, simply offer to take their name and number and explain that the boss prefers to schedule his or her own "personal" appointments.

And some bosses prefer to call back and schedule all their appointments, based on the telephone information you supply.

Additionally, when you schedule appointments, know your boss's preferences for times. Some bosses prefer to work uninterrupted in the mornings and see visitors in the afternoon; others prefer morning visitors and uninterrupted time in the afternoon. Some prefer to see visitors on certain days; for example, they will see vendors only on Fridays. Some have set times they want all appointments scheduled: 10 A.M. or 4 P.M.

Also, consider scheduling appointments at odd hours, such as 9:10 A.M. or 3:40 P.M., so as to let the visitor know that you keep a tight schedule and that your boss's time is limited.

In general, Monday mornings and Friday afternoons are inconvenient appointment times; on Mondays, the boss is planning her week's schedule and on Fridays, she may be winding up unfinished projects or may decide to leave early on the spur of the moment. Also, be careful to schedule so that appointments that run late will not interfere with the lunch hour, will not keep your boss at the office later than usual, or will not conflict with other scheduled meetings.

However, as a matter of time management, neither is it a good idea to scatter appointments throughout the day. Just when your boss is getting into her work day or a certain project, she will have to stop, lay things aside, and change tracks for the appointment. Rather, try to schedule appointments in blocks of time and leave consolidated, uninterrupted work time free.

Also going over the boss's schedule with her at the beginning of the week and again each day to coordinate and discuss exceptions to be made is always a good idea. Remember, of course, to tell callers who are seeking appointments that your scheduling is tentative and that you will call back to confirm.

Refusing an Appointment

When you determine that it would be a waste of your boss's time to see someone, rather than telling the caller "no" flatly, you can offer to take his name and number and tell him that you will give the information to your boss, who will get back to him about a convenient time *if he's interested*. If the visitor calls again to see why the boss didn't return the call, explain politely then that your boss expressed no interest in the subject, project, service, product, or whatever.

Most callers will prefer that you be honest about the lack of interest so they won't waste time in follow-up attempts to make the appointment. Here are several polite ways to turn people down for appointments:

"We thank you for your call, but Mr. Hartz is not at all interested in this matter at the moment. I would hate for you to waste your time in calling on him."

"Mr. Johnston is extremely involved in a major project right now and I'm afraid seeing him at this time would just increase your chances for a turndown."

"Although I don't think Ms. Freeman is the one you need to see (or would be interested), I suggest that you contact representatives of XYZ Company. Perhaps they have more need (or a larger budget) for that service."

"Ms. Chelton has suggested that you write a letter requesting an appointment and giving a few more details. Then she will be able to decide if you two should talk further or if she would be wasting your time."

Handling Visitors Without Appointments

A few people who haven't figured the price of an office visit lately or have never heard of time management may still drop in to see your boss unexpectedly. And, of course, there are always those visitors who happen to be in the office to see someone else and decide to drop by to say hello as a friendly gesture.

Again, as with those who call for an appointment, don't make snap judgments about whom your boss may or may not wish to see. Appearances are particularly deceiving; some very important visitors are described by some as "mousy," unassuming people.

You have six options for handling the unscheduled visitor: Give him a direct "no"; direct him to another person; offer to make an appointment; suggest that he write a letter; offer to help him yourself; or ask him to wait until the boss is free. A good secretary must make a judgment call.

But whatever you decide about the visitor, be careful not to be brusque. We all have our "blah" moods, hectic days, and rush projects; but never give the visitor the impression that he or she is a bother. Avoid opening comments such as "Did you want something?" Or, "What do you need?"

In other words, make the visitor feel welcome, not just tolerated.

Handling Those Your Boss Doesn't Want to See

A direct no is sometimes more gracious that you think in that it keeps your visitor from wasting his or her time. Refer to "Refusing an Appointment" above for tactful wording.

If you direct the visitor to another person in the company, offer to call and see if that individual can see him before he goes all the way to the fortieth floor. Such helpfulness makes your boss seem at least accommodating, if not accessible.

If you suggest that the visitor write, hand him one of your boss's business cards and note any specific key information such as a mailstop number. Give the visitor the attitude that writing is his best bet and that you fully expect him to do so.

If you think that you can help with the matter yourself by locating information or passing on information, offer to do so. You may reassure him that you are truly your boss's representative in these matters and what you say counts: "Ms. Cline prefers that I make the decisions about office equipment; perhaps you would like to talk with me about your product." Or, "I generally conduct first interviews for job openings; perhaps you'd like to sit down and tell me a little about yourself."

If the visitor is asking for a donation for a charity or civic organization, explain that your boss already contributes to a long list of causes and that you will be happy to discuss the matter with him but that you trust that the visitor will understand if he can't include any others. If the collector has the information available (and he usually does), you may ask if your boss contributed in previous years and what the amount of the donation was. All this will be helpful information in your boss's later decision.

Do take notes on conversations or underline key points on any printed materials a visitor leaves with you to reassure him that you will indeed state his case completely and fairly.

Even if you can't actually help an angry visitor with a problem, you can perhaps help defuse his anger and get him in a more receptive state to speak to whoever must deal with him next. Try something like, "Why don't you sit down a moment and explain the situation to me. I'll see if I can help or make some suggestions." (Then take notes and listen while he calms down.)

It may help you to retain your courteous manner even when the visitor is rude or angry if you understand that the visitor is not necessarily annoyed with you—but rather angry that the boss is unavailable, that her own plans have gone awry, or that his schedule is messed up for the day.

Handling Those Your Boss May Want to See

Explain that the boss has asked not to see anyone for thus-and-so reason, but explain that she may perhaps be able to make an exception. Take the visitor's name, organization, and purpose of the visit into your boss—out of earshot of the visitor. Or, if that's not possible, put the information on a slip of paper, hand it to the boss, give her time to read it, and then back away and ask if she can see the person. The boss then has the option of a yes or no, and the visitor can hear the boss's own turndown and reason.

Refuse to be manipulated into using your influence with the boss by a salesperson who prides himself on "conning" the secretary. A salesperson may call you by your first name and pretend to be your long-lost brother, offer you a free gift, or try to engage you in chitchat as if it were the cocktail hour. Make sure you don't use undue influence in getting him in to see the boss unless you think the boss will benefit from the visit.

If the boss says that he cannot or doesn't want to see the visitor, handle the situation as above under "Handling Those Your Boss Doesn't Want to See."

If you must turn down a visitor that your boss, under other circumstances, would have enjoyed seeing, you may tactfully express that sentiment:

"My boss says that although he would like to discuss the matter with you, it's not fair to you that he can't give you his whole attention at this time. He asked me to tell you that the next time you're planning to be in town, please make him aware so that you can arrange a time to get together."

Or,

"Mr. Simmons is heavily booked this afternoon and he wouldn't want to waste your time having you wait all afternoon and then perhaps not even get to see you. So, if you'll let me know next time when you're going to be in the building, I'll be glad to arrange an appointment."

When offering the visitor a later appointment, don't permit him to dally between making an appointment and waiting until the boss is free. Rather, give him options only about the appointment time: "Which day would be better for you—next Thursday or Friday morning at 10?"

Another option that you may want to suggest to your boss is that he walk out to the reception area for a short visit, one that allows more control and that can be ended more easily.

If the boss says that she will see someone without an appointment, be sure to tell the visitor how long it may be before the boss is free and give him the option of waiting or making an appointment for later.

You'll soon discover, if you haven't already, that some bosses who have "open-door" policies in theory may not actually practice that rule. For appearances' sake, your boss may grant easy access and then may expect you to protect her by discouraging the more inappropriate interruptions. When she's heavily involved in a project, for example, you may want to get up and close her door or suggest that she go to another conference room away from her office to get her project finished.

To Chat or Not to Chat

Making the visitor welcome does not necessarily mean you should try to engage her in conversation. Some areas of the country or some industries tend to be less formal and more friendly than others. Some more reserved visitors may consider "Hello, may I help you?" too informal, while others would be put off with a more traditional "How do you do?" upon their arrival.

Therefore, when and how you chat with visitors will depend on your business, your organization's desire to project a certain image, and community standards.

Also, whether you chat with the visitor who is waiting to see the boss will depend much on your role in the organization—how you see yourself, how your boss sees your function, and how the visitor perceives you. If you consider yourself someone who has specific assigned responsibilities separate from those of your boss, you probably should not try to carry on a conversation with the visitor. The purpose of the call and the details will be unknown or uninteresting to you.

If, on the other hand, you and your boss see yourself as a team fully involved in each other's projects, then you will feel more at liberty to carry on a conversation with visitors as equals.

However, if you are in doubt about how your visitor understands your role in the organization, perhaps you should take your clue from the visitor. If he or she initiates a conversation, feel free to respond.

You will probably find it safer to keep the conversation to neutral topics—the weather, sports, current events, office arrangement or decor, mutual acquaintances.

Avoid comments that give away confidential information (see Chapter 7, "Confidential Information") or show disloyalty to the company. Never complain about your organization in any way or express lack of confidence in its services or products. Also, avoid comments that may be interpreted as too personal—comments about dress, weight loss, age, disappointments, etc.

Seeing a Visitor In and Out

If greeting visitors is a regular part of your job, never leave your desk unattended without displaying a sign that says when you will return. Arriving visitors do not know whether to wait, go to a phone and call the boss, or simply announce themselves to the boss.

When visitors arrive, never see them into the boss's office or tell them to go in themselves without first checking to see if your boss is ready to talk with them. The boss may need time to go to the restroom, make a call, collect information, collect his thoughts about the upcoming visit, or regain composure from a previous appointment or phone call.

When you must go out and greet a visitor in another reception area, introduce yourself: "Mr. Lemons? I'm Martha White, Ms. Hinzt's secretary. Will you come with me, please?" Or, "I'll show you in now." Or, "Mr. Harvey can see you now."

When you introduce the visitor to the boss, always call the name of the one to be honored first; that is, introduce a younger person to an older, a less prominent person to a more prominent one. This relationship may get sticky when dealing with those outside your company. For most, a customer or client should be the honored one, no matter your boss's title. Examples:

"Mr. Top Executive, Mr. Mid Manager."

"Ms. Customer, I'd like you to meet Mr. Jason, our vice-president in charge of overseas sales."

Don't feel that you must make explanations about unusual relationships if there is more than one visitor. For unmarried live-ins, for example, just say: "Mr. Burrows, this is Jean Carter and Bob Black." If it is relevant—for example, one visitor is the other's supervisor—that relationship will become apparent in the course of the conversation to follow.

If your boss and the visitor or visitors are unacquainted, you may want to add a comment to break the ice, give them a conversational start, or jog your boss's memory about the reason for the appointment. Examples:

"Mr. Brown, this is Pete Marks about the XYZ problem."

"Mr. Smith, this is Marshall Graham...He was just telling me on the way in that he had trouble finding our building because of that sign that's still overturned on the corner."

"Ms. Cummings, this is Mark Shapiro. (Pause for them to shake hands.) "May I get you two some coffee before you begin your discussion?"

When the visitor leaves your boss's office, stop your work and acknowledge his departure in some way—either by a smile, a nod, a "good-bye," or a handshake if he initiates that. If necessary, show him out: "This way, please, and I'll show you to the elevators." In some cases, your showing the visitor out may be company policy for security reasons.

Serving Refreshments

Always offer your visitor available beverages during his wait or at the beginning of the appointment. Serve your visitor first and your boss last because you are hosting on his or her behalf. Remembering preferences such as black coffee only or hot tea with lemon makes a good impression on visitors.

Telephone Calls for Visitors

Tell the caller that the visitor and your boss have already begun their discussion and then ask if the caller wishes you to interrupt them. If he does, announce the caller and suggest that the visitor may want to take the call in your office or in the sitting area. Then remain in the boss's office so as to ensure privacy for the visitor's call.

If the caller does not want to be put through but merely wants you to take a message, ask if the message should be delivered immediately or if it can wait until the appointment is over. If the caller asks you to interrupt the appointment, then type the message, take it in to the boss's office, and wait for any instructions or answer the visitor may have for you.

How to Interrupt a Conference

Either knock on the door or buzz your boss on the intercom. Apologize for the interruption briefly (don't take 30 seconds, which is more of an interruption than the quick question you have to ask), and relay the message. Have available any further details, figures, or files before you interrupt so that you can quickly answer any questions the boss has about the situation and respond to his or her instructions quickly.

Also, remember that when you buzz the boss on the intercom, he or she may have the speaker set so that the visitor can hear what you say. If that may be a problem, interrupt personally and hand your boss a note, waiting for the reply.

Try to avoid, if at all possible, leaving your desk while your boss has someone in her office. During this time, you may be needed to screen interruptions, provide information, or make phone calls that the ongoing conference entails. When your boss is interrupted by a continually buzzing phone because you are away from your desk, that is a direct reflection on you as host. You put your boss in the position of having to be rude to the visitor and ask him to wait while she takes the call or having to be rude to the caller, saying she has someone in her office. (The caller may find this hard to believe since the boss answered the phone at a time when a secretary should most certainly be screening.)

Helping Your Boss End Appointments Promptly

When you see that an appointment is running longer than expected, interrupt your boss to remind him of another appointment or meeting he has scheduled. If he is ready to terminate the appointment, he will take it from there.

If he says he needs more time with the appointment, offer to handle the details of his being late to other meetings or appointments. Call ahead and explain that he "has been detained and will be coming shortly" or explain that "something has come up that he could not avoid, and he will be unable to attend." Offer to attend yourself as a representative, collect information for him, or suggest that the boss will be in touch later to reschedule or discuss the matter.

If you think the appointment is running late against your boss's wishes (some bosses don't know how to bring an appointment to an end), you may want to offer him an "excuse" for ending the conference by buzzing him to remind him of the time. At your announcement that it's 1:45, he can tell the visitor whatever he wishes about where he has to be when.

Canceling Appointments Due to Emergencies

When you see that your boss will be unable to see a scheduled visitor for whatever reason—he or she hasn't returned to the office from a meeting, his or her plane is late, he's tied up with another visitor—try to catch a scheduled visitor before he leaves his own office for the appointment with your boss. If your boss is away from the office and you know how to reach him when an appointment time is fast approaching, try calling him at the meeting to see if he would like you to reschedule the appointment.

When it is impossible to reach the visitor and cancel the appointment before he arrives, try to accommodate him the best way you can by taking information from him, directing him to another person, or offering to phone your boss at the meeting for a brief conversation.

Always apologize for the inconvenience and explain that the delay couldn't be avoided—that he was "called away suddenly," "became ill," "had transportation problems," "had an emergency situation develop," or "got caught in a longer-than-usual meeting and couldn't get away."

Never act as though the "no show" is only a minor inconvenience or something that happens frequently with your boss. A visitor may have scheduled her entire week around this appointment, spent hours en route, or worked long overtime hours to finish a project to be discussed at the canceled appointment time.

Relatives Who Visit

Whether yours or the boss's, visiting relatives get special treatment. If your spouse or another family member shows up at the office unexpectedly to handle a personal matter, make the visit brief and don't let it interfere with your getting back to your job.

Be particularly careful, also, that if clients or customers are waiting, you do not show special treatment by taking care of the relative's needs before your client's or customer's needs. In fact, it is best if the observer does not realize you are dealing with a relative; that detracts from the professional image you want to convey on the job.

If, on the other hand, your spouse or another family member is visiting for the first time or for a special event, you will make more of the situation. Introduce the relative, of course, to your boss and colleagues and make a few comments to help them begin a conversation. Be cautious, however, that your comments about "how great the boss is" aren't interpreted as insincere flattery.

Use your office as "headquarters" to make other introductions. In other words, rather than taking your relative in tow around to other offices to introduce him, wait until others come to your office for the introduction. If colleagues don't know your relative is in the office, phone them and give them the option of stopping work and meeting the relative: "John, my husband, Tom, dropped by my office to take me to lunch. I was wondering if you had a moment to come down and meet him?" That gives the colleague the option of saying "he'd love to, but," of controlling how long the meeting takes by coming to where you two are, or by suggesting that you bring your relative to his office for a moment.

Also, using your office to make all the introductions prevents your offending by leaving someone out. If a co-worker says she is sorry not to have met your husband, you can always say, "So am I. He was here only about five minutes, though. Several people did happen through about that time. I wish I'd have known you were free to stop by."

When the visiting relative is your boss's, follow your boss's lead about what a "to-do" you should make. If the boss includes you in the visit, offer to drop what you're doing to serve them refreshments, watch the kids, oooh over newly made portraits or whatever. If he merely ushers the relatives into his office, return to your work as normal, merely acknowledging their arrival and departure.

Accepting and Refusing Gifts from Visitors

From time to time you will be the recipient of a gift from an outsider—a client or customer.

Generally, any gift that is given to a secretary rather than the decision-maker is inexpensive; nevertheless, the ulterior motive is there and usually makes one feel manipulated—an effect that most salespersons don't realize. Although it is permissible to accept an inexpensive gift such as a personalized coffee mug or memo pad—particularly if all the secretaries in the company or your department have been given one—you certainly may feel free to refuse more expensive items such as free theater tickets or an invitation to dinner or lunch.

If you are the decision-maker in a particular selling situation and are invited to lunch, feel free to accept or reject. If you feel manipulated or put on the spot, decline: "Thank you, but I don't think so. I think I'd prefer to talk here in my office—about 2:15 if that's okay?" (You don't owe an explanation for the turndown.)

If, on the other hand, you do want to accept the gift and if your company has no policy against this, make it clear to the salesperson that your acceptance will in no way affect your decision. Of course, you will not bluntly say so, but you may convey that feeling tactfully: "Yes, I am free for lunch, but let me tell you up front that the discussion may be a waste of your time because we simply are not in the market for another word-processing package at the moment."

If the salesperson still insists on your accepting the invitation or the gift, there's no need for you to feel guilty. He or she may find something valuable in the discussion after all—up-to-date information, customer needs for future sales, or other contacts.

Hosting VIP Visitors for Formal Functions—Extended Visits, Receptions, Parties

When you are given responsibility for planning, arranging, and co-hosting either formal or informal functions for VIPs, give thought to planning an event that is out of the ordinary. First, that entails focusing on the objective of the function, the budget, and the guest list:

Is this merely a goodwill, nonbusiness-discussion function? Or will the participants want to talk business? Do you want to formally present a new product or service to the client-visitor? Do you want to impress an upper-management visitor with your austere budget? Will participants know each other, or will they want plenty of opportunity to make new contacts? Will there be language or cultural barriers with international visitors?

All of these questions will determine whether you go with the traditional cocktail party in the company conference room, the sit-down dinner at an elegant museum or restaurant terrace, or the informal evening on the town with tickets to a sports event.

Then when you make these basic decisions, you move on to more specific details such as design, production, and mailing of invitations; confirmations of attendance; design of the location as to arrangements of tables, flowers, band, as well as color and theme; menu for food and beverages; seating plans; arrangements for speeches, product presentations, or entertainment.

And planning these details is only the beginning. You must take total responsibility that things are done as you have specified. Get exact fees—including tips, taxes, and whatnots—in writing. Don't leave it to your assistants to follow up with the caterer about details such as a room change. Double-check. If things flop, you and your boss are the ones who will look bad.

During the function itself, you are still "in charge" of service details and "atmosphere." Your boss will be using his or her time to talk business, make contacts, or receive the credit for all things wonderful.

The seating arrangement should be worked out ahead of time with your boss. You may seat men and women alternately, or seat guests by divisions, by acquaintance, or by rank. If you know your guests well, don't put outgoing people by shy people, hoping the more talkative will bring the shy person out. Just the opposite will happen—the talkative will dominate the conversation and the shy person will do all the listening. Rather, seat two shy people together, and they will strike up a conversation of mutual interest.

Be everywhere at all times. Don't simply fill your glass or sit down to eat with the rest of the guests. In fact, never sit down; that shows lack of energy and lessens your control of the events. Circulate around the room to see that everyone else's needs are met.

Problem Guests

With the *drunk guest*, don't offend by asking if he needs someone or a taxi to drive him home. Simply make the arrangements and tell him (or have another colleague or your boss tell him) what you've arranged.

With the *loudmouth* that is making a scene, calmly talk to him in a lowered voice. When you lower your voice, generally he will lower his voice to hear what you're saying. Gradually maneuver him toward a secluded spot and get help in calming him.

If you have a *complainer*, hear him out but insist that he talk with you privately away from other guests. Try to accommodate him as best you can, be as persuasive as possible to get him to cooperate—whether it be seating arrangement or the kind of music playing in the background. Your best tactic may be simply delay: "Yes, I remember what you said about the dim lights. I've called someone. We're working on that."

Impudent Service People

When a caterer, building technician, or other service person becomes impudent about what you have requested to be done, don't argue or plead. Calmly ask for his name and the name of his supervisor. (He will know why you're asking.) Make a big deal of beginning to write down the details of the situation and comments that he has made to you. Speak with authority but reserved coolness as you get this information or give orders. You may not have the liberty to make threats about his company's losing your business or his losing his job—and it is probably not a good idea to do so—but simply make inferences: Stuff the information into your file folder, handbag, or whatever is handy; go to the phone out of his earshot; or speak to your boss if all else fails to get results.

Usually, the impudent person will calm down and back down about his or her refusal to do or not do what you've asked.

And don't forget to put any complaints in writing to the service organization after the function is over. Thank-you's, of course, are in order for those who give exceptional service. Cultivate this relationship for the next big event you'll schedule.

Making Introductions, Announcements, or Presentations

You may also be in charge of explaining the events of the evening to the guests or of making necessary announcements about time, transportation, accommodations, emergencies: 1) Make notes before you start so that you don't waste their attention or omit details; 2) Get their attention before you begin to make the announcement or speech; 3) Be sure that you speak in an authoritative voice at a mike or otherwise so you can be heard all over the room.

If you are in charge of the welcome, most speeches include these points:

- Welcome to everyone, calling names of the most prominent (usually including your boss or those of your department hosting the event)

- Statement about the purpose of this get-together or that this is a "traditional" or annual event

- Schedule of activities or speakers planned

- Closing invitation for guests to enjoy themselves and come to you with any problems or needs

When introducing a speaker:

- Welcome the speaker and the guests
- Introduce the topic; tell how the speaker is qualified to speak on the subject
- If you have an embarrassingly small audience, you may offer "excuses" such as "although this topic is interesting to only a select few..." or "conflicting events..." or "bad weather..."
- Call the speaker by name and invite him or her to the front or to the podium
- Remember to keep your remarks brief; guests came to hear the speaker, not you

Bringing the Evening to a Close

Be specific about ending times when you send out invitations: "A reception to be held from 5 P.M. to 7 P.M." If, however, guests are slow about leaving, you may want to encourage them with these statements: "It was nice that you could come. I know Mr. Hanson appreciated your coming to celebrate his retirement with him." Or, "Does anyone here need transportation? I'd be happy to make arrangements for you." Or, "I'm certainly glad we caught you back in town and that you were able to come tonight."

Informal Get-Togethers

If you have arranged for a simple restaurant meal, a sports event, or another local attraction, your hosting duties will be much simpler. If you have trouble in deciding what to plan, you will not offend your guests at all by asking: "Since this is your first time to visit XYZ city, is there something special you would like to see or do?" Or, "Since you visit XYZ city so often, is there anything you haven't seen or would like to do this time? How about a favorite restaurant where you'd like to dine?"

If you are entertaining international guests, they probably have already seen all the civic attractions; perhaps they would appreciate a quiet evening at a local restaurant or at the home of your boss.

When leaving the final decision up to your guests, however, it is best that you make some suggestions so that they will know your budget for the evening.

If you are not going along on the outing, handle everything you can beforehand for your boss—transportation to and from, billing, tickets for the theater, etc. Then write the information down for him or her—including times and locations of meeting places.

When Your Boss Is the Visitor

Make sure that you encourage your boss to follow up with the appropriate acknowledgments—a note, flowers, a small gift. But if the event was a special one, try to be more personal and thoughtful. Suggest a coffee-table book, a novel, food or beverage, golf balls, personal stationery, or a desk ornament.

For the contents of a thank-you note prepared for the boss's signature, see Chapter 9.

chapter 9

CORRESPONDENCE

Management guru Peter Drucker writing in *People and Performance*, (p.263), says that the ability to express yourself in speaking and writing is perhaps the most important of all the skills you can possess. Although Drucker is directing his comments to the managerial-level employee, how much more important is writing and speaking well to the secretary! After all, those are her two primary functions—handling correspondence and dealing with others face to face. In those two skills, writing and speaking, secretaries must shine.

And ultimately, writing skills outweigh verbal skills; by its very nature, a written document is more permanent. The following letter surfaced in one of my secretarial workshops; received by one of the class participants, it had already been the object of amusement in several departments:

Dear Mr. & Mrs. Wyatt,

Enclosed please find Hutner Ins. Co. loss draft #32116 in the amount of $4,562.32. I am unable to endorse this draft and return to you because the investor requirement require that specific requirements be met before we can release First Mortgages interest in this draft. Please sign the draft and return to this office so we can deposit it to escrow. Please forward a copy of the adjustors work sheet that itemized the loss that the company paid the loss on.

A copy of the signed contract—if a contractor is being used. Please have noted the amount that is needed down to start the relpairs.

If the work is being done by yourself forward a billing from the company where materials are to be purchased and we will forward a check payable to you and to the company where the material is being purchased.

After completion of the repairs please advise the undersigned in order that an inspection can be made of the repairs. When we have received approval, we will then complete the claim.

If a contractor is being used please request that he furnish us with a lien waver for the money paid to hime.

ENclosed is a certification fo repairs form to be signed and returned when the work is complete.

If you have any questions, please contact the undersigned at 1/800/224-6122 Ext 1494.

Very truly yours,

What do you think of this secretary's skills? Your writing is your "face" on the page.

When to Write Rather than Talk

Generally, a phone call is faster and cheaper than a letter or memo. (That is, if you can catch the person by phone and if the call is not long distance.) Also, a phone call or face-to-face discussion is preferable when you must negotiate something or exchange ideas and plans and want immediate response—for example, negotiating a delivery date for equipment or selecting a menu for a seminar luncheon.

Additionally, a phone call may be preferable when there is a chance you may offend. Remember that tone and body language have much to do with how you communicate. Written messages, of course, devoid of these "communication helpers," may come across flat, humorless, blunt, or aggressive when no such tone was intended. For example, a pun, an intended remark that you would have said with raised eyebrow and a smile, may seem offensive in print.

Remember, too, that whatever you write is a matter of record for all to see. When your memo or letter is passed around to others in the department, you may have escalated a problem significantly.

Finally, one other danger in writing is that when you send too many memos, people tend to ignore them; your judgment about what's important and what's insignificant comes into question.

So when should you write?

1. Write when you have multiple readers and one form letter or memo can take the place of several phone calls.

2. Write when you are simply conveying information such as reminding, confirming, announcing, or explaining, and expect no immediate response.

3. Write when the person will need the document for later reference.

4. Write when you want to ensure accuracy of details that are lengthy, complex, or technical.

5. Write when your reader will have to distribute the information to others—by your writing the message, you will more often ensure accuracy, completeness, timeliness, and ease of distribution by photocopying your own wording of the message.

6. Write when you need a permanent record.

The Personal Touch

Organizations spend millions of dollars each year on television, radio, and print advertisements trying to convey the impression that they care personally about their clients or customers—that they are not some bureaucrats off in the clouds.

Why should their employees undermine that effort with writing that sounds as though it comes from a machine and is addressed to

"Occupant"?

Be conversational: To choose the appropriate style for most correspondence, consider how you would express your ideas in conversation with the same reader or readers. If you wouldn't say to the person on the phone, "This call is to acknowledge receipt of your telephone message of October 16 about meeting for lunch to discuss options open to us with regard to..." then don't write that way. Instead try, "I received your phone message yesterday about our meeting for lunch to discuss plans for the..."

Many secretaries adopt a "foreign tongue" when writing because they perhaps feel insecure in their writing skills and, therefore, try to copy what some call an "official" or "businesslike" tone. The trend for the last two decades has been away from an overly formal writing style in business correspondence. If you're trying to emulate an older, higher-up's phraseology that seems stuffy and stilted (and outdated), don't.

For the most part, write your message as you would say it. Be careful, of course, to omit repetitious details, choppy sentences, grammatical errors, or colloquialisms that you may use in speaking.

Use a person's name and spell it correctly: "Dear Ms. Jordan" sounds more cordial than "Dear Madam." And if you would do so in conversation, call a person by his or her first name. Be careful, of course, that the person prefers your using first names; as noted earlier, some people, especially older ones, may be offended at overfamiliarity. Note the way a person refers to himself or herself on the phone or in face-to-face conversation.

If you are unsure about spelling a name, call a receptionist or check the phone directory. If you don't think people care about your misspelling their name, I can pass on several comments from those in my writing workshops who say they don't read mail in which their name is misspelled. A missing or misspelled name tells the reader he or she is not too important to you.

If you cannot possibly find a name, use a title: "Dear Program Director."

Use appropriate salutations:

Dear Sir
Dear Madam
Dear Sir or Madam
Gentlemen

Ladies
Gentlemen or Ladies
Dear Dr.
Dear Mr. or Ms.

"Dear" is the most accepted greeting and not to be taken literally any more than other social phrases such as "How do you do?" "Fine," or "Yours truly." You may, however, drop the "Dear" and begin with only the title or name of the reader.

Make your closings fit your letter: The most formal closings are "Very truly yours" and "Yours truly." To be less formal, try, "Sincerely," "Cordially," "Best regards," "With best wishes," or "Thank you."

Avoid opening with a warm-up drill: "This letter acknowledges receipt of your February 6 inquiry about the equipment shown in our catalog and our previous discussions on January 10 and January 22 when you phoned to explain that..." constitutes a warm-up drill and sets up an impersonal and stuffy style. This letter acknowledges? Why don't you? Summarizing all past correspondence and phone conversations suggests that the reader's memory or files, or both, aren't very good.

Remember that busy readers prefer to control their own reading time. That means that they need your "bottom-line" message up-front—then the details. With this arrangement they can read as much or as little as they need to understand what you're saying or do what you're asking.

"Dear Mr. Smith:

The software package "Matrix Mate" that you wrote about February 6 is no longer being distributed. We have had difficulty..."

With the main message up-front, the reader then can decide if it's necessary to read the remainder of the document.

Include pleasantries: Mention upcoming holidays, refer to past conversations, or express congratulations or praise when in order. But be sincere; overstatements sound sarcastic or phony.

Watch "fight" words: Mistaken, failed to, misled, ignored trigger an adverse gut reaction. Even the word *must* sometimes raises hackles. Consider the difference in these two statements: 1) "You must come into our Main Street office for that information." 2) "If you will come into our Main Street office, we can give you that information." If you're writing to request corrective action, such fight words will thwart your purpose.

Include courtesy words: Words such as *please, appreciate,* or *thank you* are never out of order. They motivate. Without them, your writing may seem blunt, directive, cold.

Use simple words, not pompous ones: Dignity, closely aligned with simplicity, means a writing style appropriate to subject matter, void of colloquialisms and grammatical errors. Pomposity, on the other hand, means excessively ornate or elevated, exhibiting self-importance. Don't use words that call attention to themselves rather than the ideas they express. That is not to say that you avoid complex words altogether—especially if the complex word says exactly what you mean. But don't overlook the simple word in an effort to sound "businesslike." A writer who continually uses pompous words and phrases when simple ones will do is an amusement to the reader.

The Pompous Word	*The Simple Word*
utilization	use
obtain	get
assistance	help
endeavoring	trying
parameters	scope
procure	buy
modification	change
initiate	begin
subsequently	next, later, then

Keep people in your writing: That generally means using active voice rather than passive voice; put the "doer" at the beginning of the sentence:

Passive voice: These forms should be reviewed for...
Active voice: Please review these forms for...

Passive voice: Arrangements will be made to...
Active voice: We will make arrangements to...

Passive voice: Schedules should be received by the...
Active voice: You should receive your schedules by...

Passive voice: It is requested that you bring...
Active voice: Please bring... (or, We ask that you bring...)

Note, too, that active-voice constructions are always clearer because they say who does what.

Never tell someone what he or she thinks or feels. Comics know better than to tell an audience, "The funniest thing happened the other day..." The listeners are set up for disappointment. Instead, they tell the story and let the audience decide for itself how funny it is. Likewise, leave it to your customers to make their decisions about your message or action:

Not: "XYZ no longer carries the item you ordered; however, we have shipped a replacement that has the same features and think this will meet your needs equally well."
But: "XYZ no longer carries the item you ordered; however, we have shipped a replacement that has the same features and hope this will meet your needs. If not, please feel free to return it at our expense."

Don't be arbitrary: When possible, give sufficient reason for actions or requests. People with a reason tend to cooperate better—even when they don't agree.

Don't be patronizing: Do not give unnecessary explanations or talk down to your reader: "Although you obviously were unaware of the various branches associated with..." emphasizes your superior knowledge and the reader's ignorance.

Don't be indifferent or careless: Answer all the reader's questions promptly; avoid giving details you think he or she needs while omitting others as privileged information—unless, of course, the information is truly confidential.

Avoid clichés: Clichés such as "If you will be kind enough to..." "Pursuant to our discussion..." "Enclosed please find..." or "If you have other questions, please do not hesitate to call" mark you as a lazy thinker.

Such clichés make your writing sound like a form letter—as though someone merely touched the "print" button of the computer. Certainly, form letters have a place in the business world. But when you want to influence your reader favorably, give careful thought to phraseology and take time to address his or her special concerns in a personal way.

Be careful with humor: Humor is a subjective matter that will vary from reader to reader. Remember that with a letter or memo, you don't have a smile, twinkling eye, or voice inflection to tell your reader how to take what you've written.

The Thinking Process for Effective Writing

Before you begin to draft a memo or letter, think:

- *Who is your audience?* Do you have a single reader or multiple readers? Rank them in order of importance: The most important reader gets his or her information first; lesser-ranking readers must read further into the document to get the information they need.

- *How will the reader use the information you're sending?* In other words, what's the message of primary importance to him or her?

- *How much does your reader already know about the subject?* This answer will tell you what terms, acronyms, or abbreviations you can use and how many or how few details you need to include.

- *What special problems do you anticipate in your reader's reaction?* Will he be skeptical or angry? Are you creating extra work for him? Will he tend to procrastinate about the action? Is this a low-priority item or action for him? Will he lose face accepting what you say? Are you suggesting a change that will be difficult to master?

If any of these are problems, plan how you will overcome the obstacles: With careful wording? With elaboration on the necessity of the action? With details about consequences of inaction? With a motivating, goodwill statement? With accompanying step-by-step directions?

Finally, outline your message in a functional, easy-to-understand format before actually writing the first draft. (See basic formats that follow.)

Many business letters and memos coming from your office deal with "routine" matters. When that's the case, you would do well to memorize or file on your computer "stock" paragraphs to draft certain correspondence. Once you have become accustomed to your boss's style and preferred phrases, you can make any necessary changes, vary and personalize these "stock" ideas, and then prepare most correspondence ready for your boss's signature. If you are working for a new boss, study his or her files for stock ideas, phrases, and paragraphs.

There is a place for form letters and memos in business writing; however, on most occasions you create a much better impression outside the company when your letters sound original and personal. Therefore, work to vary the phrasing of even your "form" correspondence.

Responding promptly also creates a good impression. If your boss is away from the office or if you cannot get complete information for your own response, at least acknowledge receipt of the other person's letter or memo. You can promise complete details when your boss returns or when you've had time "to check into the matter." Never, of course, reveal in your reply anything your boss may consider confidential and never commit yourself or your boss in any way until you have studied the matter and have been given an okay for such a reply.

Formats for Routine Correspondence

When your boss has given you the responsibility to compose a first draft of his or her correspondence and when you're writing letters and memos for your own signature, learn to think in what I call the Functional Format, or the MADE Format.

Eighty to 90 percent of all business correspondence should follow this basic organizational structure:

M: What's the message? Narrow, one-to-three sentence summary of your "bottom-line" message.

A: So what action next? What action do you plan to take? Or, what action do you want your reader to take based on the message you have just given?

D: Details: Who? When? Where? Why? How? How Much? Not all will be necessary for every memo; avoid mentioning the obvious. Usually, the *why* and *how* details will be the most significant and require elaboration. If the who, when, where, why, and how details can be stated briefly in the first two sections, don't repeat them here. Rather, necessary elaborations of these details follow here.

E: Optional evidence: Mention any form, table, chart, diagram, map, or copy of previous correspondence you have attached or enclosed to make the message clearer and the action easier.

Let's review each of these four sections more closely:

M: What's the message? After focusing on your specific reader or readers, you should be able to summarize briefly the significant information in a sentence or two: "We are updating our files of RUX regulations and need your help in locating missing publications." "To serve you better, the construction office phone system has been changed." "The time-management seminar I attended at University of Texas, June 6-9, presented me with valuable tools that should enhance my job performance."

A: So what action next? When you intend to take action based on the message you have given, state it: Do you plan to schedule a follow-up meeting for next month? Will you choose vendors for the new food-service facility? Will your division begin testing new equipment in October? Will you correct your records as shown on the last invoice?

Or, you may want action from the reader; if so, state what you expect. Do you want her to return the attached, completed form by February 18? Do you want her to be more accurate when doing safety inspections? Do you want her to approve your attendance at a computer-training program in Atlanta? Do you recommend that accounting procedures be changed to eliminate duplication of effort?

When the message *is* the action, this section and the first section become one. And occasionally, you send a message only to inform. If that's the case, make sure your reader knows *no action* is required.

D: Details: Who? When? Where? Why? How? How much? After the reader has "the big picture" from your beginning statement and knows what you plan to do or what you expect him to do, then he can read the details with understanding and purpose.

Of course, if the idea regarding who, when, where, why, how, or how much can be given in only a word or a phrase, you will probably have already stated such information in the opening-message sentence or sentences:

> Department liaison persons helping to plan the headquarters move to 2011 Mainstay are scheduled to attend a meeting Tuesday, July 6, at 9:30 A.M., in Conference Room 203. Doug Pharmon will explain packing procedures and answer questions about your particular department's equipment and files.

In this case, all pertinent details become a significant part of the message statement; you can give them briefly without elaboration.

In general, this third section of your memo or letter contains those details that need elaboration—usually *why* and *how*. If you anticipate a special problem in the reader's reaction, here is where you address that problem. If you expect skepticism, add authority to your position by elaborating on how thorough your investigation has been. If you expect hesitancy about a due date, impress upon the reader the importance of meeting the deadline. If you have claimed that hiring a new typist will save you money normally spent on temporary help, give the *how much* of your calculations. If you must point out someone's error, tactfully allow possible reasons the mistake may have occurred.

E: Optional evidence: Not always, of course, will you have attachments or enclosures with your correspondence. But attachments can make your message clearer or the action you expect easier to do. If you're asking for monthly data, can you send your reader a sample format to follow? If you want her to note discrepancies in past and present years' vendor contracts, can you attach a copy of the old contract so that she doesn't have to go through her files to make the comparison? If you're asking for replacement of a stolen expense-reimbursement check, can you enclose another copy of your earlier-submitted expense form?

The only time you may possibly begin a letter or memo with statements such as "Attached is..." or "Enclosed you will find..." is simply when you're writing a transmittal.

This four-part basic Functional Format (MADE) outlined above saves much time for the reader. At his discretion, he can stop reading as soon as he has all the desired information. Further, the message-first format aids in comprehension of the details and attachment. Finally, outlining in this format gives you, the writer, a straight path to follow, helping eliminate irrelevant, repetitious, and obvious details.

To understand better how this format applies to your specific writing tasks, study the following memos and letters:

To: Freda Smith
From: Marian Weymer
Subject: Health Fair Planning Committee

You are cordially invited to be a member of the Health Fair Planning Committee for Hintz General Hospital employees. If you are interested in serving on this committee, please contact Sylvia Brown, M.A., General Health/Support Service Instructor, at 823-1444.

These health fairs give people an opportunity to practice preventive medicine, receive medical screenings in various areas, and develop a health-conscious attitude. By donating your time, you will have an opportunity to contribute your suggestions and ensure that the Health Fair is a success for your own fellow dieticians. As committee chairperson, I estimate that our planning will require about 20 hours of your time over the next four months.

I'm enclosing a copy of last year's program so that you can get a general idea of what the fair entails. I look forward to your reply about serving on this committee.

To: All Department Managers
From: Marion Honess
Subject: IDRT Disk-Space Shortage

The IDRT currently has a disk-space shortage. At present there are over 10,200 datasets or about 87,000 tracks of allocated space that have not been referenced in over 120 days.
Would you please review the following datasets for your area and delete those that are no longer required?

PR	.Trofv	1/6/8-
PR	.Trofvnn	2/4/8-
PR	.PL378	2/6/8-
HS	.AD257S	4/6/8-

We appreciate your assistance in freeing this space.

Dear Ms. Markson:
Sally Doe, who worked for you from June 198-, to September 198-, has given your name as a reference. Would you take a few minutes to give us your opinion about her typing skills, her ability to get along with others, and her experience in handling clients?

We have enclosed an evaluation form for your convenience; however, please feel free to reply by personal letter or phone (123-4567).

Thank you for your time and opinion.

Sincerely,

With memos and letters that get to the point quickly and efficiently, you show respect for your reader's time and also make your message clearer.

Following are additional tips for specific, frequently written letters and memos.

Apologies

Do's

Focus immediately on positive action taken to rectify the situation rather than recall the damage done by your error.

Apologize with actions, not words. Is there something you can do to ease bad feelings? Take someone to lunch? Submit the next report a week early? Send over temporary typing help? Hand-carry the drawing to the client? Make a phone call to the manager and assume your part in the problem and ease the strain on your reader? In other words, can you go the Biblical second mile in salvaging the situation, relationship, or project?

Briefly, in a positive way, explain how the mistake happened. Not to do so is inconsiderate. Let the reader know that your mistake was not intentional or due to unconcern or carelessness.

Make the reader feel that his or her goodwill is valued.

Assure the reader that you will guard against future mistakes. (Avoid guaranteeing that something will never happen again. Murphy's Law will make you a liar, and then the reader will be doubly disappointed.) Mention that you are making a note on your calendar so you will not forget the next meeting; say that you have instructed your receptionist to put future calls from the reader through to you immediately; promise that you will personally phone to follow up information you send in the future. Offer whatever assurance you can that the mistake will *likely* not recur.

Don'ts

Don't gloss over your responsibility for the error, problem, or situation. ("We're sorry for any inconvenience this may have caused"—cliché that sounds insincere.) If the situation is important enough for the other person to mention, it's important enough for a sincere apology. When you are at fault, admitting guilt disarms the reader and makes him or her much more willing to accept your apology and explanation charitably.

Don't remind the reader again at the end of your letter about the problem or disappointment. Instead, suggest that the matter has been corrected and that goodwill has been restored.

Appointments

Do's

State the scheduling, cancellation, or delay/refusal up-front.

Always give some indication about the subject of the appointment when scheduling so that the reader can prepare beforehand any thoughts, data, or questions.

Let the reader know if the appointment is mandatory or optional and how to contact you if there's a conflict.

Give enough details about the appointment date, time, subject, location, and duration when setting or canceling an appointment. Even with cancellations, this information prevents misunderstandings about exactly which meeting or appointment you are referring to.

State any available information about rescheduling.

Express concern for the other's inconvenience when canceling.

Be sure to give reasons when delaying or refusing an appointment. If possible, point out why the appointment would not be beneficial to the requester or in the best interest of others concerned. Suggest alternatives for handling the problem, situation, or decision.

If delaying or refusing an appointment, state any conditions under which you or your boss will reconsider your answer.

Don'ts

Don't sound arbitrary, as if you are refusing or delaying an appointment on a whim with no concern for the other's inconvenience or problem situation. Offer alternatives when you can—is there someone else the person should see?

Confirmations

Do's

Use the basic Functional Format, stating what you are confirming in a simple up-front statement or two.

Repeat *all* the details of the appointment, course, meeting, speaking engagement, transaction, or whatever: date, time, place, enclosures, amounts. In short, don't rely on any previous oral or written information; repetition of details is one of the main purposes of the written confirmation.

Mention the date or manner of any initial phone, personal, or written contact.

Unless routine or obvious, suggest a method to contact you in case the confirmation note reveals some error or misunderstanding.

Don'ts

Don't confuse a confirmation with a follow-up. Confirmations need to confirm all details, not just remind of key points.

Congratulations

Do's

Mention the event or honor immediately. Don't keep the reader in suspense about your reason for writing.

Be personal without being too familiar. Avoid general, stilted phrases that make the memo or letter sound like a form message sent to all employees or customers. Inserting names rather than vague nouns such as "your child" or "your new bride" will go far in personalizing your wishes. However, avoid familiarities such as mentioning age in a birthday wish, a past divorce in a wedding note, or a physical handicap in a note about a new baby, or past difficulties in a congratulatory letter about a promotion.

Be specific in your congratulations on achievements such as promotions or awards. The reader wants to know that you understand all that the achievement or honor entails—time, effort, creativity, intellectual accomplishment. Elaborating on these specifics gives the reader time to "enjoy" your attention.

Be sincere. An effusive display of flattery makes even a great accomplishment seem small or undeserving of your notice.

Call names when congratulating more than one person. Calling names lets the readers of the memo or letter know that you understand their personal achievement or contribution to the effort.

Don'ts

Don't imply that you or someone else could have earned the same honor or achieved the same result, given the same time, or resources, or circumstances.

Don't mention negatives—even negatives that have nothing to do with the congratulated person himself. Negative comments, even though general or directed at other people or events, detract from the good feelings that the letter proposes to evoke on the part of the reader.

Don't talk about yourself, your boss, or the company; focus on the other person.

Errors

Pointing out someone else's errors:

Do's

Begin on a neutral note. Then "creep up" on the error if you can. Or, perhaps try a "there are problems" approach: "I received a copy of the forms we were supposed to fill out; however, there seems to be one column missing on Side B. Was this an oversight or should the form be reprinted to include..."

Focus on what you have done or what the reader should do to correct the problem rather than trying to assign blame.

Emphasize the importance of accuracy, giving reasons or repercussions of errors. However, don't be overly dramatic about a small matter. Whenever you overstate, the reader will tend to downplay the importance of the mistake.

If the matter is one that will likely arise again, suggest precautions against future problems.

Show diffidence and humility; never use a self-righteous or aggressive tone. Watch "fight" words such as "failed to," "ignored," "misled," "carelessly omitted."

Don'ts

Don't patronize. Even the insertion of courtesy words such as "please" and "appreciate" fails to compensate for sarcasm or a self-righteous attitude. Avoid showing your "tolerance" in overlooking or correcting another's error. Also, to avoid "screaming" in print, watch unusual punctuation marks such as exclamation points or rhetorical question marks and underlining.

Don't assume the error is intentional or due to carelessness. Consider the possibility that your instructions have been unclear or that circumstances prevented compliance or perfection. At the very least, consider that the reader may not have been aware of the importance of accuracy. Assume some of the responsibility for the error yourself.

Don't focus on the error to the exclusion of how the matter should be corrected. Your memo should not be a game of "Gotcha."

Admitting Your Own Error:

Do's

State the error and correction immediately.

Evaluate the seriousness of your mistake; then explain and apologize accordingly. When the situation has political undertones to your disadvantage, play down the error with a matter-of-fact tone. After all, everybody makes mistakes. On the other hand, a poor-me approach can work sometimes. That is, exaggerate the seriousness of the error and be profuse in your apology so that your reader must console you that things "aren't that bad." Don't, however, "bleed" all over the memo or letter for a minor error; such profuse apology sounds insincere.

Take responsibility for errors that come from your office; don't pass the buck to subordinates or your boss even though they may have made the error. If you are correcting someone else's error, use statements such as, "We should have never let that out of the office; I'll correct it immediately." Or, "I don't think I personally handled that assignment, but I'll be glad to track the problem and get back to you with a correction."

Follow-Ups

Do's

Restate your original message and request for action up front.

Identify the first communication by subject rather than date alone. (Not: "I never received the information I requested on February 10.") If an original memo or phone message was lost, misplaced, or misrouted, the reader will not know what you're talking about.

Offer an excuse for your reader's failure to reply—one that will allow him or her to save face for having failed to respond by the specified date or to acknowledge receipt of your request or message. Even a phrase such as "Could you let me know the status of...?" implies some progress.

If appropriate, use the if-I-don't-hear-from-you-by approach; state your next action if no response is forthcoming. "If I don't hear from you by June 16, I will assume you have no other names to add to the guest list and will mail out the invitations according to the attached list from our office."

Repeat all details—about who, what, when, where, why, how, how much—that were included the first time around. Don't rely on past correspondence that may not have been received.

Emphasize the critical need for response. If you can, find reader incentive for the action you want.

Enclose a copy of the original memo only when the subject is too long or complicated to be repeated easily in the present reminder. Otherwise, doing so seems to be "proving yourself" or documenting the reader's failure to reply or comply.

Don'ts

Don't imply that the reader is negligent or incompetent.

Don't sound self-righteous.

Don't use a whining or threatening tone.

Don't take away all the reader's excuses. Leave your reader room to excuse his delay or failure; your only concern should be that he follow through with the project now that you have reminded him.

Information, Requests for

Do's

Focus immediately on the information you need. Don't make your request a by-the-way item toward the end of the memo or letter.

Be specific in all questions you want answered and, if important, state the format in which you want the information provided. If you can provide a form, questionnaire, or some other example, do so.

Tell why you need the information if the reason is not obvious. Occasionally, when readers don't understand the necessity for some action or information, they "pick and choose" what data they think you need rather than respond with what you want.

Emphasize due dates. Phrases such as "at your earliest convenience" may be intended as a courtesy, but they invite procrastination; if you have a due date in mind, say so. Be careful to avoid the double-due-date effect. That is, if you are requesting information that you, in turn, will incorporate into your own work and then supply to someone else, don't state both dates. Such an explanation lets the reader know the "grace" period built in for yourself. The two dates, therefore, become leeway (in the reader's mind) for getting the information to you. For special emphasis, put the due-date detail in a paragraph by itself.

Anticipate the reader's steps in preparing the information. The more questions you can answer before they're asked, the sooner you'll get your information.

Provide incentive for the reader to cooperate. Remember the usual mound of paper your memo must compete with for attention; make your requests stand out.

Invitations

Do's

Mention the event and/or occasion immediately: retirement dinner for Betty Burton, monthly staff meeting, lunch discussion, or relocation plans.

Request a confirmation of attendance or acceptance of invitation to speak by a certain date, not "as soon as possible" or some other vague time.

Consider all details attendees may need such as date, time, place, cost, reservations (state if or if not required), map or travel directions, and contact name and number for more information.

When inviting someone to speak, mention specific topic guidelines, time restraints, other speakers and their topics (to prevent overlap), question-and-answer period, equipment needs and availability, audience type and size, expenses or honorarium, and any follow-up expected.

Give the agenda. Remember that readers may make a decision about attendance solely on the basis of the program or meeting information given in your memo. Also, the agenda gives necessary information for those who may have to come late or leave early; they can decide if attending only a portion of the event would be worthwhile. Even in a personal luncheon invitation, agenda or "purpose," details allow your reader to think beforehand so that your later discussion is productive.

"No" Replies

Do's

Begin on a positive, or at least neutral, note—even if simply a restatement of the request or assurance that you have carefully studied the situation. The "bottom-line" message in a "no" reply should not come up front because it hits the reader too hard; some audiences would not even bother to read your following explanation.

Build up with your criteria or reasons for your forthcoming "no." In this fashion, you are asking the reader to examine the evidence with you and to accept your reasoning and conclusion. Don't prolong the explanations to the point that you sound defensive or pleading; however, don't make your explanations so brief and general as to be unconvincing.

State your "no" in a positive way in the internal part of a paragraph or at the end of a paragraph—"We will *be unable to take advantage* of your presentation next week." Or, "Changing our attendance list at this time would not, I'm afraid, *accomplish your objective of having more SER people attend.*"

Mention any conditions under which you will reconsider. For

example: "When the current project has been completed...," "When business improves...," "If you do not feel this will meet your needs equally as well..."

Offer any alternative "yes" willingly, not begrudgingly.

End on a positive note. At least thank the reader for her interest or effort. Leave her with a back-to-business-as-usual feeling.

Don'ts

Don't use the basic Functional Format. A "no" reply requires special arrangement; you need to give the reader time to adjust to what's coming.

Don't begin on a negative note: "Why does this proposal not include maintenance costs as I stipulated in our bid request?" sets a reprimanding note for the remainder of the letter.

Don't hide behind "company policy" or a that's-the-way-we've-always-done-it explanation. Even if company policy or experience is a valid basis for your response, explain the reasoning behind the policy or past action.

Don't be wishy-washy with your answer.

Records, To Check and Correct

Do's

State immediately that you want to verify, question, or correct such-and-such record.

Give full details about the records to which you refer, not simply the one item you need to check. With only one identifying detail, the reader may have trouble locating the information or may overlook other discrepancies that neither of you knows about.

Ask for a response so that you know your message was received and your requested action taken. If your verification is routine, you may use the "unless I hear from you" approach. Caution: What happens if your intended reader is out of the office for two weeks?

Assume a tone of mutual responsibility and competence. Never imply that your records could contain no error and that the reader's records are always the incorrect ones. Avoid comments such as, "Our records show that...; would you please correct yours accordingly." Rarely is it necessary to place blame for the error; rather focus on verifications and/or corrections.

References, To Request

Do's

Mention the dates the applicant worked at the previous company and the name of the immediate supervisor, if the letter is not addressed to that person specifically.

Give the reader specific information about the job for which the applicant is applying, and highlight particular abilities or traits on which you would like comments. In other words, help the reader think; point out the necessary duties that would be required of the applicant for the desired job. Otherwise, you're likely to get the routine reference that basically says, "Jill is a nice person."

Make the reference easy to give—supply a form, a questionnaire, a list of questions to be answered easily, or a phone number in case the reader prefers to call.

Thank the reader for his or her efforts in responding. Remember that this request, often considered a personal rather than a business matter, takes time away from other (to the reader) more important tasks.

References, To Supply

Do's

Include the facts of the employee's work—major responsibilities and dates under your supervision. Then, check company policy with regard to giving further details.

If company policy permits, you may include both strengths and weaknesses in job performance. However, when mentioning weaknesses be careful to avoid judgments and outright statements about incompetence. Instead, to point out a problem, you may say:

> Mary has had a problem with tardiness while working with me. My records show that she has been tardy 20 percent of the time, and for our department this creates a work-flow problem. Perhaps this tardiness, however, would not be a significant problem in your company. Also, let me add that Mary has gone through a recent divorce that may have had some effect on her initiative to get to work on time. In a new job, perhaps she would be more conscientious about punctuality.

Comment on personal characteristics that make the individual a good employee.

Keep in mind legal safeguards: Be honest; make sure you have proof of what you say; bear no malice. If you cannot give a strong recommendation, perhaps you can defer to someone "who can give a stronger recommendation than I can." But don't let personal feelings affect your evaluation of a person's abilities; keep in mind that people react differently to various supervisory approaches. Remember that often the employee transferring to another department or company may see your comments.

Verify the reason for the employee's leaving your department. Be brief.

Solicitations for Financial or Personal Involvement

Do's

Use an upbeat first statement or paragraph to get attention and compete with more pressing tasks. Then state your request for participation.

Be explicit in what kind of response you expect; give the details the reader needs to respond. Make things easy.

Elaborate on incentives for involvement. Mention specific personal benefits when you can; suggest departmental or company good-will when you must be general.

Give testimonials, if possible, from higher-ups or other clients or customers who intend to participate and/or who support your efforts. If not sheer enthusiasm, then obligation and politics may provide the necessary incentive.

Show personal enthusiasm for the project; don't make your involvement sound obligatory or "just part of my job."

Write in a light, informal style on most occasions. Personal involvement most often results when people who care about people convey personal warmth and concern. Don't make this a routine or business-as-usual letter or memo. You need to get attention by your style of writing or by other motivational tactics.

Don'ts

Don't take for granted that your reader will understand the benefits of participation. Remind him or her what they are.

Sympathy

Do's

Mention the tragedy about which you are writing, but avoid

going into detail about the situation and its consequences or how you heard of the incident.

Let the reader know that you understand his or her loss by mentioning specific details and praise of the deceased. When you don't know the deceased well, speak of "hearsay" evidence or remind the reader of complimentary things he himself has said of the loved one: "I've heard you say that Mary had contributed so much to your own promotions." Such comments help the reader to praise the loved one and to work through his own grief.

If you offer to help, be specific. General offers of "if there's anything we can do to help" sound insincere. If you are willing to take on one of his projects while he's out of the office, say so specifically.

If you can do so, express your sympathy with action (donations, flowers, referrals, whatever).

Thank-You's

Do's

State your "thank you" immediately as the primary reason for writing.

Be specific in detailing the "whys" of your gratitude. In other words, let the reader know that you understand and appreciate the efforts she put forth. Mention the good results of the reader's information, advice, or project. What benefits did you or someone else derive?

Name names; thank individuals, not groups. Let them know you are aware of their personal contribution to the success.

If you can be sincere, offer to return the favor, hospitality, referral, or whatever.

Don'ts

Don't comment on negatives. Mention of any disastrous results detracts from the thanks or commendation.

Don't couch your thanks or commendation in vague clichés: "Thank you for your valuable contribution to the project." Or, "Your assistance with this information is sincerely appreciated."

Transmittals

Do's

Mention the information you are transmitting first; this proposal, contract, illustration, printout, check, invoice, or report is the major message of interest. (Ordinarily, as I stated earlier in the Functional Format MADE explanation, you mention attachments or enclosures last.)

List all enclosures specifically to discover errors with regard to missing or improperly routed documents.

Tell why the document is being sent. Is it at the reader's request? For information only? To verify your own records? For processing? For approval? For distribution? For review and comment?

Give a brief summary of the significant information contained in the attached or enclosed document. Depending on the document, this summary may mean only the amount of a check or invoice and its purpose or a lengthy paragraph about major findings or facts contained in a complex report or proposal.

Anticipate and answer possible questions about the attachments: Are there unusual figures or facts that the reader may question? Are there omissions? If so, why? Will there be exceptions? If so, what are they?

Give your opinion, when appropriate, about the enclosed information. Do the enclosed contract drafts show progress in the negotiations? Do you think the entire project will be completed by the target date? Do you agree with the disputed invoice you're submitting? In other words, prepare and/or interpret for the reader.

If you're not sending everything the reader needs or has asked for, tell him or her why not. Then let the reader know when to expect further information or documents.

(For a complete discussion of writing and editing and samples of these and many other formats, see my earlier books *Would You Put That in Writing?* and *Send Me a Memo*.)

Who is Responsible for Editing?

When I conduct writing workshops for corporate clients, I frequently hear engineers, accountants, data analysts, and lawyers express different views about whose responsibility is what in writing their memos and letters. Some writers say they specify every comma and paragraph, tell what should be capitalized or in lower case, and even spell difficult words. And they expect the final copy returned to them exactly as dictated or written.

Other writers, however, say they concentrate only on the

content and organizational structure of their correspondence and expect their secretaries to correct all grammatical errors and clarity problems without bothering them again about such changes.

Either arrangement is fine—as long as both writer and secretary know what it is and are capable of fulfilling the expected role. But problems develop when the boss has not told the secretary about these expectations of her expertise.

If you work for a boss who has not made it clear what he or she expects from you in the editing process, you should ask about those responsibilities immediately. Secretaries feel frustrated, however, when they must send out a letter in which there is an unclear or grammatically incorrect statement simply because the boss doesn't know better and won't allow her to make changes. And bosses become frustrated when they turn this editing for clarity and grammar over to secretaries who do not have the expertise to handle the job.

The finished product is improved if both boss and secretary are capable of effective writing; two proofreaders are always better than one.

If you have observed that your boss lacks effective writing skills or does not want to or does not have time to handle correspondence, perhaps you can begin to assume this editing responsibility by showing him what you can do in one of three ways: You may begin to prepare answers to incoming correspondence and pass them on to the boss, with the incoming letter, ready for signature. He then can either make changes and/or sign immediately. If he makes extensive changes in the actual structure of your sentences and your organization of ideas (rather than simply adding or correcting content), then you can safely assume that he still prefers to write his own letters and that you should edit only with his permission.

A third approach to learn your boss's preference and also to let him know of your competent writing skills is simply to type what he has dictated or written, make necessary grammatical or clarity changes, and then call them to his attention with a comment such as, "I reworded this statement to eliminate a grammatical problem." You can then see if he seems appreciative or offended.

No matter which arrangement you both decide on for editing, do not send out a letter in which you have made changes without having your boss review it. Often when you attempt to restructure someone else's words, you change the entire meaning of the sentence by simply moving, adding, or deleting a phrase. Always get a final reading from the writer.

If your boss always makes changes in what he writes or what you write, doing a perfect copy is a waste of time. Prepare a rough draft and let him revise before you type the final copy.

Editing for Content, Conciseness, Grammar, and Clarity

Layout

When you rework a draft of a lengthy document, remember that the layout you choose is a courtesy to the reader. Always allow adequate white space and headings.

Paper is inexpensive compared to your reader's time. Informative headings allow your reader to skim material to see what's there for later reading, and they also allow a reader to relocate information later without having to reread the entire document. An "informative heading" is not a generic term such as "Discussion." Discussion of what? Instead think "newspaper" for informative headings: "Discussion of Operating Lease" or "Advantages of Operating Lease Over Capital Lease." Finally, make sure heading placement and size are consistent throughout the document.

Watch paragraphing also. Comprehension decreases with paragraph length; after 10 lines the reader's attention wanes. After 14 lines, attention drops off drastically. A short paragraph of even one sentence can be effective to introduce a new direction or to call attention to a specific detail. For example, if your readers tend to miss deadlines, try giving due-date information in a one-sentence paragraph.

When appropriate, use lists instead of paragraphs—bullets, asterisks, numbering, or lettering. Lists are easier and quicker to read because they break down complicated information into small bits. However, you don't want to go to the extreme so that your entire document is simply one list after another.

Accuracy and Completeness

Always recheck figures, dates, titles, names, costs, or any other statistics. Errors most often creep in at these points. And don't put off checking until "later." Frequently, when you question something and then put off verifying its accuracy, you forget to do so. Then after the boss reads and signs the final draft, you assume she has checked the information; she assumes that you did the double-checking. Result: Nobody verifies.

Finally, have all facts or concepts been sufficiently illustrated? Could you improve overall appearance, acceptance, or understanding with a chart, graph, or copy of past correspondence?

First-Choice Words

In school, your teacher may have emphasized that you should not use the same word over and over—that you should choose a synonym. For example, instead of your saying "advantage" in every sentence, the teacher may have suggested that you vary your wording by writing "benefit," "vantage point," or "another plus." In some cases, that advice may be appropriate.

Most of the time, however, switching terms for the same thing leads to clarity problems. You call something a "seminar," then a "workshop," then a "conference." Or you refer to the attached "contracts," and then later call them "arrangements." When such switches occur, your reader wonders if you're still talking about the same event or item.

Choose the best word and stick with it.

Grammar

In my earlier book, *Would You Put That in Writing?* I introduced "The 10 Commandments of Grammar," the 10 most frequent errors in business writing. Abide by them.

- Thou shalt not dangle verbals.
- Thou shalt not write fragments for complete sentences.
- Thou shalt use parallel structure.
- Thou shalt make pronouns agree in number with their antecedents.
- Thou shalt make verbs agree with their subjects.
- Thou shalt not change tenses and moods unnecessarily.
- Thou shalt punctuate correctly.
- Thou shalt choose appropriate words and phrases.
- Thou shalt spell correctly.
- Thou shalt not clutter with capitalization.

Nothing influences your image like grammatical errors in written communication. And grammatical errors usually create clarity problems. Be a nit-picker.

Readability and Clarity

Keep sentences to a readable length—between 15 to 20 words. That does not mean, of course, that every sentence should be exactly the same length; vary the pattern and length. Follow a long sentence with a short one. When you have to use complex, technical words, compensate for the difficult ideas by using even shorter-than-normal sentences.

Prefer concrete words and phrases: Not "significant increases" but "an increase of 73 percent." Not "new facilities," but rather "new warehouse." Not simply "inadequate" but "inadequate in size" or "inadequate access" or "inadequate climate control."

Circumlocutions

Prefer active-voice verbs to shorten your sentences and make them stronger. Not: "It has been concluded by our investigators..." (seven words). But: "Our investigators concluded..." (three words).

Dig buried verbs out of noun phrases. Not: "This is for the purpose of your evaluation." Rather: "Evaluate this for..." Not: "We will take into consideration..." Rather: "We will consider..."

Avoid adjective and adverb clutter, repetitious details, and padding phrases such as "at this time" (now), "with regard to" (about), "in view of the fact that" (because).

Sexist Language

Because the English language does not have a neuter third-person singular pronoun other than *it*, writers face a dilemmna in deciding how to avoid sexist language. In the past, *he* was the only acceptable singular pronoun for people of an unspecified gender. Today, writers who follow this style offend many readers.

Here are several suggestions for handling the pronoun problem:

Use plurals when you can: Say, "Employees must show their ID badges," rather than "An employee must show his ID badge."

Substitute nouns for pronouns when possible: Write "The authorized person approving the entry is indicating that the *approver* has ..." rather than "The authorized person approving the entry is indicating that *he* has..."

Alternate the words "he" and "she" throughout the document. Under one heading use he for the singular pronoun, and in the next section, she. Or, alternate from situation to situation randomly. Be careful, however, not to alternate when to do so would confuse the meaning.

Use both—he/she or he or she: This arrangement is fine if you are not making reference more than once or twice a page. Frequent use of this wording, however, is cumbersome.

Use s/he or s(he) or (s)he: This reference allows readers to read whichever pronoun they choose. Writers have been using the slash and parenthesis for years to indicate plural and singular choices: "Record all absences of your employee(s) on Form 2162." (The slash or parenthesis, however, is less formal than the other choices.)

Proofreading

Always allow sufficient time for your writing to "cool off" before trying to proofread. When your material is fresh, you cannot even catch typographical errors; you simply read what you think you wrote or typed. With a short document, leave it for a couple of hours before you try to proofread it. With something longer, let it sit for a day or two before you edit.

Also, never try to proofread for too long in one sitting. Your concentration cannot be at its peak for much longer than half an hour or an hour at most. If you must edit hurriedly in a short time, take frequent breaks to improve concentration.

Below are several tips for proofreading accuracy:

1. Force yourself to read one word at a time by using a pointer to guide and slow you down. This method, particularly, should help you catch omitted words.

2. Read the document backward from end to beginning.

3. Turn the document upside down to read it. You will generally be able to recognize the words, but the slowness of the method will force your eyes to examine one word at a time.

4. Have someone read aloud the document you typed from as you follow along on the original.

5. Have someone who knows nothing about the subject read what you've written. If she has questions about clarity and phrasing don't simply fill her in verbally. Those questions are a warning sign that you should reexamine your wording; your reader, even with the appropriate background knowledge, will probably have the same questions.

6. Proof for specifics, one step at a time. That is, on first reading, check only names, dates, numbers. On second reading check for punctuation. On third reading, check for omitted or repeated words. Then, read for smooth sentence structure, and appropriate transitions. Finally, check paragraphing, layout, headings.

part three

PREPARING YOURSELF TO MEET THE CHALLENGES

chapter 10

CREATING YOUR IMAGE

When you talk to someone on the telephone, you begin to get a mental picture of what he or she looks like even though you've never seen the person. Young. Old. Gray. Balding. Plump. Tall. And then when you finally have an opportunity to meet that individual, you find out how right or wrong that mental image was.

In much the same way, secretaries, even through limited exposure to other departments or outsiders, create an image that others carry with them—a thumbnail sketch, if you will, of their personality and, more importantly, their expertise in the job. Have you ever walked into a department store and dealt with a salesclerk for only five minutes and then walked away wondering how that person ever manages to get out of bed in the morning? Perhaps you simply caught the salesclerk on a bad day; nevertheless, the impression is there to stay.

Secretaries, as with most all occupational groups, have been stereotyped. Below are some of those thumbnail sketches created in the minds of coworkers and customers:

Secretarial Stereotypes

Bear Bertha: She responds to people as if they have come into her life to make her eat spinach. "What do you want?" is her normal greeting; silence or an unintelligible mumble is her closing. Any request for information from her is treated with the utmost suspicion for the requester's need to know.

Slow Sarah: Slow Sarah eats molasses for breakfast and is sluggish for the rest of the day. Correspondence and reports coming from her office are collectors' items before they get to the recipient; in fact, her colleagues regularly build in a "late" period for any deadlines they give her. By the time she picks up the phone on the eighth ring, the caller has already hung up—and just as well; she doesn't have time to talk. If she does take a call from someone who's persistent, the caller could have delivered it in person by the time it takes her to record the message. If she ever has an errand on the fifty-ninth floor, she takes a picnic lunch.

Disorganized Diane: Disorganized Diane's motto for the files is, "Don't touch anything; it'll surface on its own sooner or later." She creates her own Grand Central Station confusion by scheduling a salesperson's visit, a meeting of the Accident-Prevention Group, and lunch with her husband for the same hour. She *reminds* her boss of his missed meetings. Callers may be left holding while she runs to the bank to make a deposit.

Flirty Freda: Freda gazes into male eyes as if she hadn't had a night on the town in weeks. She takes work breaks rather than coffee breaks, spending most of her time visiting from desk to desk about what she did the night before and cooing that she may just be free again the next evening. She's on a first-name basis with every Tom, Ted, and Todd from mailroom clerk to the CEO. The pen, pencil, phone, and note pad on her desk have been replaced with hairbrush, lipstick, and nail polish.

Sloppy Susan: Sloppy Susan looks as if the cat fed and dressed her for the day. On ordinary mornings she appears wearing jeans; when dignitaries are to be in the office, she adds sequins. Her desk looks as though nine people have just finished a barbeque—half-filled Styrofoam cups, crumpled napkins, mustard, tissue paper, empty soft-drink cans, lipstick-coated plastic forks, and a pickle or two. When she gets up from the desk and treks to the files, she's stocking-footed—with runs. Documents leaving her office frequently carry her seal of approval—a couple of typos and a coffee stain.

Whiny Winnie: Whiny Winnie's voice sounds like an untuned violin, and the lyrics aren't much better. She hates the file system, the food in the cafeteria, the slow elevators, the sunlight streaming through the windows, the dark restrooms, the rigid hours, the unrelenting workload, the monotony, her vacation plans, the word-processing package, the stock-option plan, the traffic on Highway 6, and her mother-in-law. No one ever gets word to her about changes in policies and procedures. Her boss has "no idea how hard she works," and others in the office take advantage of her "good nature."

Personal-Problems Paula: You can't help feeling sorry for Personal-Problems Paula. If her youngest isn't having asthma attacks, her unemployed uncle has come to stay for four months. A tornado took the roof off her grandmother's barn, and her car needs four new tires. Friday afternoons she has to take off early to take her oldest child to the psychiatrist; and when she's late on Tuesday and Thursday mornings, it's because her cat threw up all over the carpet. And "when you've got more time," she can really give you the details.

Champion-of-a-Cause Cathy: Champion-of-a-Cause Cathy has more important things to do than type and file while she's on the job. As head of the Toys-for-Tots Drive, she's checking collection boxes for donations. Schedules for the annual blood drive have to be posted at the elevators; clients get her attention only when they themselves are bleeding. She makes rounds monthly for donations to the Save-the-Snail Foundation. If anybody expresses interest in installing a PA system on the parking lot, Cathy'll have a rough-draft petition ready for signatures by 5 P.M.

Prying Priscilla: No snicker or sniffle is too insignificant for Prying Priscilla; she'll not allow you to leave her office until you confess to going outside in the snow in your pajamas. Her boss's mail marked "Personal—to be opened by addressee only," she reads just "to make sure." Tell her what kind of raise you got, and you'll hear it from the new receptionist by the time you get to the other end of the hall. Spending a lot of time around open office doors, she always knows exactly what Mr. Brown said to Mr. Smith on the golf course, how much Sharon Sladdle owes on her Master Card bill, and why Tony Cangelose no longer picks his wife up for lunch.

Spacey Silvia: Spacey Silvia doesn't know when to come in out of the lobby. She looks at her desk each morning as if it had just been shipped in from Siberia. Clients and customers wave objects before her eyes to make sure the smile is meant for them; then they proceed with caution in giving her details of a problem, writing down for her all important names, dates, and figures. Her telephone messages read like hieroglyphics. When the repairman shows up, she has forgotten why she phoned him.

If any one of these stereotypes fits, don't wear it; change it. Your career is at stake. Examine the following habits, traits, or attitudes that top secretaries consider essential in creating a professional, efficient secretarial image:

Dress

When asked how much an attractive appearance has to do with liking or noticing someone, most people underemphasize it. But numerous research studies show that looks *do* count in social situations and particularly on the job. You yourself know that dress is important if you've been to a play rehearsal where actors were out of costume or have heard a lawyer advise her client how to dress for the courtroom. Attractive, well-dressed people are judged to have more desirable character traits, to be smarter, and to be more efficient on the job (Kleinke, *First Impressions*, pp. 14-16; Berscheid and Walster, *Psychology Today*, March 1972, p. 46).

And that appraisal carries over to the boss. John Malloy, "dress for success" advocate, has done considerable research in linking a secretary's dress to how successful others judge her boss to be. A secretary can dress for either her boss's or her own success or failure. An inappropriately dressed secretary shows little respect for her own work or for her boss.

Appearance is indicative of mental outlook. Specifically, then, what does proper dress entail? Of course, you must dress to fit the image of your total office and appropriately to your part of the country. But generally speaking, bosses and top secretaries give these guidelines:

Suits and nice dresses are top-of-the-line. Jacketed pantsuits are appropriate in some offices, not in others. Jeans are never permissible. Dresses should not be too tight, too short, too long, too low-cut, or too off-the-shoulder. Men serving as secretaries should match the boss in dress—preferably suits.

Jewelry should be conservative. You don't want to jangle as you walk. Wear a light perfume or cologne or wear none at all. Hair styles and makeup, too, should be appropriate for the office—not too fussy or partyish. Take time to freshen makeup at lunch or at breaks so that you don't look "worn out" by the end of the day.

The most expensive, stylish, and well-pressed suit or dress will not make much difference on an obese person. Our society is prejudiced about obesity and judges the overweight person to be lazy, self-indulgent, and undisciplined. True or not, the stereotype remains.

Your *attitude* about your dress is also important. Once you arrive at the office looking your best, don't continually primp. Keep your mind on your work rather than your appearance throughout the workday.

Mannerisms

Avoid obnoxious habits such as chewing gum, cracking knuckles, interrupting, coughing and sneezing on others and their possessions, scratching your head or your nose, talking and laughing loudly, using obscene language, slinking rather than walking, or blowing smoke on others. When people don't have ashtrays in their work area, chances are they don't want you to smoke there.

Work Environment

Avoid making your work space or desk look like a bulletin board in a college dorm. Don't tack up personal clippings, vacation scenes, obscene specialty items, certificates of membership in the YMCA, or an excessive number of family snapshots. (One or two family photos are okay, but don't turn the desk top into a collage.)

Make sure your desk top doesn't look like a picnic with empty cups, spilled coffee, crumpled napkins. If you eat your lunch there, consider how the food smells, how your chewing sounds, how appetizing the leftovers look to clients and customers.

Don't spread out into neutral work space with your purse, folders, lunch, books, trash. Why sit on someone else's desk while you proof a letter when she could be working there?

If your company doesn't hire a janitorial or plant service on a daily basis, take care of the household chores yourself—talk to the plants and dust the cobwebs from the visitors' chairs!

Borrowing

Of course, you're not worried about running up a sum equal to the national debt, but a dollar here and a quarter there adds up. When you must borrow money from someone, make a note of it on your calendar and repay it the next day.

Especially, don't borrow money from the petty cash fund or allow others to do so. If you feel like a guard at Fort Knox, so be it. Explain that you are responsible when the fund doesn't balance and insist that all transactions be arranged through you—you yourself record the expenditure on a petty-cash voucher and be the money-changer.

When it comes to equipment and supplies, whether it be paper clips or typewriters, return what you borrow. If you mess it up, clean it up. If you break it, fix it. If you move it, put it back.

Punctuality

Do not shrug off tardiness. Don't think that if your boss doesn't come in some mornings until 9:20 A.M., no one should complain if you are a few minutes late from time to time. Nothing could be further from the truth. First of all, your boss probably does not always leave at 5 P.M. and may in fact carry work home in the evenings and over the weekend. And even if she does, she is not being paid for the actual time put in, but rather for the results.

On the other hand, you are being paid for the actual hours you are on the job—in other words, your availability. You are paid to be at work between certain hours "just in case"—in case the phone rings, in case a client calls early, in case there's an emergency, in case of anything that requires a live body to make a response or a decision.

No matter if other, older employees take advantage with long lunches or coffee breaks; don't follow their pattern. Their tardiness may be tolerated, or it may be taken out of their paycheck or responsibilities. But when your new boss or co-worker has little knowledge of your skills or expertise accordingly, they judge you on attitude and punctuality.

Of course, everyone has occasional emergencies such as unusually snarled traffic or illness, but the boss has heard them all—probably too often.

Absenteeism

In school you could always get makeup assignments or copy someone else's class notes when you were absent. But at work, things generally can't wait. Somebody else has to take up the slack, and sooner or later that person, be it a co-worker or a boss, will get resentful. Your absence interrupts others' work schedules, leaves customers hanging with half-solutions, and costs overtime or temporary salaries.

Frequent absences on your part create a "tentative," panicky attitude all around—even when you are present. When the boss or co-workers leave a project in your hands at 5 P.M., they go away with a panicked feeling that maybe you won't be there the next day to finish it.

Almost everyone awakes one morning out of five "feeling bad." To determine how sick you really are, ask yourself if you'd be able to go with a friend who called you to say she had tickets to a special matinee and lunch. A sleepy, sluggish, headachy feeling usually dissipates in a few hours on the job.

Unless you're headed to the doctor or a funeral home, go to work.

Proper Grammar

Bad grammar is like bad breath; even your best friends won't tell you. Why? Our reaction is usually defensive because we think proper grammar is something we should have learned in grade school and any hint that we need improvement comes across as a suggestion for remedial work.

Nevertheless, we categorize ourselves socially and occupationally when we use bad grammar either in oral or written communication. And articulate bosses cringe at the thought of having a secretary/representative who says to a client, "We don't hardly have any calls for that." If you have a problem because you had chicken pox when your seventh grade teacher taught subject-verb agreement, arrange to attend night classes at your local junior college. In the meantime, read your secretarial handbooks as if they were your Bible.

Dependability

If you start something, finish. If you promise, deliver. If you are responsible, take charge. It's easy to be responsible for things you control, but your true measure comes when you have to be responsible for other people and situations that you can't control. If you fail, don't look for excuses.

You can't let the details take care of themselves; they often don't. Carry out the intent and the spirit, as well as the literal meaning, of the assignments and directions you are given. Never adopt the attitude: "I'm here until more money or marriage do us part" or "It's just a job."

Here is how some high-ranking secretaries describe their penchant for being dependable:

"I go into a job with 110 percent. I want to know exactly what's expected of me; how to do it and why I'm doing it. I want to do it exactly right. I'm not a perfectionist in other areas of my life, but I am in my job."

"Details—that's how my mind operates. I operate one step ahead of my boss. I usually have the answer letter prepared for his signature before I show him the incoming letter."

"I go all the way to the period. I follow up everything and everybody."

Self-Control

Consider these Biblical proverbs:

"A man without self-control is as defenseless as a city with broken-down walls." "It is better to have self-control than to control an army."

We've just passed through two decades of let-it-all-hang-out philosophy, which employees have brought to the job—to their detriment. Researcher Carol Tavris in her book, *Anger: The Misunderstood Emotion,* Simon and Schuster, 1982, writes that letting anger out is no more healthy than holding it in. She cites many studies to show that people who let out their rage do *not* have lower blood pressure or other physical reactions that are necessarily better for the body.

But her conclusions are the same as others who take the opposite, let-it-all-hang-out position: When you are angry, find out why and then decide if anger is the right reaction to get the response you want.

If it's not, control it.

Self-control involves much more than losing your temper at work; it may also involve leaving your good times at home. Your personal life at the office creates one of two problems for you: Either people are too interested in whom you dated last weekend, or they're not interested enough. Someone who's always taking and making personal phone calls, running errands to the cleaners, and talking about family problems can't have her mind on her work.

If that's the case and you really have personal problems that are affecting your work, you need to let your boss know. Ask for his or her patience while you seek a solution, and then try to cover your emotional upheaval as best you can.

And if you're so angry or so hurt that you feel as though you are going to cry, disappear to the restroom until you regain composure.

Does that mean that you have to be Miss Merry Sunshine all the time? Is this a case of phoniness? No on both accounts. People are expected to go about their jobs with a business-as-usual attitude in all occupations: The waitress doesn't tell you about her knee surgery when she brings your entree; the ticket-taker at the movie theater doesn't cry and tell you how the picture reminds him of his recent divorce; nor does the lawyer tell you that her mortgage holder is foreclosing on her house.

Keep your mind on your work.

Loyalty

Know when to keep your mouth shut. Never express to anyone but the boss reservations about what you're doing. (Unless, of course, the issue is a moral one; and then you may have to go to top management or resign.)

I once had a telephone installer come to make some adjustments to my phone when I added another business line. Prompted by a simple informational question from me, he began to relate how the phone company overcharged for his services, how defective their equipment was, and how terrible their office recordkeeping system was. By the time he left, I felt like pulling the phone out of the wall and forgetting to pay the bill.

And if you have difficulties with a specific person to the point of sabotaging organizational goals and projects, go directly to that person to discuss the issue—not some third or fourth party, who may relay all kinds of garbled messages. Bitterness and pettiness are unflattering.

Goodwill

"...Goodwill to all men" is no problem; it's goodwill to all women that's a problem for some secretaries. Some women, primarily due to cultural conditioning, still think of women in the work force as inferior to men. They are jealous of other women who get promoted above the secretarial level, making snide remarks such as, "She got that managerial job simply because she's a woman and they have a quota."

Congratulate others as they move up; send a written note if you know them.

Nothing creates a worse image for you than mean-spirited attitudes, actions, and words to a successful or fortunate co-worker.

Industrious Spirit

Never fill your empty hours with personal tasks or pleasures such as knitting a sweater, painting your nails, talking to a friend on the phone, trading jokes with the service repair representative, or reading a book or magazine. When you have a slack workload, offer to help out someone else, ask your boss for more work, or take initiative in doing nonroutine chores that you never have time to do otherwise.

Particularly, show enthusiasm when your boss asks for things in a kind, nondirective way: "Do you know where such-and-such file is?" from the boss shouldn't get the answer, "It's over there." Get up and get the file yourself; the request is a polite one but should be handled with as much industry and eagerness as the more directive, "Get me the such-and-such file."

Initiative

On occasion, *not* doing what you're told is a matter of good judgment. An elderly man suffering from pulmonary lung disease and wearing an oxygen mask stepped inside an office building and asked the receptionist to direct him to the nearest restroom. Having been told by her boss that people "off the street" shouldn't be allowed to use the company's restroom facilities, the receptionist refused to give him directions to the men's room unless he had an account with the company.

Incensed, the man explained that he did indeed have an account there and that his wife was on another floor transacting business. But because the man did not have account identification with him, the receptionist still refused to page the wife, check the account, or permit the man admission to the restroom!

Sounds ridiculous, doesn't it? Yet some people lay common sense aside when they see a company policy statement or hear a department rule.

Take initiative. Think. Could this particular situation be "the exception"?

Those kinds of employees, though they certainly can be given accolades for doing what they're told, haven't discovered their true potential to the boss. You, too, can increase your value to your employer if you learn to take initiative in your job. That does not mean, of course, that you will authorize a $10 million expenditure without the boss's approval!

Management experts have described several levels of initiative: The lowest level is waiting to be told what to do. The next level is asking what you can do. The next level is recommending things to be done that you see as particularly helpful or needful. Fourth is acting and then telling your supervisor immediately what you've done in time for him or her to "undo" it if necessary. Finally, you can act and then report what you've done at some later time.

Certainly, you cannot take the same initiative in all tasks, problems, or assignments because potential for disasters varies from situation to situation and supervisor to supervisor. But observe what others in positions similar to yours are doing to make their supervisor's job easier. What are his problems that you could alleviate? What doesn't he like to do himself that you could handle? In other words, assume that your boss is a very busy person who doesn't have time to answer every question, look for every error, handle every problem, or tell you what to do next.

Test what authority and responsibility you have for different tasks by first asking and doing; then, the next time, doing and reporting back. For example, ask your boss if you can write a letter for her signature or if you can phone the people involved in a project and explain the change of procedures.

Be observant of what goes on around you; learn new skills; ask the "why" behind things you're asked to do. Your work will be more accurate, more enjoyable, and more valuable. And when the occasion arises for you to take initiative, your boss won't have to outline every step.

But there are pitfalls in taking on too much responsibility: You may overstep your authority and anger your boss about projects, problems, and situations where she wants complete control. Second, you may take on tasks for which you haven't been sufficiently trained and, as a result, do a poor job. For these reasons, take initiative one step at a time.

Secretaries with initiative report that they have been able to take on additional responsibilities (responsibilities that weren't part of the job when they were hired) in the following functions: teaching the boss a skill such as use of the computer or phone equipment; reorganizing the filing system; requisitioning supplies; changing the decor and layout of the office; completing expense reports;

handling accounts receivable; writing and placing ads in newspapers and journals; preparing the budget; scheduling work sheets and vacations; scheduling and hosting board meetings; dealing with service companies for purchases, maintenance, and repairs; handling personnel problems; handling charitable contributions; writing all correspondence; compiling monthly reports; keeping minutes for meetings; and screening job applicants.

What can you do to make your boss's job easier and make yourself look good?

And don't forget the little things. Rather than tossing a misaddressed letter back into your "out" basket for the mailroom to reroute, look up the address yourself and add it to the envelope so that the letter will get to the addressee sooner. Going the extra mile always puts you out in front of your peers.

Assertiveness

You've probably run into your share of people who need *non*assertiveness training—the cleaning woman who says she doesn't do windows, the IRS representative who says you owe another $326, and the baby sitter who tells you what time you have to be in on school nights.

But basically, people fall into three broad classifications, with variations in each: The *submissive* person does not reveal her true feelings or values. She allows others to violate her rights. They cart off her typewriter when she needs it; they tell her she's coming in Saturday afternoon to work; they blow smoke in her face while she flinches and wheezes. She talks in a weak, almost inaudible voice, avoids eye contact, permits others to interrupt her, moves away from others when they approach, obeys without question, tiptoes around almost unnoticed. She passes on all credit to someone else and assumes all blame for herself. She reacts rather than acts.

The *aggressive* person carries out her wants and likes at the expense of others. She argues to make her point about things that don't matter. She belittles, hurts, and manipulates others to her advantage or at least to their pain. She talks loudly, stares, interrupts, crowds others' space, glowers, stalks. She obeys grudgingly after having all the reasons, takes all the credit for others' work and passes her failures on to co-workers. She believes her methods are best, insists on them, and refuses to compromise.

The *assertive* person falls between these two extremes. She reveals what her values and needs are and goes about meeting those needs while exercising self-control where others' rights come into play. She says what she thinks without intentionally humiliating or hurting others. She acts and reacts, moving to get her needs met but retracking into a problem-solving mode when the other person needs to meet his needs. She speaks at a moderate speed and pitch—distinctly and precisely. She does not discount her successes nor take credit away from others. When she fails, she assumes responsibility and outlines a plan for improvement or correction.

Bosses want and need assertive secretaries for several reasons:

A submissive secretary can't exert the authority needed in dealing with co-workers, customers, or clients. She can't protect her boss's time; she can't get the service rep to repair the copier; she can't persuade a co-worker to accept her solution to a problem.

On the other hand, an aggressive secretary offends and often creates "people" problems even while settling production problems.

All this is not to say that secretaries should be totally assertive in every situation. But rather, assertive secretaries choose what manner is best in which situation. If the CEO comes for a visit, complaining about "the whole world living on caffeine," she may choose to change her hosting routine and serve only fruit juices in the CEO's presence. That's not nonassertiveness; that's politics. But if a customer insults her with obscene language and she doesn't remove herself from the situation, that's humiliation.

Sense of Humor

If you have to tell someone you have a sense of humor, you probably don't.

Not everybody can tell a good joke all the way to the punch line or turn a witty phrase. But one can train herself to see the amusing side to life, learn to laugh at herself, and laugh with, and not at, others. Having a sense of humor is the kind of attitude that makes you, when watching a wrecker pull your car from the ditch to the mechanic shop, remark, "I bet this beats the gas mileage I've been getting." Humor can make a bad situation better or a heavy disagreement lighter.

But be careful about being flippant or cute with superiors, clients, or customers; you don't want to offend by getting too personal or to become known as the office clown who doesn't take the job seriously. Neither do you want to laugh at "how much money your company wastes," "policy inconsistencies," or "other incompetent employees"; that comes across as disloyalty.

Positive Mental Attitude

Some people never feel good about themselves or their job because they have neurotic needs and goals: an excessive need to be needed; a compulsion to have another's approval (worse yet, everyone's approval) at all costs; a drive to accomplish more than their abilities will allow.

A more recent neurotic drive is what Elizabeth Ames, in her article "So You Think You Work Hard" (*Savvy*, May 1983), calls "overwork chic." She defines this goal or need as the tendency to be a martyr, a superwoman, and a threat to colleagues. But simply because one keeps longer, "harder" hours does not necessarily mean she produces quality results. In fact, the need always to be excessively busy may simply mean she's unorganized and inefficient.

Rule One: Develop a positive mental attitude simply by throwing away such neurotic goals. Learn to get your basic needs for security, love, and approval met in other, more acceptable ways and places. Believe in yourself and you will inspire others' confidence in you.

Rule Two: Don't look at visitors, phone calls, and people as "interruptions"; they are your job.

Rule Three: Stay away from negative people; their pessimism is catching. Instead go for the good, the positive, the uplifting, the improvement, the solution. Expect to win.

Rule Four: Don't dwell on mistakes. Even computers make mistakes; allow yourself some "downtime." Some of the very best secretaries admit to sending out an important document with a typo, letting someone take the only file copy, giving the boss a wrong time and place for a once-a-year luncheon, being too flippant with a client on the phone, and undercharging a customer for hundreds of dollars.

But look at disappointments and errors as the exceptions of life, not the norm, and see what they can teach you for the future.

Rule Five: Recognize stressful situations and take steps to cope. The National Institute for Occupational Safety and Health (NIOSH) lists secretarial work as one of the most stressful in the nation. Why? Secretaries have a heavy responsibility and yet not much corresponding authority. Additionally, they have short deadlines; unclear, hurried communication and instructions; varying priorities; constant interruptions; few assistants to which to delegate; limited resources; lack of information; perhaps interpersonal conflicts with co-workers; and perhaps procrastinating, incompetent, or indecisive bosses.

Even when you enjoy your job immensely, there can still be stress. To alleviate this job stress, try to devote more attention to your physical well-being—eat better, exercise more, get adequate rest, spend time meditating.

Second, deal with boredom, a chief stressor, to avoid burnout:

- Expect the routine in any job and lower some of your expectations for job self-actualization. Even best-selling authors and award-winning actors get bored with repetitious interviews; professional athletes get bored with practice drills; politicians get bored with filibusters.

- Try glamorizing your job to yourself and to a friend. What interesting people do you get to meet? What great minds do you get to listen to? What important information are you privy to? What policies and procedures do you help set? What travel do you do? What important functions do you get to attend? Secretaries tell of meeting prime ministers and cabinet members, of handling a boss's financial estate of millions, of delivering a college tuition check to a foreign student flown to the U.S. at her boss's expense.

- Vary your schedule. Come to work an hour early; take an alternate route; eat lunch at a different time or place; change the order of your daily tasks.

- Take your vacation days a few at a time throughout the year rather than in one block. A long weekend rejuvenates.

- Change or expand your job responsibilities. If you can't assume more tasks from your boss, can you expand into other departments or help a co-worker?

- Develop your skills. Ask to attend both in-house and outside seminars, workshops, or lectures. Ask for "cross-training" in others' jobs as a replacement in case of emergency.

- Develop interests outside your job. Buy something new. Commit yourself to a new relationship, or devote more time to an existing one. Compete in some event. Learn a new hobby or sport.

Rule Six: Don't work down to others' level of mediocrity. Be outstanding; model the most talented in your organization and in your profession. Our society is moving away from the autocratic authority that says respect and power are based solely on title. Your superior knowledge and abilities, despite your job title, can put you in a position to influence productivity and people.

Rule Seven: Take control of your life and your job. Plan your work; developing a system alleviates that feeling that you're "down under." Have energy and enthusiasm for what you do. Some people have little energy because they have no interest in anything, no ambition, no cause, no hobby, no friends. Make a commitment to a job, a person, or a cause and carry it out. Live in the present, not the past. Change the way you talk to yourself; don't see yourself as a victim, but rather as a survivor and an achiever.

Managing Time

You can't control time, but you can manage it. And most essential in time management is how you manage other people—their procrastination and inefficiencies—and how your relationships with others improve as a result of taking charge of your time and tasks.

Be aware of the difference between efficiency and effectiveness: If you need to find the middle initial of the president of a client corporation for the year 1953, it is *efficient* to phone that company's library and ask someone to check an old annual report and get back to you the next day. Or, you may perhaps take an hour to go to the public library and look up the information for yourself.

But it's *effective* to get the information from your boss, who happens to play golf weekly with the individual in question. Consider the importance of the material you need, as well the amount of salary involved in your spending the time to complete the task.

Always ask, Is there a better, faster way?

Where You Spend Your Time

If you have little idea about where your time goes, keep a log for a day or a week and jot down what you're doing every 15 minutes. You'll soon discover your own time-wasters and time-savers among the more common ones mentioned in the following pages.

Long-Range, Weekly, and Daily Routines

Long-range planning includes putting major events and projects (conventions, seminars, vacations, annual and quarterly reports) on your calendar, along with accompanying mini-deadlines by which various steps leading to those events and projects should be completed.

At the end of the week or the beginning of the next, check your schedule and that of your boss's for upcoming work. Get a head start on reports due on Thursday by phoning for necessary information on Monday. Block the week out so that appointments or intentions to "have lunch with Betty" get assigned to a specific time slot and so that discretionary time is bunched together.

Then compare schedules daily with your boss. Give him or her last-minute details about hotel or travel arrangements; reconfirm or reschedule appointments; ask your list of questions (see Chapter 1) to prevent later interruptions of both your workdays.

Set time frames for most everything you do, or tasks will expand to fit the time you allot for them.

Priorities

Make sure you know what your boss's priorities are for the week and the day and then rearrange your schedule accordingly. If you have a choice, always tackle complicated tasks before simple ones. Otherwise, you tend to waste time, energy, and thought dreading and procrastinating the complex chore.

Remember the 80/20 rule originating with the Italian economist Pareto: Twenty percent of the work produces about 80 percent of the results. Don't spend two hours composing a memo that will be read by only two subordinates across the hall, frittering time away on the trivial.

And remember that your boss's opinion of what's trivial and significant is what counts. Draw a line between striving for excellence and striving for perfection.

Communications with the Boss

Not only is it a waste of your time and theirs but it's a constant source of irritation to bosses that secretaries continually interrupt their work to ask questions, get instructions, or verify information.

Much of your communication can be written directly on the document in question. Underline the statement in a letter that says the boss is invited to a retirement luncheon and write in the margin: "Would you like for me to make reservations?"

Keep a running list of questions or issues that need to be discussed with the boss and then set up daily conferences—be they 30 seconds or 15 minutes—to get or give the information you both need.

Phone Calls

Think before you dial to prevent your having to call back because you forgot something. Jot notes to yourself about all the points you need to cover in the phone conversation.

Think twice before you leave your number and ask someone to return your call. Do you want to be interrupted with the return call when you're in the middle of another project, or had you rather call again yourself on your own schedule? Also, when you keep control of the contact, you avoid waiting for information while someone delays in getting back to you or forgets altogether.

Think a third time before you place one call now, one call later. Instead, make all or most of your calls in one sitting. And make this a time when you'll likely get to talk to the person you want. Early morning, right before or after lunch, and late afternoon are good times to catch busy executives but difficult times to catch lower-level employees.

When callers need to speak to your boss and insist on calling back rather than having him return the call, suggest a specific time when callers are likely to catch him.

When you place calls for your boss, leave complete messages about the purpose of the call so the caller will have all the necessary information when he returns the call; also suggest the best times for returning the call.

Do other things requiring little concentration while you talk on the phone—paper clipping or stapling, signing letters, putting in a typewriter or printer ribbon, filing.

Encourage your boss to signal you to pick up your extension when he wants you to hear details that you must attend to from a specific conversation. Getting the information first-hand saves the boss's time in having to fill you in later and prevents your missing details or background information necessary for you to do a complete job.

Mail

Handle the mail only once before filing it, passing it on to the boss, rerouting it, or throwing it away.

First, sort the mail into categories—correspondence; bills or statements; ads or circulars; newsletters, magazines, journals.

Second, open all correspondence or stapled "junk mail" and make sure you attach any enclosures to the basic documents. Be sure to check envelopes for return-address information that is not on the primary document. Be careful about destroying "junk mail"; your boss may want to see it merely to stay informed of new products or services. After all, when junk mail is opened appropriately, the boss can toss it away in about two seconds.

Third, route the mail. Send documents such as job resumes or invoices to the appropriate department or person. Place what you can handle yourself into your in-box. Prepare your boss's mail.

In preparing your boss's mail, always put the most urgent on top of each category. Make important notes on mail as you read it. Underline key points and details. Jot down things you need to check: "Isn't this the same date as the PSDA convention?" Also, underline key details and points and add your comments, such as: "Should I make your hotel reservations for this?" Or, "I've already discussed this with Selma and have her information." Or, "This date has been added to my tickler file."

Be just as meticulous with outgoing mail: Lay urgent correspondence and reports in the center of the boss's desk for immediate signature and don't forget to see that they get a signature at the earliest possible moment.

When documents are returned to you, make sure you include all enclosures in the envelopes or send them in separate packaging immediately.

Be aware of all the special mail services offered by the Post Office and private companies—services such as overnight express, registered mail, special pickups, and the like.

Also be aware of the average time it takes first-class mail to travel to and from cities you frequently mail to and also the length of time required for materials to get through from department to department within your own company. Many employees have no idea that some pieces of correspondence take days to get from the top floor to the bottom. Mail accordingly.

Errands

Rarely should you do errands one at a time. If you have to go to the fortieth floor to take something to the mailroom, gather up all the information for copying, the telephone message for Ms. Whitfield, the contracts for Legal, and do all the tasks on one trip.

Also, take a moment to confirm things before you run the errand. Before you make a special trip to get something to the printer before five, call to see if he will get to the task any sooner than if you come in the next morning. Before you deliver the contracts to Ms. White's office for signature, phone to make sure she's there.

Correspondence

Rather than force others to compose letters or memos to answer yours, have them check an answer or simply sign your letter or memo at the bottom: "If the above figures are correct, would you please verify by signing your name at the bottom of this memo." Or, "If you want to add any names to the guest list, please add them to the bottom of my list and return it to my office."

This speedy reply saves time in several ways: You don't have to wait for a procrastinating recipient to get around to writing a lengthy letter or memo; you save your reader's time; you save "middle-person" (i.e. clerical) time.

Also, make sure correspondence originating in your office is written in plain English, not bureaucratic gobbledygook. It takes much longer to compose and read a sentence such as,

"Management has become cognizant of the desirability of the issuance and utilization of proper identification to all personnel upon their entrance of company facilities," than, "We plan to issue you ID badges for entering the building."

Dictation/Typing

Develop a habit of typing long telephone messages as they are given to you and typing out notes or instructions to your boss or co-workers. Trying to read sloppy handwriting, along with the resultant mistakes in decoding, wastes time.

Encourage your boss, if she dictates, to dictate to a machine rather than to you personally. She will get her thoughts on paper about six times faster (handwriting 20 to 30 words per minute versus 150 words per minute at the normal speaking rate) than writing by longhand. And you can be doing other things while she talks, rambles, repeats, and changes her mind. She can talk twice as fast as the normal secretary takes dictation. And a secretary can transcribe from a machine 33 percent faster than from longhand or shorthand. (MacKenzie, *The Time Trap*, p. 74). Therefore, have your boss "tell it to the machine."

Posting Information

Many secretaries waste hours a day answering the same questions from different people. When you can, type and post on bulletin boards information that is frequently requested of you—policy and procedure matters; safety rules and regulations; dates, locations, and times of regularly scheduled meetings and classes; job openings and requirements; telephone numbers for service, purchase, or repair; equipment operating instructions.

To those who don't come by your office personally for the information, prepare written material and offer to mail it. That's much faster than repeating the same song and dance to every caller.

This-Is-How-We-Do-It Records

After you finish major projects, particularly ones that occur infrequently, take a few minutes to record what you did and how you did it. Such records will save you much time the next month, quarter, or year when you have to repeat the performance.

Lists

Write things down:

- Who to call about what and accompanying phone numbers
- How to prepare the annual report from first to last
- What steps are involved in hosting the annual sales meeting
- Old guest lists
- Menu suggestions
- Directions for repairing or maintaining equipment

Proper Equipment

Some secretaries handle complex tasks with inadequate equipment and supplies, much as though trying to cut the lawn with a pair of scissors. Buy appropriate rubber stamps. Use quality copiers. Select software packages with the proper functions for your applications. Develop and print forms to collect information. Install good telephone equipment with adequate lines.

Grouping Related Activities

Few would consider collating pages to a manual by walking to the copier and photocopying one page then returning to their desk to hole-punch the page and place it in the binder before beginning to copy page two.

But many people handle other activities in such an inefficient manner. A phone call here, a phone call there; a contract delivered here, a computer search there. Instead, do related activities at one time to avoid the wasted effort in deciding what to do next, in moving to the appropriate location for the task, and in gathering the necessary equipment.

For example, make all outgoing calls, then run errands, then discuss a subordinate's work with her, then handle correspondence first drafts, then read what's in your boss's outbox.

Avoiding the Work-Wait Pattern

In all offices, there are peak and off-peak hours, days, and weeks. But if you merely "go with the flow," you will find yourself bumping up against deadlines. And contrary to what most people say, they don't work best under pressure. They may work faster at that moment for that project, but do they really work better? Usually accuracy goes down; decisions are hasty ones; details go by the wayside.

To avoid crises and the work-wait pattern, set your own personal deadlines a few hours or days before others set deadlines for you. In other words, if you have a routine report due on May 15, set your own deadline of May 10 for information requests to others and perhaps May 13 for your first draft.

When major deadlines are imposed on you, start at that date and work backward on your calendar, setting mini-deadlines for various steps and stages.

And remember to follow up to see that others on whom you are depending meet their deadlines.

Finally, keep a handle on the amount of time you wait on your boss—for her to get off the phone, to get on the phone, to sign a letter, to receive a visitor. Try to accomplish small chores while you wait rather than simply sit or shuffle.

Reading

Read and underline key points for your boss so that he can merely scan and get the gist of an article or correspondence. Write your questions or comments out in the margin, so he knows why you thought he'd be interested in the information.

If the boss prefers, you may prepare a typed synopsis containing only the essentials—"big-picture" message; expected action—his or the reader's; important details—usually the how and why; any attachments he needs to examine.

When reading articles, newsletters, and such for your own information or career growth, preread by glancing at blurbs, captions, illustrations, and headings. Either underline topic sentences or summarize in the margins key points of long paragraphs. Then save the material in a reading file for later reference. If you need key information later, you don't have to do much rereading.

Consolidating and Using Discretionary Time

Try to block out your daily and weekly schedule so that you leave yourself a block of time when you can set your own priorities. If that is an impossibility due to frequent calls, visitors, or instructions from your boss, rearrange your schedule and work while everyone else is out of the office—during the lunch hour or first thing when you arrive in the morning. Rather than making the coffee, watering the plants, and uncovering the office equipment, sit down and concentrate on compiling the report statistics. Then go back to the tasks that require less concentration as others start to appear.

Most find that having enough "free" time is an infrequent luxury on the job, not a problem. But when you finish the routine projects, tackle some of the chores that you keep postponing until "someday."

- Work on your files. Check completeness and arrangement. Move appropriate files to the inactive drawer or section. Type and affix new labels. Throw out old paperwork, or at least move it to an inactive file so you won't have to keep looking through it to get to what you want. Various records management experts estimate that 80 to 95 percent of all files are *never* needed after original filing.

- Scrutinize standard office forms. Are they outdated? Can you eliminate some items? Do you need to add others for more complete information?

- Check your supplies and order what you need.

- Update your telephone files. Throw out old numbers or move them to an inactive file. Add new ones.

- Bring desk manuals up to date.

- Revise and update your job description and that of your subordinates.

- Clip articles from journals and magazines that you think your boss, co-workers, clients, or customers would like to see. Underline key points and send copies.

- Look for someone else around the office who has extra work and offer to help her out.

- Educate yourself. Study the competition—their product or service pamphlets. Read professional or organizational journals and newsletters. Attend workshops and committee meetings as a participant or observer.

Prime Time

Everyone "peaks" at different times of the day or week. Some people are more alert and energetic in the morning, while others operate best at the end of the day. Some like to dive into projects "first thing Monday morning," while others like to work into their serious projects about middle week.

Discover your prime time and schedule your most difficult tasks then. Your energy and accuracy will be higher, resulting in a quicker, better product or service.

Decison-Making/Problem-Solving

Follow these generic steps to a faster decision or solution: Define the problem. Generate possible solutions or options. Evaluate each solution or alternative in light of the available facts and circumstances. Choose whichever solution or option meets the most, or most important (there is a difference), of your criteria. Plan how to put your decision or solution into effect. Work your plan.

Meetings

Avoid meetings when you can. Can the information be dispensed just as effectively through a memo or by phone? Cancel meetings when you know key people will be absent. Otherwise, you'll have to spend time filling them in or conducting another meeting for the same purpose.

If you need a meeting, schedule it for an "off hour" so that people know your time is important—say, 10:20 A.M. to 10:40 A.M. With such scheduling, people tend to take starting times more seriously.

Try stand-up meetings around your desk. Meetings where people have to stand tend to be shorter.

When you must attend others' meetings, take other work with you to do while you wait on stragglers and when no-agenda meetings wander.

Procrastination

Time experts Alan Lakein (*How to Get Control of Your Time and Your Life*, Edwin Bliss (*Getting Things Done*), and Dru Scott (*How to Put More Time in Your Life*) suggest several ways to psyche yourself out of procrastination: Consider the unpleasant results of your delay. Focus on the rewards of finishing your project. Take large tasks and divide them into small steps, forcing yourself to do "one little thing" now. Don't allow yourself to "dawdle," doing everything but the necessary. Isolate yourself in a prime work location away from interruptions of any kind. Catch yourself in a high mood and pull out the work. Commit the results and the deadline to another person—someone to whom you will be embarrassed to report that you have not finished the project. Reward yourself for progress—take five minutes longer on your coffee break or treat yourself to a big lunch.

A few people have trouble with what I call procrastination "in reverse." Because they can't stand the pressure of a deadline or because they are well-organized and hate to "waste time," these people often do things so far in advance that they end up doing much extra work and, at times, work that turns out to be unnecessary altogether.

For example, as soon as the boss accepts an invitation to speak at the next year's sales convention, the secretary begins collecting information for drafting his speech. Then two months before the event, he has to cancel due to other conflicts. Or, a secretary may spend an hour composing a guest list for a certain function, when two days later she gets a "mandatory list" from her boss's superior.

As much as I hesitate to say this, there is such a thing as planning too far in advance.

chapter 11

YOUR FUTURE

You wouldn't think of asking a lawyer what her plans are for moving up to judge, or ask a violinist what his chances are for moving up to orchestra conductor. Yet, many people assume that all secretaries are marking time until they get transferred, promoted, or married.

Not so. Many in the secretarial field are quite happy where they are; they enjoy their role as support staff for important executives—roles that enable them to use their organizational and communications skills to the fullest, to mix with great minds, to be involved with top-level policy, and to observe corporate life from a close insider's view of the board room.

That is not to say, of course, that all secretaries work for top executives and find their jobs varied and interesting. That's where "moving up" or "moving on" comes in. Although in my interviewing and other researching I've discovered many secretaries who have moved up and out of the secretarial role, far more say they have no desire to do so. What they do aspire to is being the most outstanding secretary in the organization, working for higher-level executives and expanding their skills and expertise in other areas.

Nevertheless, those who have made secretarial work their career choice must deal with a common prejudice or stigma about being "just a secretary". Here's what some say:

"But yes [there's a prejudice], as far as attitude toward 'secretary.' I just make a judgment about their [those who have this patronizing attitude] mentality. Those who know me, know my capabilities; and those who don't, I don't have time to educate them. I just twit them off and make them feel a little foolish."

"People say, 'What do you know? You're just the secretary.' My boss corrects that by referring these people who try to bypass me back to me anyway for the information they need. And sometimes my boss will throw away a message, if a person wouldn't talk to me to get the information he needed. Usually people with little responsibility do this—it makes them feel superior."

"A secretarial job is what you make it; that's like saying, 'Oh, I'm just a housewife.' You can improve typing skills, communication skills, telephone skills. The job can grow if you want it to."

"I don't have any problems because I know they [bosses and others in the organization] need me a lot. And that makes me feel that I have power over them."

As with any other prejudice, be it sexual, racial, or occupational, you have to work to educate others to the facts rather than the stereotypes.

Getting Your Boss to Delegate More Responsibility to You

To keep rising to your level of competence and to keep your enthusiasm from waning, take initiative and ask your boss for more responsibilities. Find out what his problems are and see how you can go about alleviating them. Where does he spend most of his time? How could you help him save some of that time, or at least give him more time for a particular function or task? Observe what needs to be done and begin doing it.

Or ask for projects, reminding your boss of what you've been able to accomplish in the past with little or no instruction. Competent people recognize competent work.

When your boss assigns you a project, spend some time helping him help you. Ask questions: "What is the ultimate purpose, goal, or desirable end product? What are the deadlines involved? What resources—finances, personnel, information—are available to you? To whom can you go with questions and for further detailed instructions? What authority do you have and at what stages should you check back with the boss?

If you do well, you will be rewarded with even more responsibilities.

Letting Your Boss Know You're Ready for Promotion

You should let your boss, co-workers, and personnel know of your desire to be promoted to new responsibilities—either within your present department or outside. Make your boss aware of special training as you receive it and how your skills are progressing in areas she may not be in a position to observe closely. And don't necessarily give her only the glowing reports of major triumphs that were easy for you; mention problems and snags you hit and explain how the solution was a learning experience for you. Additionally, keep your personnel file updated for review when new job openings are posted.

And don't feel that you should know how to do a certain job before you get a promotion. As long as you have proven yourself where you are, you are eligible to be taught the new job. Rarely should you expect to know a job before you are hired or promoted to it.

A former secretary with a large school district explains her rise: "I have had four major job category changes because I got bored and asked for more. I take initiative and show that I'm capable."

Another former secretary, who is now office manager of 30 employees, explains: "I outline the responsibilities I have and how I have accomplished them. Then I mention areas I would like to learn and work into. Then I explain why I have the ability to do that. Then, I leave them [bosses] with that to think over."

In talking with your boss, tell her what parts of your job you don't enjoy, as well as what you do enjoy. That knowledge will enable her to assign you new projects or promote you to the "right" areas. And if you're offered a "promotion" that you don't want, say so. For example, a boss may assume you'd like to move into a certain division simply because the branch office is closer to your home. If that transfer is not in line with your career goals, speak up.

Occasionally, you may not have to "move" at all to be promoted. You may discover that under the title of secretary you've already been performing tasks requiring independent judgment, decision-making, and follow-up with your boss's supervision. If so, ask for a title more in line with what you actually have been doing. "Supervisor of...," "Director of...," "...Manager."

If you find that you can take absolutely no more responsibility or tasks from the shoulders of your boss, ask him if he objects to "sharing you" within the department. Expand your functions and responsibilities with others who have more than they can handle, who aren't doing a good job with what they've been assigned, or who want to do as little as possible for the same paycheck. The more you do, the more chances for notice and reward by someone higher up the ladder. The longer you stay in one slot with the same responsibilities, the more others, your boss included, tend to peg you and think you too specialized to broaden your horizon.

Why should a boss be willing to promote you? Promotion is less expensive than training someone new from outside the company; you'll learn the job quicker since you already know company philosophies and the general ways things are done. Additionally, you have already proven yourself.

There is, however, one hang-up: the boss who hesitates to promote you because you have proven yourself *so well* you have become indispensable to her. Therefore, it's imperative that you don't let anyone see you as indispensable—for your own career's sake. Use your spare time to tell co-workers and your typists/clerks what you know. On occasion, give them a chance to help with your projects while you observe and give them further instructions and feedback. Leave adequate instructions and complete desk manuals for times when you're away from the office so that your replacement can do an adequate job. In fact, when you ask for a promotion, having a replacement already trained can be just the encouragement a boss needs to give you the go-ahead.

Finally, you may run into the boss who won't give you a promotion because he doesn't want to lose you no matter what. Don't permit a boss to trap you with flattery or loyalty; it's nice to have your contributions valued—but not to the extent of a stymied career. You may have to get a promotion laterally and then take an alternate route up the ladder. Although you may be disappointed to find out that your boss has held you back for selfish reasons, you can still give your old boss credit for hiring, training, and developing you into a valuable employee.

How and When to Negotiate a Raise

A 1983 survey conducted by Professional Secretaries International entitled, "Secretaries...Who Earns What? And Why?" reveals some startling facts:

- Pay is based on seniority. Length of time with an employer has more impact on salary than skills, education, or even job title.
- Staying with the same boss can be harmful. Compensation does not keep up when one stays with the same supervisor too long, unless that supervisor is promoted.
- Employers don't pay for experience. Starting secretaries earn only $1,000 a year less than those with 20 years' experience.
- Usually there's no financial advantage to changing jobs, but those new to the field benefit from the shortage of secretaries.
- A better title is worth about $1,000 more a year.
- Except for those without a high school diploma and those with a master's degree, education does not affect salary.
- Those with 45 years' experience actually earn less than someone just starting.
- All other things being equal, heads of households earn more than their counterparts.
- The majority of secretaries see no advancement opportunities, but having a career discussion with one's supervisor helps.

In my interviewing, as well as that of well-known management experts, I've found that many secretaries "have not because they ask not." Most simply take cost-of-living or pay-grade raises as they come along; few ever ask for a raise.

Why is that? Most secretaries offer reasons such as they have a good relationship and they don't want to "put the boss on the spot"; they fear being turned down; they think the boss will notice what they do and give them what they deserve without their having to ask.

My response to them: If you and the boss have a good relationship and if you're doing a good job, why would the boss turn you down? How long can the pain of being turned down last? If you don't think you deserve more, why should your boss think so? When you go to the dry cleaners to pick up a suit, do you pay more than the asked fee simply because your suit is pressed well? When you're satisfied with what you're making, why should your boss offer to pay you more?

A merit, not a cost-of-living, across-the-board, raise is feedback for how well you're doing in the job. Ask.

How to make your request then? Outline your accomplishments, increased training or education, and problems solved since you had the last performance review. Then decide on what raise amount you think is reasonable. (Most management consultants say that companies can live with 15 percent increases in good times; taper accordingly.)

An executive secretary to the vice-president explains her preparation to request a raise:

> I keep a list of things I've done. I do a lot of reading. I practice asking for the raise. I talk into a recorder to make sure my voice isn't shaky and that I don't sound like I need a raise. I give specific reasons and usually ask after I've done some big thing he didn't think I could pull off. I know when the company is doing well and when there's money. He'll ask me how much I think I deserve. And I give him what others in equivalent positions are making and then tell him what I think I should get according to that. He usually gives me what I ask.

When you set up an interview with your boss to ask for the raise, begin with your reasons and follow up with your request. Base your request on your own qualifications, accomplishments, assumed responsibilities, and goals. Always try to quantify past results—money saved, increased production, special contacts made, technical knowledge gained, comments of goodwill from customers or clients.

If you can't claim any such accomplishments, base your request on the very monotony of the job or its significance to the company. For example: "The very monotony of these tasks makes money my only reward; therefore..." Or, "Since I'm the only secretary who has dealt with our overseas operations on these matters and personally know the proper foreign government regulations, I'd like to suggest a salary increase of..."

Try to find out and focus on your boss's standards for measurements. What does he place the most value on? The quantity of work you do? The creativity you bring to the job? The way you handle clients and customers? Your willingness to stay overtime until projects are completed? Your punctuality and attendance record? Mentioning that you deserve a raise because you have accomplished something the boss doesn't consider valuable gets little attention.

Emphasize the symbolic meaning of the promotion/raise rather than focusing on the money. For example: "This increase, of course, will allow me to feel to that I really am contributing to your effectiveness and your goals."

Name your specific amount, being sure that the request is the highest figure in the appropriate range for your industry and level. At least this will be a starting point for negotiation; and if the boss comes back with a lesser offer, you still won't be too disappointed.

Make sure your body language agrees with your words. Keep good eye contact; get the jitters out of your voice; and make your posture show confidence.

Now, for some don'ts. Don't ask for a raise simply because someone else has received one. Such a request falls into the category of playing little red schoolhouse, where Mary asks teacher to give her a "B" because Susan got a "B." Someone else may have received a raise because her work far exceeded yours; to be told such won't be flattering.

Don't ask for a raise based on financial need. Because supervisors cannot very well verify true needs (even needs related to heavy medical expenses, etc.), they will often react against heartstring manipulation.

Don't whine: "But I've been doing this same old job and everybody else gets the best projects." Or, "But you promised me last year that if I...so I am...so why don't you...?"

If after your best efforts, your boss still says he cannot give you a raise, ask for other substitutions in lieu of a raise: "I understand, then, that all raises are frozen now; but perhaps you would consider some small token such as membership in the health club around the corner." Or, "Perhaps, then, since you're not at liberty to approve the raise, you could manage to give me a few extra days off—say one Friday afternoon a month."

Perks that secretaries I interviewed have been granted include membership at a country club, a car allowance, paid parking, two free tickets to see her family overseas, invitations to special civic and organizational functions attended by the top-level executives, and liberty to take off in the middle of the day when work is slack.

Playing Positive Politics

The term *politics* has a negative connotation for most people but politicians. Episodes like Watergate and Abscam come to mind, with their sordid investigations, harassments, lies, bribes, and cover-ups.

But positive politics we've been playing all our lives. You speak to the mail-carrier, hoping he or she will pay particular attention not to leave your oversized packages out in the rain. You buy from your neighbor's son when he comes around selling candy for the school band. You go out of the way to speak to your professor at night school, hoping she will remember you when grading time comes. You campaign for your friend's school board election because you think he will vote to buy computers for your child's school.

When most employees say they don't "play politics," they mean not overtly so; they mean that they are neither deceiving nor manipulative. But they do play politics by doing an outstanding job, by identifying the results that get rewarded with money and verbal recognition, and by cultivating a personal support system.

How does a secretary play positive politics?

First, by making her boss look good. An alert secretary reads magazines and journals and clips articles that would be of interest to her boss's colleagues and passes them on to the boss to forward to the peer, superior, or client. She marks special dates on her calendar—birthdays, employment anniversaries, promotions—and reminds her boss to send a note, card, flowers, or to schedule a lunch. She makes her boss look good by the speed and accuracy of the information coming from their office. She makes her boss look good by her constant availability and willingness to do the "extras" for visitors.

To bring attention to her own accomplishments, a secretary learns to ask the right questions; she learns the why behind things so she can make independent judgments when necessary. She asks for frequent job reviews from her supervisor, so he knows what skills she is acquiring and the magnitude of her contributions to the team effort.

Occasionally, when the information is not confidential, she lets others know of worthwhile contributions by the boss to the organization—either by casual conversation or in memos.

When either she or the boss gets a note or memo of appreciation from a higher-up or a client, she circulates it around her department to those who have contributed to the project with a personal handwritten note of thanks to those involved. Or, she may wish to prepare a letter for her boss's signature, thanking a particular client or customer for his business, his confidence, and his "kind words" about something she has done. If the compliment to her is a verbal one, she passes it on to her boss: "I thought you might like to know that Customer Jones was pleased about the delivery of our last order. In fact, he complimented me yesterday, saying..."

She understands and respects the chain-of-command rather than trying to thwart it. Although she studies organizational charts and knows the formal structure, she also listens to the grapevine and observes who are the real powers that be in the organization. Passing that information on to her boss, she can help him or her align people who support specific ideas and projects.

Additionally, a secretary can make herself and her boss look good simply by being visible in the organization. She offers to serve on volunteer projects such as the blood drive, the United Way, the Committee for Increased Police Protection or whatever. She shows up at company functions. She is personally available for large functions for which she had made all the arrangements so that she can take care of any problems or special needs—and also take credit for a job well done.

She is a visible participant in meetings. By helping to facilitate the group's progress and keeping everyone on target, she calls attention to her communication skills. She may also gain recognition for contributing ideas.

If the boss is in a meeting and gets an important call that he wants to take, she doesn't merely call the conference room and have someone else deliver the message; she takes the message into the meeting herself so that she is identified with that executive.

If possible to alter her transportation arrangements for lunch, she offers to stay and cover the phones during her boss's important meetings. And she doesn't rush out the door immediately at quitting time if a meeting is just breaking up. She stays around to be visible to those just leaving.

Visibility may be as simple as speaking to high-level people. In fact, executive secretaries report that the top officials are often the loneliest at any organizational gathering because most people are afraid to strike up a conversation with them. A secretary to the CEO for a large oil company advises, "Speak to the people who are your higher-ups. Gradually they will begin to notice you and then ask someone your name. Sometimes it's the higher-ups who never get spoken to, and they appreciate it."

Get people to notice and remember your name by using both your first and last name in self-introductions: "Clare Burns speaking," not just, "Ms. Burns." Also, if you can think of a witty twist, add a phrase or a memory peg to help the co-worker or client remember your name: "I'm Susan Sweet—but I won't harm your teeth." Or, "I'm Terry Wakefield from Wakefield, Indiana." If the name is different, spell it or explain it: "That's Booher—with an 'h'; most people assume the 'h' is a typo and substitute a 'k' as in Booker."

If you've met the other person before, help him recall: "Oh, yes, we met at the annual lawyers meeting out in Phoenix a couple of years ago. I was then an assistant to James Larkson, if you remember him?" Finally, you can help people remember your name if they can see it as well as hear it. You'd be surprised how many can't remember a class instructor's name until they see it written on a brochure or a book cover. Keep a nameplate on your desk.

Finally, positive politics involves loyalty—to your co-workers, your boss, and your organization. Of course, bad-mouthing company products, services, or policies to outsiders is a no-no, but such negative comments even inside your own company put you in a rather negative light also. Statements such as "this is how we did it back at my old job" are invariably taken as a putdown to your new boss and co-workers.

Occasionally you'll find the loyalty line even less visible when you must make decisions about situations where you feel torn between loyalty to a peer, to a boss, and to the common good of the company. Situations involving an incompetent boss, a moral issue, or an unfair dismissal all create inner turmoil.

Here's what secretaries report about such conflicts of loyalty:

"We had an officer who was abusing his power for personal gain. I kept listening to details about the situation although I was witness to none of the wrongdoing. But I thought there was merit and there was a little key to the whole thing. I asked, 'Hey, whatever happened to such and such an account that we set up for our employees who do such and such? Did they ever make use of that?' My boss then instructed me to look into it because he became curious. Well, I spent a lot of hours answering his question. And we wound up with a major dismissal. And no one knows to this day how it was all discovered...I wasn't trying to hurt that person but to protect the people that were being abused."

"I once had an alcoholic boss. He kept doing his job with a flair; the only repercussion was that his treatment of me was terrible. I prayed about how to handle it and thought of quitting. He would never have reported his problem, but he wasn't always sure he could deal with the problem personally. He would have had to quit if someone hadn't encouraged him to get help."

"We've had an employee who has been here as long as I have. This person has problems and she's going to lose her job this summer. I hate that. She has worked very hard for this company, worked her rear-end off. But she can't get along with people. It's not fair to others to have to walk on eggshells with her. It's not fair to her to be fired after she's given so much to the company. It's not fair to the others who have to put up with her."

"When you have an employee with a problem, you identify with their wanting an immediate answer. But my boss has to go to his boss sometimes, and that delays things. I identify with both. I see the management decision-making process and the time it takes, but I also see the immediacy of the situation for the employee."

When you are asked to take sides in situations such as the above, the problem gets stickier because your own integrity is at stake. First, tell your boss how you feel about the unethical or unfair situation without blaming, name-calling, or judging.

For example: "I understand the instructions you gave me for doing thus-and-so, but I don't feel I can carry that assignment out. Would you please pass that on to someone else?" (You don't say anything about the matter being immoral, unfair, a deception; he will know all those terms himself.) Such a simple I-message will put the ball in his court to either rethink or reexplain his position, change his mind, or let you off the hook by assigning someone else.

Keep a record of the situation as it develops—dates, assignments, instructions, your comments and refusals, and any threats from the boss.

If you decide to go to a higher authority or department in the company, make sure it's the correct one rather than telling the situation to whomever will listen.

If you do not want to go above your boss's head, you have the choice of going along with her instructions or resigning. You can also check with the Department of Labor or the Equal Employment Opportunity Commission if you feel you are being harassed or fired for saying no to an unethical assignment. If you choose to resign, make sure your personnel records show the correct reason you chose to leave the organization.

To Find or Not to Find a Mentor

Although a relatively recent concept in the corporate world, the mentor-protégé relationship has been around for a long time. Artists, athletes, philosophers, and educators have had masters to teach, model, and encourage them in their work.

For many secretaries, their bosses have been their mentors. Bosses have a close working knowledge of their secretary's capabilities and of where those talents may fit into the organization. If they become an effective team, they may both rise through the organization together.

In the absence of a boss who is capable and interested in your career, you have several other options—peers with more experience in your company, peers working in other organizations, past bosses, or other retirees.

An administrative assistant in a large construction company explains,

> Most of the bosses and many officers of this company are my mentors. It's nothing for me to get on the phone to one of them and say, 'Mr. So-and-So, when you have time I need a lesson.' And when they can, they'll give me a call and say they have time and they're delighted to explain the *whys* behind a

new report or something. And then I'm an overnight expert. They get a better employee out of the relationship. But also I have played on the fact that most intelligent people are not selfish with their knowledge. They feel good to share.

What a mentor can do for you, of course, depends on whom you choose as a mentor. In general, they can show you better ways to do your job, introduce you to other people in the organization, share information about company politics, tell you what mistakes others have made in their careers, give you a different perspective on your projects and problems, advise on training needs, and possibly reward you with promotions.

Recent research, however, suggests that boss-mentors, and even mentors in general, may tend to hold their protégés back from promotions (Inroads, Inc., studies reported in *Savvy*, December 1984; Blotnick, *The Corporate Steeplechase*). Therefore, if you decide a mentor can indeed take you where you want to go, choose wisely and know when to ease out of the relationship.

Professional Organizations and What They Can Do for You

Although some secretaries see their own professional organizations as mostly social, others find them beneficial for several reasons. First, they provide networking opportunities—a chance to talk with others outside your own company who perform the same occupational roles you do. Such networking allows you to gain new perspectives on problems you have, to learn of leads to other resources to handle your job better, and to make contacts for promotions and job changes.

The organization itself provides through its publications, seminars, and national and local speakers valuable information as to specific skills, on-the-job problems, and salary ranges for those of your specific expertise and experience. Speakers at regular monthly meetings talk about both job and personal matters of interest—time-management, stress, physical well-being, career growth. These organizations also provide opportunity for members to develop management skills as officers or committee leaders or members. Finally, such organizations promote and enhance the role of secretary to the general public.

Below are names and addresses of the more prominent secretarial organizations:

American Society of Corporate Secretaries
1270 Avenue of the Americas
New York, New York 10020

Executive Women International
965 E. Van Winkle, Suite One
Salt Lake City, Utah 84117

National Association of Executive Secretaries
3837 Plaza Drive
Fairfax, Virginia 22030

Professional Secretaries International
(formerly The National Secretaries Association)
301 East Armour Boulevard
Kansas City, Missouri 64111-1299

BIBLIOGRAPHY

Adams, Linda, *Effective Training for Women*. Wyden Books/Simon & Schuster, 1979.

Albrecht, Karl, *Executive Tune-Up: Personal Effectiveness Skills for Business & Professional People*. Englewood Cliffs, New Jersey: Prentice-Hall, 1981.

Anastasi, Thomas E. Jr., *A Secretary Is A Manager*. Medfield, Massachusetts: Delvin House, 1976.

Anderson, Ruth I., Dorothy E. Lee, Allien R. Russon, and Jacquelyn Wentzell Crane, *The Administrative Secretary*. McGraw-Hill, 1974.

Atwater, Eastwood, "I Hear You," *How to Use Listening Skills for Profit*. Prentice-Hall, 1981

Azibo, Moni, and Theresa Crylen Unumb, *The Mature Women's Back-to-Work Book*. Chicago: Contemporary Books, 1980.

Baird, John E. and Patricia Hayes Bradley, "Styles of Management and Communication: A Comparative Study of Men and Women," *Communication Monographs*, June 1979, pp.101-11.

Barnahas, Bentley, *Develop Your Power to Deal With People*. West Nyack, New Jersey: Parker Publishing Company, 1971.

Beach, Dale S., *Managing People at Work: Readings in Personnel*. MacMillan, 1971.

Becker, Esther, and Evelyn Anders, *The Successful Secretary's Handbook*. Barnes & Noble Books, rev. ed., 1984.

Becvar, Raphael J., *Skills for Effective Communication: A Guide to Building Relationships*. Wiley, 1974.

Belker, Loren B., *The Successful Secretary: You, Your Boss and the Job*. American Management, 1982.

Bennett, Dudley, *Transactional Analysis and the Manager*. New York: AMACOM. 1976.

Berkman, Harold W., *The Human Relations of Management*. Encino, California: Dickenson Publishing, 1974.

Bermont, Hubert, *How to Become a Successful Consultant in Your Own Field*. Consultant's Library, 1978.

Berne, Eric M.D., *Games People Play*. Ballentine, 1964.

Berscheid, Ellen, and Elaine Walster, "Beauty and the Best," *Psychology Today*, March, 1972.

"Better Temper that Temper!", *Newsweek*, January 1983, pp.42-43.

Bird, Caroline, *Everything a Woman Needs to Know to Get Paid What She's Worth*. McKay, 1973.

Blake, Robert R., Jane Srygley Mouton, and Artie Stockton, *The Secretary Grid*. New York: AMACOM, 1983.

Blau. P. M., "Cooperation and Competition in a Bureaucracy," *American Journal of Sociology*, 59:530-35, 1954.

Bliss, Edwin C., *Getting Things Done: The ABC's of Time Management*. New York: Bantam Books, 1976.

Blotnick, Scrully, *The Corporate Steeplechase*, New York: Facts On File, Inc., March , 1983.

Bolles, Richard Nelson, *What Color Is Your Parachute?* Berkeley,

Bolton, Robert, *People Skills*. Englewood Cliffs: Prentice-Hall, 1979.

Booher, Dianna, *Getting Along With People Who Don't Get Along*. Broadman Press, 1984.

Booher, Dianna, *Would You Put That In Writing?* New York: Facts On File, Inc., 1983.

Booher, Dianna, *Send Me a Memo*. New York: Facts On File, Inc., 1984.

Bormann, Ernest G., Ralph G. Nichols, William S. Howell, and George L. Shapiro, *Interpersonal Communications in the Modern Organization*. Prentice-Hall, 1969.

Bosticco, Mary, *Etiquette for the Businessman*. London: Business Publications Limited, 1967.

Bradford, Leland P. Ph.D, *Making Meetings Work*. LaJolla, California: University Associates, 1976.

Bramson, Robert M., *Coping With Difficult People*. Anchor Press/ Doubleday, 1981.

Broaded, Charley H., *Essentials of Management for Supervisors*. New York: Harper and Brothers, 1947.

Burgoon, Michael, Judee K. Heston, and James McCroskey, *Small Group Communication: A Functional Approach*. New York: Holt, Rinehart and Winston, 1974.

Business Etiquette Handbook. West Nyack, New York: Parker Publishing Company Editorial Staff, 1965.

Catalyst, Staff, *Making the Most of Your First Job*. New York: Putnam's Sons, 1981.

California: Ten Speed Press, rev. ed., 1979.

Catalyst Staff, *Marketing Yourself: The Catalyst Women's Guide to Successful Resumes and Interviews*. Putnam, 1980.

Catalyst Staff, *What to Do With the Rest of Your Life: The Catalyst Career Guide for Women in the '80's.* New York: Simon & Schuster, 1980.

Cermak, Laird S. Ph.D, *Improving Your Memory*. McGraw-Hill, 1976.

Cohen, Herb, *You Can Negotiate Anything: How to Get What You Want.* Lyle Stuart, Inc., 1980.

Crain, Dr. Sharie, *Taking Stock: A Woman's Guide to Corporate Success.* Contemporary Books, 1977.

Daniels, Diane, *The Professional Secretary: Skills and Techniques for Recognition and Success*. New York: AMACOM, 1982.

Danziger, Kurt, *Interpersonal Communication*. New York: Pergamon Press, 1976.

Davidson, James, *Effective Time Management*. Human Science Press, 1978.

DeGise, R. F., "Recognizing and Overcoming Defensive Communication," *Supervisory Management*, March 22, 1977, pp. 31-38.

Douglass, Merrill E., and Donna N. Douglass, *Manage Your Time, Manage Your Work, Manage Yourself*. New York: AMACOM, 1980.

Doris, Lillian, *Complete Secretary's Handbook*. Prentice-Hall, 1983.

Doyle, Michael, and David Straus, *How To Make Meetings Work*. New York: Wyden, 1976.

Drucker, Peter F., *The Changing World of the Executive*. Times Books, 1982.

Drucker, Peter F., *Management: Tasks, Responsibilities, Practices.* Harper & Row, 1973.

Drucker, Peter F., *People and Performance*. New York: Harper & Row, 1977.

DuBrin, Andrew J., *How to Deal with Problem People in Key Jobs*. New York: Van Nostrand Reinhold, 1976.

DuBrin, Andrew J., *Survival in the Office: How to Move Ahead or Hang On.* Mason/Charter, 1977.

DuBrin, Andrew J., *Winning at Office Politics*. New York: Van Nostrand Reinhold, 1978.

Dunsing, Richard J., *You and I Have Got to Stop Meeting This Way*. AMACOM, 1978.

Fallon, William K., *Effective Communication on the Job: A Guide for Supervisors and Executives*. American Management Association, rev. ed., 1963.

Farnsworth, Terry, *On the Way Up: The Executive's Guide to Company Politics*. London: McGraw-Hill (UK) Limited, 1976.

Fear, Richard, *The Evaluation Interview*. 2nd ed., McGraw-Hill, rev. ed., 1978.

Ferner, Jack D., *Successful Time Management*. Wiley, 1980.

Fisher, Roger, and William Ury, *Getting to Yes: Negotiating Agreement Without Giving In*. Boston: Houghton-Mifflin, 1981.

Fries, Rowe, Travis, and Blockhus, *Applied Secretarial Procedures*. McGraw-Hill, 1974.

Fulmer, Robert M., *Practical Human Relations*. Homewood, Illinois: Richard D. Irwin, Inc., 1977.

Glasgow, Robert K., "High Achievers Are Made, Not Born," *Data Forum*, Vol. 1, No. 1 (Fall 1982), pp. 7-8.

Girard, Joe, *How to Sell Yourself*. Simon & Schuster, 1979.

Goffman, Erving, *Behavior in Public Places: Notes on the Social Organization of Gatherings*. Free Press, 1963.

Goldberg, Philip, *Executive Health*. (Business Week Books) McGraw-Hill, 1978.

Golde, Roger A., *What You Say Is What You Get*. New York: Hawthorn, 1979.

Goldfein, Donna, *Everywoman's Guide to Travel*. Millbrae, California: Lew Femmes Publishing, 1977.

Greenburger, Francis, and Thomas Kiernan, *How to Ask for More and Get It: The Art of Creative Negotiation*. Doubleday, 1978.

Grossman, Jack H., "Are Your Messages Provoking Conflict?" *Supervisory Management*, November, 1970, pp. 2-6.

Harragan, Betty Lehan, *Games Mother Never Taught You*. Warner Books, 1977.

Harris, Thomas A., *I'm Okay, You're Okay*. Harper & Row, 1967.

Harrison, Jared F., *Improving Performance and Productivity (Why Won't They Do What I Want Them to Do?)*. Reading, Massachusetts: Addison Wesley, 1978.

Hart, Lois Borland, *Moving Up! Women and Leadership*. AMACOM, 1980.

Hegarty, Christopher, and Philip Goldberg, *How to Manage Your Boss*. New York: Rawson-Wade, 1980.

Henderson, George, *Human Relations from Theory to Practice*. University of Oklahoma Press, 1974.

Henley, Nancy, *Body Politics*. Prentice-Hall, 1977.

Hewitt, Jay, and Morton Goldman, "Effectiveness of Various Reactions to a Hostile Attack," *The Journal Of Social Psychology*, 96, 1975, pp. 245-253.

Higginson, Margaret V., and Thomas L. Higginson, *The Ambitious Woman's Guide to a Successful Career*. AMACOM, 1975.

Hoffman, William G., *How to Make Better Speeches*. New York: Funk and Wagnalls Company, 1976.

Huseman, Richard C., Cal M. Logue, and Dwight L. Freshley, *Interpersonal Communication in Organizations*. Boston: Holbrook Press, 1967.

Hutchinson, Lois, *Standard Handbook for Secretaries*. New 8th ed., New

York: McGraw-Hill, 1979.

Ilich, John, and Barbara Schindler Jones, *Successful Negotiating Skills for Women*. Addison-Wesley, 1981.

Imundo, Louis V., *The Effective Supervisor's Handbook*. New York: AMACOM, 1980.

Irish, Richard K., *Go Hire Yourself an Employer*. Anchor Press/Doubleday, 1972, rev. ed., 1978.

Irish, Richard K., *If Things Don't Improve Soon I May Ask You To Fire Me*. Doubleday, 1975.

Januz, Lauren R., and Susan K. Jones, *Time Management for Executives*. Scribner, 1981.

James, Muriel, *The OK Boss*. New York: Addison-Wesley, 1975.

Jeffrey, Wendell E., *Essays in Interpersonal Dynamics*. Homewood, Illinois: Dorsey Press, 1979.

Johnson, David W., *Human Relations and Your Career*. Prentice-Hall, 1978.

Jongeward, Dorothy, and Philip Seyer, *Choosing Success: Transactional Analysis on the Job*. Wiley, 1978.

Jongeward, Dorothy, *Everybody Wins: Transactional Analysis Applied to Organizations*. Reading, Massachusetts: Addison-Wesley, 1976.

Jongeward, Dorothy, and Muriel James, *Winning With People: Group Exercises in Transactional Analysis*. Reading, Massachusetts: Addison-Wesley, 1973.

Kelley, Robert E. *CONSULTING: The Complete Guide to a Profitable Career*. New York: Charles Scribner's Sons, 1981.

Kets de Vries, Manfred F. R., "Managers Can Drive Their Subordinates Mad," *Harvard Business Review*, July-August, 1979, pp. 125-134.

Kisiel, Marie, *Career Strategies for Secretaries: How to Get Where You Want to Be*. Contemporary Books, 1982.

Kleinke, Chris L, *First Impression: The Psychology of Encountering Others*. Englewood, New Jersey: Prentice-Hall, 1975.

Koehler, Jerry, *The Corporation Game, How to Win the War with the Organization and Make Them Love It*. New York: MacMillan, 1975.

Koile, Earl, *Listening As a Way of Becoming* Waco, Texas: Word, 1977.

Korda, Michael, *Power! How to Get It, How to Use It*. Random House, 1975.

Korda, Michael, *Success! How Every Man and Woman Can Achieve It.* Random House, 1977.

Kotker, Zane, "Happy Endings," *Savvy*, January 1983, pp. 31-32.

Laird, Donald A., Dr., and Eleanor C. Laird, *Sizing Up People.* McGraw-Hill, 1951.

Lakein, Alan, *How to Get Control of Your Time and Your Life*. Peter H. Wyden, Inc., 1973.

Langer, Ellen J., and Carol S. Dweck, *Personal Politics: The Psychology of*

Making It. Prentice-Hall, 1973.

Lathrop, Richard, *Who's Hiring Who*. Ten Speed Press, 1977.

LeBoeuf, Michael, *Working Smart: How to Accomplish More In Half the Time*. McGraw-Hill, 1979.

Lefton, R. E., Ph.D, V. R. Buzzotta, Ph.D, and Manuel Sherberg, *Managing Productivity Through People Skills*. Cambridge, Massachusetts: Ballinger, 1980.

Levinson, Harry, "The Abrasive Personality at the Office," *Psychology Today*, May, 1978, pp. 78-84.

Lieberman, Harvey, and Erwin Rausch, *Managing and Allocating Time: Industrial*. Didoctic Systems, 1976.

"Life According to TV," *Newsweek*, December 6, 1982, pp. 136-140.

Likert, Rensis, and Jane Gibson Likert, *New Ways of Managing Conflict*. New York: McGraw-Hill, 1976.

Linkletter, Art, *Yes, You Can!*. Simon & Schuster, 1979.

Loeb, Robert H. Jr., *Managers at Work*. New York: Association Press, 1967.

Loftus, E.F., *Memory*. Reading, Massachusetts: Addison-Wesley Publishing, 1980.

Lorayne, Harry, *How to Develop a Super-Power Memory*. New American Library, 1974.

Lopez, Felix S., *Personnel Interviewing*. McGraw-Hill, 1975.

Lovely, Yvonne, *Practical Secretary's Manual and Guide*. New York: Parker Publishing, 1978.

Mackenzie, Alec R., "How to Make the Most of Your Time," *U.S. News and World Report*, December 3, 1973, pp. 45-54.

Mackenzie, Alec R., *The Time Trap*. New York: AMACOM, 1972.

MacKinnon, Catherine A., *Sexual Harassment of Working Women: A Case of Sex Discrimination*. New Haven, Connecticut: Yale University Press, 1979.

Marshall, Christy, "A Cross Reference," *Savvy*, November 1982, pp. 30-33.

Maslow, A. H., "A Theory of Human Motivation," *Psychological Review* July 1943, pp. 370-396.

Martin, Judy, *Miss Manners Guide to Excruciatingly Correct Behavior*. Atheneum, 1982.

McGonagle, John H. Jr., *Managing the Consultant: A Corporate Guide*. Radnor, Pennsylvania: Chilton Book Company, 1981.

McGregor, Douglas, *The Human Side of Enterprise*. New York: McGraw-Hill, 1960.

Miller, Gerald R., *Explorations in Interpersonal Communication*, Sage Publications, 1976.

Minirth, Frank, Paul Meier, Frank Wichern, Bill Brewer, and States Skipper, *The Workaholic and His Family*. Grand Rapids, Michigan: Baker Book House, 1981.

Molloy, John T., *Dress for Success*. New York: Peter Wyden, 1975.

Morgan, Henry H., and John W. Cogger, *The Interviewer's Manual.* New York: Drake Beam Morin, Inc., 1980.

Morris, John O., *Make Yourself Clear!*. McGraw-Hill, 1980.

Morrow, Jodie Berlin, and Myrna Lebow, *Not Just A Secretary: Using the Job to Get Ahead.* John Wiley & Sons, Inc. 1984.

Murphy, Dennis, *Better Business Communication.* McGraw-Hill, 1957.

Murphy, Elizabeth R., *The Assistant.* AMACOM, 1982.

Neilsen, Eric H., and Jan Gypen, "The Subordinate's Predicaments," *Harvard Business Review*, September-October, 1979, pp. 133-143.

Newstrom, John W., Robert M. Moncza, and William E. Reif, "Perceptions of the Grapevine: It's Value and Influence," *Journal of Business Communications.* Spring 1974, pp. 12-20.

Nierenberg, Gerard I., *How to Give and Receive Advice.* Simon & Schuster, 1975.

Nalfeh, Steven W., and Gregory White Smith, *Moving Up in Style: The Successful Man's Guide to Impeccable Taste.* St. Martin's, 1980.

Oates, Wayne E. *Confessions of a Workaholic.* New York: World, 1971.

"On Human Relations," *Harvard Business Review*, Harper & Row, 1979.

Oncken, William Jr., and Donald L. Wass, "Management Time: Who's Got the Monkey?" *Harvard Business Review*, November-December 1974, pp. 75-80.

Orlick, Terry, *Winning Through Cooperation.* Washington, D.C.: Acropolis Books, 1978.

Parker, Willard E., and Robert W. Kleemeier, *Human Relations in Supervision.* McGraw-Hill, 1951.

Parlee, Mary Brown, "Conversational Politics," *Psychology Today*, May 1979, pp,. 48-55.

Peale, Norman V., *The Power of Positive Thinking.* Fawcett, 1956.

Perry, Pascarella, "How Can I Keep the Boss Happy?" *Industry Week,* October 13, 1975, pp. 38-43.

Peter, Laurence J. Dr., and Raymond Hull, *The Peter Principle.* William Morrow, 1969.

Peters, Thomas J., and Robert H. Waterman, Jr., *In Search of Excellence.* Harper & Row, 1982.

Pietsch, William V., *Human Be-ing.* New York: Lawrence Hill & Company, 1974.

Pinkstaff, Marlene A., and Dick Pinkstaff, *Personal Skill Building for the Emerging Manager.* Boston, Massachusetts: CBI Publishing, 1979.

Pleninger, Andrew, *How to Survive and Market Yourself in Management.* AMACOM, 1977.

Porat, Frieda, and Mimi Will, *The Dynamic Secretary: A Practical Guide to Achieving Success as an Executive Assistant.* Prentice-Hall, 1983.

Press, Aric, "Abusing Sex at the Office," *Newsweek*, March 10, 1980, p. 81.

Quick, Thomas L., *Person to Person Managing.* New York: St. Martin's, 1977.

Quick, Thomas L., *Understanding People at Work*. Executive Enterprises Publishers, 1976.

Rardin, Rich, "Correcting Common Discussion Leader Mistakes," *Training and Development Journal*, December 1982, pp. 14-15.

Reber, Ralph W., and Gloria Van Gilder, *Behavorial Insights for Supervision*. Prentice-Hall, 1972.

Reeves, Elton, *How to Get Along with (Almost) Everybody*. AMACOM, 1973.

Ringer, Robert J., *Winning Through Intimidation*. New York: Fawcett, 1973.

Robbins, James Gambrell, and Barbara Schindler Jones, *Effective Communication for Today's Manager*. New York: Lebhar-Friedman Books, 1974.

Roche, Gerard R., "Much Ado about Mentors," *Harvard Business Review*, 57, No. 1, January-February 1979, pp. 14-16, 20, 24, 26-28.

Rogers, Carl, and Betty Stevens, *Person to Person*. Lafayette, California: Real People Press, 1971.

Roseman, Ed., "How to Become a Better Teamworker," *Product Management*, January 1976, pp. 17-20.

Rosenthal, Robert, et al, "Body Talk and Tone of Voice: The Language Without Words," *Psychology Today*, September 1974, pp. 64-68.

Ruben, Harvey L., M.D., *Competing*. New York: Lippincott and Crowell, 1980.

Ruben, Harvey L., M.D. *Competing, Understanding, and Winning the Strategic Game We All Play*. New York: Lippincott and Crowell, 1980.

Rusk, Tom N., and Randy A. Read, *I Want to Change, But I Don't Know How*. San Diego, California: Blue Pacific Books, 1978.

Rutherford, Robert D., *Just In Time: The Inner Game of Time Management*. Wiley, 1981.

Saint, Avice, *Learning at Work*. Nelson-Hall, 1974.

Saline, Carol, "How Not to Crumble Under Criticism," *Redbook*, August 1980, pp. 19, 177, 178, 181.

Sayles, Leonard R., and George Strauss, *Human Behavior in Organizations*. Englewood Cliffs, New Jersey: Prentice-Hall, 1960.

Sayles, Leonard R., and George Strauss, *Managing Human Resources*, 2nd ed., Englewood Cliffs, New Jersey: Prentice-Hall, 1981.

Schenkel, Susan, Ph.D., *Giving Away Success: Why Woman Get Stuck and What to do About It.* McGraw-Hill, 1984.

Schmidt, Peggy J., *Making It on Your First Job*. Avon, 1981.

Schrader, Constance, *Nine to Five*. Prentice-Hall, 1981.

Scott, Dru, Ph.D., *How to Put More Time in Your Life*. Rawson Wade Publishers, 1980.

Selye, Hans, M.D., *The Stress of Life*. McGraw-Hill, rev. ed., 1975.

"Sexual Harassment Lands Companies in Court," *Business Week*, October 1, 1979, pp. 120 +.

Shafiroff, Martin D., and Robert L. Shook, *Successful Telephone Selling in the 80's*. New York: Harper & Row, 1982.

Shook, Robert L, *Ten Greatest Salespersons—What They Say About Selling*. Harper & Row, 1978.

Shook, Robert L., *Winning Images*. MacMillan, 1977.

Silcox, Diana, and Mary Ellen Moore, *Women Time*. Wyden Books, 1980.

Simon, Sidney B., *Negative Criticism*. Niles, Illinois: Argus Communications, 1978.

Simpson, Marian G., *Tested Secretarial Techniques for Getting Things Done*. West Nyack, New York: Parker Publishing, 1973.

Skelton, Marilyn Brock, and Jerald M. Jellison, "Beware the Sainthood Trap," *Savvy*, January 1983, pp. 17-18.

Steele, Addison, *Upward Nobility: How to Win the Rat Race Without Becoming a Rat*. New York: Times Books, 1978.

Steele, Fritz, and Stephen Jenks, *The Feel of the Work Place*. Reading, Massachusets: Addison-Wesley, 1977.

Stockard, James G., *Rethinking People Management: A New Look at the Human Resources Function*. AMACOM, 1980.

Stone, Janet, and Jane Bachner, *Speaking Up: A Book for Every Woman Who Wants to Speak Effectively*. McGraw-Hill, 1977.

Sussman, Lyle, "Communication: What are Your Assumptions?" *Supervisory Management*, June 1976, 21, pp. 35-37.

Swindoll, Charles R., *Improving Your Serve*. Word, 1981.

Tacey, William S., *Business and Professional Speaking*. Dubuque, Iowa: William C. Brown Company, Publishers, 1970.

Tarrant, John J., *How to Negotiate a Raise*. New York: Van Nostrand Reinhold, 1976.

Tavris, Carol, *Anger: The Misunderstood Emotion*. Simon & Schuster, 1982.

Thompson, Margaret H., and J. Harold Janis, *Revised Standard Reference for Secretaries and Administrators*. MacMillan, 1980.

Torrington, Derek, *Face to Face: Techniques for Handling the Personal Encounter at Work*. London: Gower Press, 1972.

Tracer, Irving H., "Job-Stress—Women Cope Better," *Human Behavior*, January 1979, p. 34.

Uris, Auren, *The Blue Book of Broadminded Business Behavior*. New York: Thomas Y. Crowell Company, 1977.

Van Fleet, James K., *Power With People*. Parker Publishing Company, 1970.

Van Fleet, James K., *Guide to Managing People: How to Control People Through the Secrets of Dynamic Leadership and Supervision*. Parker Publishing Company, 1968.

Veninga, Robert L., and James P. Spadley, *The Work/Stress Connection: How to Cope With Job Burnout*. Boston/Toronto: Little, Brown & Company, 1981.

Vermes, Jean C., *Complete Book of Business Etiquette.* West Nyack, New York: Parker Publishing Company, 1976.

Vermes, Jean C., *Secretary's Guide to Dealing with People.* Parker Publishing Company, 1964.

Wassmer, Arthur C., Ph.D., *Making Contact: A Guide to Overcoming Shyness, Making New Friendships, and Keeping Those You Already Have.* Fawcett, 1978.

Walsh, Richard J., "Ten Basic Counseling Skills," *Supervisory Management,* July 1977, pp. 2-9.

Webber, Ross A., *Time Is Money! Tested Tactics That Conserve Time for Top Executives.* Free Press, 1980.

Weisinger, Hendrie, Dr., and Norman M. Lobsenz, *Nobody's Perfect: How to Give Criticism and Get Results.* Los Angeles, California: Stratford Press, 1981.

Weitz, John, *Man in Charge: The Executive's Guide to Grooming, Manners, and Travel.* MacMillan, 1974.

Welch, Mary Scott, *Networking: The Great New Way for Women to Get Ahead.* New York: Harcourt Brace Jovanovich, 1980.

Williams, Marcille Gray, *The New Executive Woman: A Guide to Business Success.* The New American Library, 1977.

Wiksell, Wesley, *Do They Understand You? A Guide to Effective Oral Communication.* MacMillan, 1960.

Wilcox, Roger P., *Oral Reporting in Business and Industry.* Prentice-Hall, 1967.

Winston, Stephanie, *Getting Organized.* Warner Books, 1978.

Wright, Milton, *Getting Along with People: A Guide to Personal Success.* Folcroft, 1977.

Yates, Jere E., *Managing Stress.* AMACOM, 1979.

Zelko, Harold P., and Frank E. X. Dance, *Business and Professional Speech Communication,* 2nd ed., Holt, Rinehart and Winston, 1st ed., 1965, 2nd ed., 1978.

Zunin, Leonard, and Natalie Zunin, *Contact: The First Four Minutes.* Ballantine Books, 1972.

Index